Researching Violence, Democracy and the Rights of People

Violence, democracy and rights are issues that are not fully addressed in research methodology literatures, yet violence is of vital interest in substantive and theoretical debates across the social sciences, education, philosophy, politics and cultural studies. Methodology needs to be informed by, and be relevant to, the debates and practices within and across these perspectives on the worlds of everyday life.

Research is fundamentally entwined with the political, the ethical and the legal. When it presumes the neutrality of method and ignores its radical roots of inquiry, it is in danger of being politically co-opted and ethically naïve. Research that reveals what is at stake politically, ethically and legally is typically open to accusations of being partisan and therefore political. It cannot avoid being political in the broadest sense of the word, and, consequently, the researcher cannot escape – through some mystical notion of being 'objective' – the political, ethical and legal consequences of undertaking research.

Research is vital to the construction of public spaces for debate, decision making and action. Hence, there is a close relationship between methodological practices, research design and the conditions under which violence, democracy and rights can be addressed.

Researching Violence, Democracy and the Rights of People explores what is at stake methodologically (both theoretically and practically) for researchers seeking to expand opportunities for people to become visible upon the public stages of debate, decision making and action, and thus make audible their experiences of wrongs and injustices, express their rights and engage democratically in processes of change.

Drawing on international contributions and contexts, this book introduces readers to the complex realities of real research and the substantive issues that their methodological approaches strive to deal with. It will benefit undergraduate and postgraduate students as well as postdoctoral and experienced researchers across a range of cultural and social science disciplines, and educational and sociological researchers. Its aim is to explore and contribute to the development of innovatory approaches to engaging in research that make a difference in the lives of people.

John F. Schostak is Research Professor of Education at the Education and Social Research Institute, Manchester Metropolitan University.

Jill Schostak is Visiting Fellow at the School of Education and Lifelong Learning, University of East Anglia, and most recently has undertaken contract research with the College of Emergency Medicine.

Researching Violence, Democracy and the Rights of People

Edited by
John F. Schostak and Jill Schostak

Routledge
Taylor & Francis Group

LONDON AND NEW YORK

First published 2010
by Routledge
2 Park Square, Milton Park, Abingdon, Oxon OX14 4RN

Simultaneously published in the USA and Canada
by Routledge
270 Madison Avenue, New York, NY 10016

Routledge is an imprint of the Taylor & Francis Group, an informa business

Typeset in Garamond by
Pindar NZ, Auckland, New Zealand
Printed and bound in Great Britain by
TJ International Ltd, Padstow, Cornwall

British Library Cataloguing in Publication Data
A catalogue record for this book is available from the British Library

Library of Congress Cataloging-in-Publication Data
Schostak, John F.
Researching violence, democracy and the rights of people / John F.
Schostak and Jill Schostak.
    p. cm.
    1. Violence—Research—Methodology. 2. School violence—
Research—Methodology. I. Schostak, Jill. II. Title.
    HM886.S38 2009
    303.601—dc22   2009025530

ISBN10: 0-415-47877-4 (hbk)
ISBN10: 0-415-47878-2 (pbk)
ISBN10: 0-203-86360-7 (ebk)

ISBN13: 978-0-415-47877-9 (hbk)
ISBN13: 978-0-415-47878-6 (pbk)
ISBN13: 978-0-203-86360-2 (ebk)

Contents

Editors

John F. Schostak is Professor at the Education and Social Research Institute, Manchester Metropolitan University. He has been involved in over 70 funded research projects, most of which have focused on innovation, institutional analysis, curriculum processes and workplace learning. He is interested in qualitative research methods generally. Recent publications include: (2002) *Understanding, Designing and Conducting Qualitative Research in Education. Framing the Project*, Open University Press; (2006) *Interviewing and Representation in Qualitative Research Projects*, Open University Press; and, with Jill Schostak, (2008) *Radical Research: Designing, developing and writing research to make a difference*, London: Routledge.

Jill Schostak is Visiting Fellow at the University of East Anglia. She is interested in contemporary philosophical debates and qualitative methodologies. She has interests in a broad range of contemporary social issues involving people's rights and freedoms, exploring these through philosophically informed approaches as exemplified in the book *Radical Research*, which she co-wrote with John Schostak, and in numerous chapters and conference papers. She has carried out qualitative research in six funded research projects, studying the experiences of consultants and trainee doctors in clinical contexts. She was recently consultant researcher for a research project on continuing professional development in the medical professions.

Contributors

Erica Burman is Professor in the Department of Psychology and Speech Pathology at Manchester Metropolitan University. Her specialist areas include: feminist critiques of psychology, critical psychology, discourse analysis, gender, 'race' and mental health, group analysis and psychoanalytic social theory and clinical practice. Recent publications include: *Deconstructing Developmental Psychology* (Routledge, 2nd edition, 2007); 'Pedagogies and politics: shifting agendas within the gendering of childhood' in: Joe L. Kincheloe, Raymond A. Horn and Shirley R. Steinberg (eds) *The Praeger Handbook of Education and Psychology*, vol. 3 (Praeger, 2007); 'Emotions, reflexivity and feminized action research' in: *Educational Action Research*, vol. 14 no. 3, pp. 315–332 (2006); '(How) can critical psychology help feminist antiracist work?' *International Journal of Critical Psychology*, vol. 18, pp. 9–33 (2006).

Jean-Louis Derouet is Professor of Sociology of Education at the Institut National de Recherche Pédagogique (National Institute for Research in Education, Lyon, France). He is also a member of the Group of Political and Moral Sociology at the École des Hautes Études en Sciences Sociales – CNRS (School for Advanced Studies in Social Sciences). He is the Chief Editor of Éducation et Sociétés, an international journal of education, and chairs the committee 'Éducation, Formation, Socialisation' for the Association Internationale des Sociologues de Langue Française (AISLF), the International Association of French-Speaking Sociologists. He also takes part in the coordination of the Network of European Experts in the Social Sciences of Education (NESSE). He focuses on the political philosophy of justice in education and training in the Atlantic space since the XVIIIth century and works on the redesign of forms of justice and the State in the context of the welfare state crisis.

Henry Giroux taught high school history in Barrington, Rhode Island from 1968 to 1975. Giroux received his Doctorate from Carnegie-Mellon in 1977. He then became Professor of Education at Boston University from 1977 to 1983. In 1983 he became Professor of Education and Renowned Scholar in Residence at Miami University in Oxford, Ohio where he also served as

Director at the Center for Education and Cultural Studies. He moved to Penn State University where he took up the Waterbury Chair Professorship from 1992 to May 2004. He also served as the Director of the Waterbury Forum in Education and Cultural Studies. He moved to McMaster University in May 2004, where he currently holds the Global Television Network Chair in Communication Studies.

Panayota Gounari is Assistant Professor of Applied Linguistics at the University of Massachusetts, Boston. She holds a PhD in Cultural Studies in Education from Pennsylvania State University. Her primary areas of interest include language policy, linguistic hegemony and immigration, critical discourse analysis, the role of language in social change and the construction of human agency/democratic spaces as well as the implications for critical pedagogy. Her publications include: *The Hegemony of English* with Donaldo Macedo and Bessie Dendrinos (Paradigm, 2003); and *The Globalization of Racism*, (Paradigm, 2006).

Kaye Haw is Principal Research Fellow at the University of Nottingham. She has spent her research career working with difficult and hard-to-reach groups on sensitive issues. Her career has been driven by a methodological interest in obtaining access to groups that have been traditionally silenced and, through a participatory research process, ensure their 'voices' are articulated and heard in arenas where this would not normally be the case. She is particularly interested in a range of educational and social issues that have affected or affect members of urban communities.

Romuald Normand is a High Certificated Teacher in Social Sciences and Lecturer in Sociology. He is currently at the Institut National de Recherche Pédagogique, Lyon, France. He is a member and a coordinator of NESSE (The Network of Experts in Social Sciences for Education) in collaboration with the General Direction of Education and Culture (European Commission). He participates also in the works of the Redaction Committee of the journal *Education & Sociétés*, and he is a member of the Scientific Committee of the French Association of Administrators in Education.

João Paraskeva is a graduate in Humanities (Portuguese, Latin, and Greek) from the Universidade Católica Portuguesa and a Masters in Education specialising in curriculum development from the Universidade do Minho. He taught at the Universidade do Minho and now teaches at the University of Massachesetts – Dartmouth. He is an author of publications in the area of education, politics and culture. His books include: *A Dinâmica dos Conflitos Ideológicos e Culturais na Fundamentação do Currículo*; *Currículo: factos e significações* with José Carlos Morgado; and *(Re)Visão Curricular do Ensino Secundário* with José Carlos Morgado.

Cathie Pearce is Research Fellow at the Education and Social Research Institute at Manchester Metropolitan University. Having been a Senior Lecturer in Education at MMU for four years, she moved to a full-time research post in September 2006. She has had a broad range of teaching experiences in inner-city primary schools and has recently completed her PhD 'Experiencing and Experimenting with Pedagogies and Research'. She has been involved in a number of research projects which have focused on community, inclusion and pedagogical issues within multi-professional contexts. Her particular research interests lie in the inter-relationships between theory and practice, research methodologies and reflexivity.

Concepción Sánchez Blanco is Professor at the Faculty of Educational Science at the University of A Coruña, Spain, in the Department for Pedagogy and Didactics. She has published papers focusing on violence and childhood, as well as books including the following: *Early Childhood Education Dilemmas*, vol. I. (M.C.E.P, 2000); *A Critique of Early Childhood Education: Reform, Research, Innovation and Teacher Training*, vol. 2. (M.C.E.P, 2001); *Physical Violence and the Construction of Identities: Proposals on Critical Reflections for Nursery Schools*, (Graó, 2006).

Gurnam Singh works in the Faculty of Health and Life Sciences at Coventry University as a Senior Lecturer in Social Work and Teaching Fellow. The central focus of his research has led him to explore the interface between theory and practice and how, in particular, anti-oppressive ideas and concepts become translated, interpreted and reflected in the actions of individuals and organizations. Recent publications include: 'Emancipatory discourses of Sikhism: a critical perspective', in: *Sikh Formations: Religion, Culture, Theory*. vol. 2, no. 1 (2006); 'Anti-racist social work and postmodernism', in: M. Todd and M. Farrar (eds) *Teaching 'Race' in Social Sciences: New Contexts, New Approaches* (BSA/C-SAP, 2006); with S. Cowden 'The "user" friend, foe or fetish? A critical exploration of user involvement' in *Health and Social Care*, 26(4)(2006); and *Supporting Black and Minority Ethnic Practice* (Teachers/Assessors: Practice Learning Taskforce, Department of Health, 2006).

Loïc Wacquant is Professor of Sociology at the University of California in Berkeley and Researcher at the Centre de Sociologie Européene in Paris. His interests comprise urban marginality, ethnoracial domination, incarnation, the penal state, and social theory and the politics of reason. His recent books include: *Body and Soul: Notebooks of an Apprentice Boxer* (2004); *Pierre Bourdieu and Democratic Politics: the Mystery of Ministry* (2005); *Urban Outcasts: A Comparative Sociology of Advanced Marginality* (2008); and *Punishing the Poor: The Neoliberal Government of Social Insecurity* (2008). He is a co-founder and past editor of the interdisciplinary journal *Ethnography* and recipient of the 2008 Lewis Coser Award of the American Sociological Association.

Introduction

If there was no violence, would nation states and all their institutional and political forms exist? Or is this the kind of question that should not be asked by researchers? If research is thought of as an empirical investigation of contemporary conditions there is no experimental design that could answer such a question. Yet, all the same, it is the kind of question that radically displaces the taken-for-granted 'reality' of the 'nation' as a normal and natural form of social organization, and opens up the possibility of other forms where violence is not the organizing force of social reality. The chapters of this book, in their different ways, radically challenge perceptions of the normal and the natural. All conceptions of the real, the right and the good are open therefore to critique, challenge and reformulation. It begins and ends in everyday experience.

What is involved in researching violence? Take, for example, how violence structures communities. In order to address a serious gang problem in the housing estates of one local area, a football 'Estates League' was set up by the local football club. Its object was:

> ... to break down the barriers between the kids, you know, across the different estates and the different areas. And it could be as simple as a road that splits the two estates and there's hostility. So you use football as the level playing field to do that.
> (interview by Schostak for Barclays Spaces for Sports 2008)

A geographical area is not simply a neutral area empirically composed through sense experiences. It is also symbolically structured. For example:

> It's all territorial. We have two Pakistani groups literally divided by one street, called Taverners Road and if you live where the MUGA [multi-use games area] is you're classed as 'top end' and if you live past [...] Road you're 'bottom end'. And top end and bottom end are constantly in conflict.
> (interview by Ramwell for Barclays Spaces for Sports 2008)

It is not just the geography and architecture of an area that is seen but its social and cultural reality as a 'picture in the head' (Lippmann 1922), a picture composed of territories defined by animosities, controlled and contested by different gangs, leaders and powers. The role of this 'picture' in relation to 'reality' according to Lippmann, who was concerned with how public opinion is formed and managed, is fundamental to how people conceive of and act in the world:

> For the real environment is altogether too big, too complex, and too fleeting for direct acquaintance. We are not equipped to deal with so much subtlety, so much variety, so many permutations and combinations. And although we have to act in that environment, we have to reconstruct it on a simpler model before we can manage with it. To traverse the world men must have maps of the world.
>
> (Lippmann 1922: 10–11)

But whose map, and in whose interests? The danger, according to Lippmann, is to be aware of when the map has already been, as it were, tampered with, and some idealized or utopic and misleading landscape has been sketched out. The task, in Lippmann's view, is to ensure that the maps or pictures that people have in their heads accord with those required by the elite groups leading and representing the people in democracies. He called it 'the manufacture of consent', a phrase later taken up by Herman and Chomsky (1988) in their analysis of the influence of the media. For Lippmann, this manufacture of consent was essential to the development of democracy because in his view any notion that there was a reality to public debate as a basis for democracy was a fantasy – indeed, the public could only be a 'phantom public' (Lippmann 1927). This view of the 'public' when linked to contemporary developments in neoliberal views of and practices of democracy is critical to formulating what is meant by radical research.

Radical research is intimately linked to the creation of public spaces where a wide range of people are able to voice their views, engage in debate and contribute to the making of decisions concerning policy and action. However, as Lippmann argued, the social, economic and political realities of life are immensely complex. People's everyday lives are riddled with contradictions. Globally they can be seen underpinning the great chasms separating the wealthy, the safe and the healthy from the poor, the bloodied and the ill. Individually, there are the hopes for fairness alongside the fear of failure, the desire for a better life as well as the anxiety that comes with ever-present risks. On each side of each contradiction, claims for universal rights are mixed with demands for special consideration. Under what conditions do experienced contradictions explode into violence? When and for whom is violence employed as an acceptable strategy of control? No such questions can be answered in ways acceptable to, and understandable by, all unless there is a methodology, a framework of research, a publicly accessible and assessable ground for critique and for describing the 'reality' of complaints, of demands and of judgements. Perhaps it is an impossible task. However, it is the aim – that is, the impossible goal – of all research that seeks to address both the plight and the potential of being alive. Can the features of a methodology sensitive enough and radical enough to the demands of such an aim be sketched and made the basis of projects that can create a difference in the lives of people subjected to 'violence'?

Look around the contemporary world. The stakes are high. Harber (2004) has described the ways in which schools around the world have created some of the conditions in which violence is engaged in and perpetuated. Or, explore the connections between political philosophy and political policy as in Norton's (2004) account of the rise of neoliberal politics and American foreign policy. Or, follow Chomsky's indefatigable production of book after book detailing the violence and injustice of state policies and corporate practices. Or, indeed, read such policy documents as the 2008 WHO report from the Committee on the Social Determinants of Health which states: "Social injustice is killing people on a grand scale". Or, simply open today's newspaper, or listen to today's news broadcast or search the Internet for news items with combinations of such key words as: 'violence', 'rights', 'power', 'corporate power', 'state power', 'communities', 'racism', 'abuse', 'war', 'terror', 'social justice' and so on.

In short, at stake for individuals, is their life.

> Akhar, he's been here a year, and it was only three weeks ago during an art lesson, a lesson about a door, "you open a door and what do you see?" He was working with one of our teaching assistants, and just suddenly opened up to her twelve months on, here's a child who came here to learn English, but that was not his only difficulty, and he started to tell the teaching assistant about doors, and how he'd hide behind doors and that his brother was arrested and taken to the police station, and was killed in there ... but it's taken 12 months for us to realise what had happened to him when he'd left Iraq ... you don't know how many years he's been told not to speak about it, he's had to come to terms with his older brother's murder, who was only about 18.
>
> (Schostak *et al.* 2004)

There is so much here. It is absolutely about the local day-to-day practice of the teacher; the singular, unique life that is Akhar; as well as the global power structures and competing universal claims focusing around national interest, religious independence and liberal democracy that have pierced his life. How can research respond to this?

The response begins in the smallest – and thereby the hardest – of all steps. It is about learning how to create the radical conditions under which the tiniest of steps may be made that bring into necessary debate the particular and the universal that is inextricably linked in every demand and to bring into action the rights of individuals in the immediate context of their everyday lives. Each of the authors of this book, in their different ways, contributes to this task. From them can be learnt the ways in which research can create the conditions for the radical.

Learning to create the conditions of the radical

Each chapter contributes to the work of the radical in two ways. The first is through adopting the form of the radical, that is, its methodological stance. The second is through the very substance of the research, its engagement with the real and how it produces public space(s) and the 'public(s)'. In order to frame the discussions of the contributors, Chapter 1 explores the political dimensions of methodological design in relation to violence and rights. Without a sense of the 'public' there is also no sense of the objective, the valid, the generalizable or universal as a framework for the generation of evidence, analysis, theory or critique. Critical to researching violence is the meaning given to 'power' from the viewpoints of (a) Power, that is, the consolidated organization of power by nation states, their governments and by the key national and transnational organizations that regulate the behaviours of people and (b) the viewpoints of individuals and the powers they have in terms of thinking, imagining, feeling, willing and acting. The experience and interpretation of an act as being 'violent' or the 'legitimate use of force' or 'only play' and so on will differ according to viewpoint. The question is whether research is to be employed to reinforce Power's control over individuals, or whether research can contribute to the development of the powers of individuals to engage with each other peacefully and justly.

In Chapter 2 Derouet considers the spaces of justice in the contexts of schooling and lifelong learning from the very different perspectives of equality and the training of competitive elites. Justice is configured variously as equal opportunities, equal outcomes, equity instead of equality, accountability and recognition of differences. But have these spaces of justice been commandeered into "concepts and instruments of the managerial state" (see p. 32) by the political machinery? What is the way forward? Is it by reconfiguring the manipulated spaces into others that orientate learning towards real-life challenges whilst "keeping the humanistic educational project aside from production imperatives" (see p. 36)? Education, it may be argued, underpins conceptions of justice and politics upon which making a critique of everyday circumstances depends. How do contemporary forms of democracy shape the practices in schools and colleges and how can education in a broader sense assure democratic practice?

The institutions of everyday life are where power is consolidated and 'naturalized' until the violence of Power is rendered invisible. How then can research make such 'naturalized' structures and processes of violence visible? In Chapter 3 Burman focuses on the service provision for Pakistani women who seek asylum, whether they are in Pakistan or within the UK, in order to provide insights into the various forms of violence that can be found in ethical-political spaces. The women are subjected to 'pathologizing gazes' from a range of standpoints, which differ between two nation states. The exploration of these ethical-political spaces, however, opens up another space, that of the rhetorical through which forms of representation render these women 'victims' by, for example, closing down alternative options towards democratic and just decision-making processes. Burman offers a principled approach to engaging in research with people.

The methodological discussion in Section *i* sets the issues raised in both Chapters 2 and 3 into a discussion of the relation of research to the production of 'public space', that is, a space in which the powers of individuals count democratically. For purposes of emancipatory practice, the nature of what counts as 'public space' is critical to the validity, objectivity and generalizability of research as it is to the notion of 'justice'.

Normand develops the theme of the space of justice in Chapter 4 with his narrative of how the headscarf or bandana of a young minority girl comes under the gaze of authority, the institution, the teaching profession and, indeed, the nation state. The perspective for his analysis is informed from an Arendtian 'space of appearance' which is "the essence of polis as a mode of living together". In "a common space known as a school", the very act of blurring the boundaries between what is an acceptable act and what is an unacceptable act conspired to destabilize and threaten justice and modes of living together.

In the fifth chapter Singh writes of black minority ethnic groups whose very existence attracts "the gaze of state authorities and professionals" (see p. 87), an almost archetypal labelling activity through the application of 'deficit models', individually or collectively, and the elision of the lives of these groups into "the 'problem' of immigration and integration" (see p. 88). How can the power relationship between researcher and subject be equalized? Can one truly give voice to the oppressed, the less dominant, the less significant? Where does interpretation end and reconstruction begin? What does "an emancipatory research paradigm" (see p. 87) look like? Can it take "degrees of ontological separation" (see p. 97) into account in a positive and emancipatory way?

In Blanco's Chapter 6, the violence in the playground that young children are subject to in schools is seen ethnographically. She calls upon notions of social justice to open up textual spaces whereby the voices and subjectivities of children come to be heard and rendered visible. It is at the level of intimate, face-to-face relationships, even in a primary school playground, where battles for equality and freedom are played out.

The discussion in Section *ii*, drawing upon Chapters 4 to 6, focuses more upon the intricacies of contestation where boundaries are challenged, Power(s) resist and categories become 'shifty'; that is, where Power is unhinged and individuals exercise their powers to redefine, transform and create the conditions for alternative social forms. In the gaps that open up, what are the methodological possibilities for the emergence of alternative 'spheres of just-ice' and thus of a new model of education and democratic practice? How may research methodology be employed to open up the spaces of questioning and critique?

In Chapter 7, Paraskeva turns to ways in which two spaces embedded in the cultures of the West intertwine and shape each other. He argues that the media is heavily implicated in how it shapes violence that occurs in schools. Further, so ubiquitous, subversive and insidious is this shaping by the media of school spaces that the boundaries between violence and non-violence have become blurred. He addresses the likely foundational motives behind school violence in order to bring about a better understanding which, in turn, will lead to "a democratization of knowledge" (see p. 125) so essential to an intricate process of meaning making.

Taking a social-action participatory research perspective, Haw argues in Chapter 8 for the need to provide a way of enabling the voice of minority communities to be heard. The research makes use of video "as a community consultation tool". This approach creates "a series of spaces for critical dialogue and action" that allow forms of agency to emerge in order to reconfigure the biological and psychological models, so dominant in criminology, that limit the lived world to a discussion of probabilities and correlations that runs along-side a language of causality. An analytic approach that looks at a 'narrative moment' of individuals relates the external lived worlds of the young people and their internal 'felt' worlds by embodying the thinking, feeling and practice of their everyday lives.

Pearce explores the configuration and reconfiguration of textual spaces in Chapter 9 by introducing the term 'violency' in order to access what would otherwise be unknown and unthought, and thereby countering the 'limiting of possibilities'. As researchers, it is essential that we avoid trapping ourselves in framings of our own making and continue to problematize our own thinking. How is it that people get identified as other than normal? Rather than either/ or, would a 'politics of emergence' drawing on the radical democratic theories of Rancière, Laclau, Mouffe and others create a place for an ethics of discord to render visible different ways of being?

Wacquant in Chapter 10 analyses the 'violence from above' through which the poor and the destitute are separated from the middle classes and the rich. The boundary between them is increasingly fragile as the gulf between rich and poor progressively widens. Something has to give. Riots may be seen as a "return of the repressed", that is, as the frustrated demands and hopes that are not realistically addressed by the many policies that do nothing to redress the inequalities of wealth.

Section *iii* explores in more depth the intimate relations between a given society and the schools and educational institutions it designs. As children bear society's hopes and fears concerning the future, so schools bear the demands to prepare children for the future. But what kind of future? Or, rather, whose future is at stake if children represent the potential for change? Do children become the battleground, the contested space, with schools as the instruments to do battle? This section further explores the spaces research methodologies can open up and the extent of political challenges that they reveal.

It is currently, in Gounari's view, as outlined in Chapter 11, a "self-constructed [...] political and ideological Dark Age" (see p. 180), where the manufacture of fear of the next big threat keeps the people in their homes, apathetic, defenceless and vulnerable. The manufacture of fear and danger justify the closing down of the universe of politics and shrink public spaces, resulting in the creation of 'anti-politics' when: "the welfare state makes way for the warfare state". In the name of 'homeland security' and what is misnamed as 'democracy' and 'freedom', pre-emptive strikes, wars, and the curtailing of civil liberties and questioning become almost an unpatriotic act. In a climate where Power exerts such legitimizing guidance and justification, we find ourselves located in that Arendtian space in which power has shifted sinisterly and malevolently into violence.

In Chapter 12 Giroux insists that a nation can be seriously threatened from inside as well as from outside. The threats from outside, whatever the form they take, are visible to all inasmuch as they are explicitly and repeatedly represented in the nation's media and thus remain in the public eye. The invisible threats from inside comprize the powerful alliances formed by corporate bodies with like-minded goals, such as: government agencies, the military and the defence industries. All of these have a vested interest in promoting and selling a very particular vision of a better world to the larger population, and the business of arriving at this vision goes on behind doors closed to the public eye, where the boundaries between 'doublespeak' and 'cover-up' are conveniently blurred, almost beyond recognition. Spaces and places of power have been quietly and systematically seized and manhandled into models of domination to infiltrate and turn higher education institutions into a "hypermodern militarized knowledge factory". Since 11 September 2001, it is argued, the persistent, steady trickle has become an acceptable two-way traffic lane and "a biopolitics of militarization" (see p. 199) has substantially emerged, heralding "a crisis in politics" and "a fundamental crisis in democracy" (see p. 205) in which spaces of critique *and* possibility are absent.

Section *iv* further explores the extent to which research, researchers and the institutions that employ them have been co-opted by Power. It also explores the possibilities for avoiding co-option by the state and engaging in strategies for resistance. It argues that in researching issues of violence, academic work involves radically opening up spaces to formulate a language of critical resistance and identify methodological strategies for action by re-imagining politics and the nature of public space.

In the concluding Chapter 13, writing as a fundamental work of research goes well beyond any concept of it being reduced to the text on a page. It is an emancipatory practice. A world is always a space of inscriptions, composed of the sounds of voices, the marks of signs. A world as a space that provides some intelligible unity and grounding to an individual's life is composed and sustained through the ways in which it can be imagined and symbolically represented publicly as well as privately and intimately. Research writing is composed through interactions and engagements with others as a project unfolds. Emancipatory practice writes against the ruling Power, opening up possibilities to create the conditions for public spaces that are inclusive of the voices of all individuals.

References

Harber, C. (2004) *Schooling as Violence: How schools harm pupils and societies*. London: Routledge Falmer.

Herman, E.S. and Chomsky N. (1988) *Manufacturing Consent: The political economy of the mass media*. New York: Pantheon Books, updated 2002.

Lippmann, W. (1922) *Public Opinion*. New York: Harcourt Brace and Company.

Lippmann, W. (1927) *The Phantom Public*. New York: Macmillan.

Norton, A. (2004) *Leo Strauss and the Politics of American Empire*. New Haven and London: Yale University Press.

Schostak, J.F., Schostak, J.R., Piper, H. and Pearce, C. (2004) 'Cultures of death: The challenge for educational action research'. CARN conference, Malaga.

WHO (2008) *Closing the Gap in a Generation: Health equity through action on the social determinants of health*. Final report of the Committee on the Social Determinants of Health, World Health Organization. Available at http://www.who.int/social_determinants/final_report/en/ (accessed August 9, 2009).

Part A

Design, values, violence
and rights

Chapter 1

Values, violence and rights

Jill Schostak and John F. Schostak

Is the function of research the creation of instruments and knowledge for the control of the world about? Or is it to create the conditions for freedom and for creatively engaging with others in order to build social worlds of mutual benefit? Although apparently contrary in aim, each question can draw upon the heritage of the Enlightenment philosophers underpinning the drive towards modernity as liberation from feudal beliefs, traditions and social organization. There was a drive towards mastery over nature, whether this was the formulation of physical laws governing natural processes or control by the mind over the body and its instincts and passions. However, there was also a drive towards liberation, whether on the model of republicanism or a more pragmatic or market form of democracy. Kant expressed the mood and intent of 'enlightenment' powerfully as:

> Nothing is required for this enlightenment, however, except freedom; and the freedom in question is the least harmful of all, namely, the freedom to use reason publicly in all matters.[1]

Furthermore, as Balibar (1994) has proposed, it makes little sense to talk about freedom without also equality as a necessary dimension. To emphasize the point of the co-existence of freedom and liberty he uses the term *égaliberté* (equaliberty). In any hierarchical situation, the subordinate has less freedom than the superior. Thus, freedom can only be attributed to all in the public use of reason if all members of the public are equal. Methodologically, freedom, equality and the use of reason in public are inextricably linked to the furtherance of social justice and democratic practices. Research design that has as its object the use of reason to explore, interpret, understand and engage in productive and creative action to form social realities to the mutual, public benefit of all must include these within its formative and framing principles. This then provides all forms of research radically committed to *égaliberté* in the use of 'reason publicly in all matters' a key criterion for critique both of its own research design and in its examination of social, cultural, political and economic issues. Without criteria statements concerning what counts as data, theories or hypotheses concerning causal relations, or what is 'natural', cannot be assessed. Take for example the following assertions by Margaret Thatcher[2] when she was Prime Minister of the UK:

> I think we have gone through a period when too many children and people have been given to understand "I have a problem, it is the Government's job to cope with it!" or "I have a problem, I will go and get a grant to cope with it!" "I am homeless, the Government must house me!" and so they are casting their problems on society and who is society? There is no such thing!

The task as she saw it, along with Reagan, the US President at the time, was to reduce the public sector and the role of government and unfetter the market because, as she repeated, "There is no such thing as society". Such views were underpinned by the arguments of Freidman and Hayek's monetarist, free market economics and in particular the views of Carl Schmitt and Leo Strauss, many of whose students made their way into positions of power in the Reagan and Bush governments (Norton 2004). Indeed, Carl Schmitt's (1996) conception of the political as formed in terms of friends and enemies can be seen in Huntington's (1993, 1996) clash of civilizations and most notoriously in Bush's 'Axis of Evil'[3] referring to those primarily Middle Eastern, Islamic countries seen as the sponsors of terror that led to the destruction of the World Trade Center twin towers on 11 September 2001.

Of significance in the research context is the antagonism, the mutual exclusivity of viewpoints that give each other no space for yet another alternative, or a possible shared public space of debate. How the 'public' is conceptualized is methodologically critical. If, at one extreme, the 'public' is a phantom (Lippmann 1927) and if, "Ours must be a leadership democracy administered by the intelligent minority who know how to regiment and guide the masses," (Bernays 1928: 127) then effectively the public is the elite, the 'intelligent minority' who manipulate the voting citizenry, which in turn is less than the total number of people of all ages and all nationalities living and working in a given nation state. If, however, the public is conceived as the totality of people, then the range of views, interests, values and demands necessarily increases. Different kinds of social arrangements for the accomplishment of debate, negotiation, decision making and action to those of elite forms of management will have to be found. And this is where research has its radical focus in the formation of those spaces where the multiplicity of voices can act to create a public fora of debate, decision and action.

The radical democracy of Laclau and Mouffe explored in their various writings provides a further attempt to understand and propose the necessary conditions under which the numerous demands, opposing views and conflicting values can be brought into a public space in such a way that the antagonisms do not break out into violence and war but are managed in a political framework where voices are treated equally and thus no elite is able to dominate, lead or regiment the 'public mind'. In the variety of ways that people organize their relations, the design of research must take into account what is at stake for people when 'value', 'knowledge', 'truth' and 'agency' are constructed, expressed, recognized, asserted and realized; or denied and rendered invisible or inaudible in political, social and cultural contexts. How research methodology is defined is critical in being able to take fully into account as 'data'/'evidence', that is, the 'visible' in terms of public/political decision making and the 'invisible' (Rancière 2004; see also Chapter 9): those who are 'rich' in resources, and those who are 'poor' (Rancière 2003). The work of radical research methodologies is to reveal the nature of the regimes underlying social organization and the extent to which they promote the freedom and equality necessary for the creation of a public space where all can be equally heard and equally taken into account – that is, the politics and methodologies of democracy.

Methodology, values, violence and rights

Research methodology cannot be extricated from questions of democracy, people's rights, and their suppression through violence. Each of the following chapters, in their different ways, deals with the substantial issues of violence (that is, content), emancipation, democratic practices and the methodological processes through which content both emerges and is explored analytically and critically and is potentially transformed through engagement in public spaces. The key terms of such radical research methodologies include:

- voice
- subjectivity
- objectivity
- validity
- reliability
- representation – qualitative, quantitative
- analysis
- meaning – interpretation
- critique
- the relation between particular or singular instances and conceptions of generalization and universalization
- evidence and processes of revealing that which is 'hidden'
- ethics
- trust
- truth/law
- action/engagement/manipulation of circumstances.

Methodology relates to the ways in which such issues as these are put together with the methods (observation, interview, artefact collection, manipulation of circumstances) through which data is constructed and analysed to produce discussions, arguments, representations, theories, models, findings and recommendations. Throughout, it is the 'use of reason publicly in all matters' that constitutes the rigour of the research.

Methodologically, the conditions for the creation of public space for the use of reason begin with the recognition of the other as co-productive of social organization of any kind. Without such recognition there is no 'social', only an 'ego' caught in a self-reflective gaze as in a mirror – all objects of such a gaze are merely reflections of the self and its experiences of subjective organization. To see the mirroring – and the mirror – would require a recognition of its 'otherness' and its co-production of the ego and its subjective landscape. Whether it is a Cartesian-like doubt, a Husserlian-like suspension of belief or a Freudian-like suspicion, the recognition of an otherness emerges, whether an otherness that can play tricks or lead astray, or an otherness that despite its trickery points always to a reality, an existence, a being that is in some way independent of any thought about it. Kant made a distinction between the 'thing-in-itself' (noumenon) and the appearance that the 'thing' takes in consciousness (phenomenon) that is both useful and problematic. It is useful in that it enables researchers to concentrate on what appears to a public and what can be made public. It is problematic because what appears (representations in consciousness) is always, as it were, empty. That is to say, the representation is always lacking. It can never satisfy in the sense that the representation of food in the mind does not feed the body.

Like food, 'voice', and not its representation by some elite group, is an essential condition of the public; that is to say, voice has the power to constitute the public and is thus fundamental to the logic of social action and therefore of any methodology for studying and engaging with the social. Voice constitutes the protagonists, the co-producers, the theatre, the validity and the objectivity of what is enacted, seen, heard and named. Essential to voice is freedom, the freedom to create itself in public. The public then is the way in which the multiplicities of speaking subjects freely making their particular demands, whether individually or collectively in groups, make a space within which they come to see themselves, in their multiplicities, as makers of a world. This 'making of a world' can be seen in the action taken by some people in Dartford who, as children in the 1970s, started skateboarding. When they grew up they were still skateboarding and collectively started a movement to build a skateboard park in their local area. Their story is told on *YouTube*: "Historically we've never had anything in Dartford to skate. There weren't any fantastic street spots. And there hasn't been anything round here to skate for, well nothing close by unless you want count London till five years ago we started up a movement to get a skatepark built in Dartford".[4]

And then the story of skateboarding in Dartford and the building of the skatepark begins as various people tell their part in it. One says, "As far as

I know people have been skateboarding in Dartford since skateboarding first became big in the late 70s". There is thus a considerable history to draw upon. From a police point of view, there were "issues of youngsters cycling round the town centre particularly around certain areas, or on their skateboards". So an approach was made by some skateboarders to the local council and "councillors actually started talking to the skate users and the, the end users, which is pretty positive". At the time "none of us on the council knew anything about skateboarding". The councillors were then invited to see what was happening. Meeting the people involved convinced the councillors. A sum of £75,000 was set aside for the project by Dartford Council. Then Groundwork indicated there was also money from Barclays Spaces for Sports available. David Smith as Sponsorship PR manager then described the role of the programme where "we really look to develop sites that reflect what communities in those areas actually want so if they want a skatepark or a BMX track then that's what we'll look to provide them with". The site as a whole cost £120,000 with £50,000 from Barclays and £70,000 from the council.

(MMU 2008)

This is a simple illustration of the creation of a 'public', where the voices of a group perceived as problematic created an audience, and demanded to be heard in a space that had not previously considered them as anything other than noise or trouble. As in most such cases, the demand was one that eventually locked into the interests of powerful others, in this case, the need to resolve a local youth problem which – fortunately – matched the corporate social responsibility agenda of a bank.

The approach employed was typical of what may be called, following Laclau and Mouffe (1985), an hegemonic strategy. That is, the interests of different groups are aligned around at least one issue in common. The more powerful the groups, the more likely the strategy is to succeed. There is a similarity here with a methodological approach to generating consensus about the features and existence or otherwise of a given object, a process often known as 'triangulation'. Triangulation involves coordinating different views and different methods that are directed towards a given phenomenon or object. In the ways that people talk about it and act towards it thus becomes 'objective' for a given public. In research terms, the objectivity, validity, accuracy of description and 'truth' of a phenomenon increases to the extent that it can be substantiated by the senses (seeing, touching, smelling, hearing, tasting), that it is common to the accounts given by multiple witnesses and that it is researchable through the use of different methods, whether qualitative or quantitative. For example, skateboarding – what is it? Is it a sport or a nuisance undertaken by young people out to make trouble? How do people talk about it? What is the range of views? Who are the 'dramatis personae' – the list of 'characters' and of 'subject positions' that they can adopt towards each other? How do they see each other – as friends, as enemies, as onlookers, as 'problems', as …? How do they act towards each other? What are the histories of events or 'things that happen' that each person can tell? Pictures begin to emerge of the different ways in which each of the protagonists 'see' the world about and the place that skateboarding has in this. It provides a way of analyzing how social and symbolic space is configured in relation to physical space. It also provides a way of seeing how people can act upon these configurations of space, place, identity and event in order to reproduce them, resist them or change them.

Such configurations are dynamic and the typical use of 'triangulation' can freeze the dynamism into fixed-frame analyses of objects as can happen in grounded theory (Glaser and Strauss 1967; Strauss and Corbin 1998) where too often data from interviews and observations is refined into increasingly high-level abstractions (Charmaz 2006). It is even more evident in statistical analyses where snapshots of opinions are taken over a particular time period, or in laboratory-style approaches where behaviours are studied out of their social context or in randomized controlled trials (RCTs) where the allocation of people and social objects to categories becomes increasingly problematic as the research focuses on cultural phenomena rather than physical phenomena, or even spurious as the dynamics and real differences and nuances relating to individuals, objects, processes and structures are overlooked, ignored or rejected.

Skateboarding and other street games provide a useful way of thinking about the dynamics of social spaces (Schostak and Schostak 2007). A pavement with its kerbs provides a safe space for pedestrians. The rules relating to being a pedestrian include keeping to the walkway and keeping moving. People – particularly young people who look 'rough' and who regularly hang around on street corners – become a focus of attention by the police who want to 'move them on'. Their act of 'hanging around' becomes a social object to be talked about and acted upon. By their presence, these young people have created territory over which they can exert their power. Similarly, some young people with a ball, kicking it or throwing it from one to another, create a space that prevents others from walking through. In each case it is a game space where one individual or one group is set against another, moves are made that can be countered. Strategies and tactics relating to the game space evolve. The space, the 'rules of play', the differences in power, the courses of action, the histories of 'what happened' can all be described, analyzed, theorized.

Going back to the Dartford example, in the early days young people would seek any surface or edge provided by the architecture of the local area as a place to skateboard. Their use of those surfaces of course contravened 'normal use' and became defined as a nuisance. It attracted the attention of the police and so various tactics had to be employed to prevent and move them on. The skateboard space could not be incorporated into public space, yet it only existed because of it. In this sense, the 'public', through which the 'normal' is defined, excluded the young people involved in skateboarding. From that point of view, their actions could only be seen as 'trouble' and a 'public nuisance'. From a research point of view, a triangulation of views as between, for example, local residents, business interests, the police and social workers would focus in on skateboarding as a problem. However, another triangulation can be made with those involved in skateboarding who would probably shift the 'problem' to a lack of facilities and perhaps a sense of harassment by police. In this simplified example, a sense of 'sides', of contest between clearly definable protagonists, emerges. To include the views of each 'side' in the process of triangulation challenges both the notion of 'normal' and the notion of the 'public' that defines the 'normal'. The 'public' is defined by the voices that are included in its ambit as those having interests or demands that can be counted as meaningful, objective and rational in terms of being legitimate, whether in the context of tradition or the law.

By involving and persuading the political elite the Dartford skateboarders expanded the range of publicly audible voices. In the process there was a modification of each identity in relation to the other. Moreover, there was a modification in the conception of the public and of the value of skateboarding itself. The 'public', then, is composed of a coordination of views towards particular 'objects'. Initially, the views were in antagonistic relationships: the skateboarders were viewed as problems by the police, or as having nothing worth saying by the politicians, and the skateboarders saw the police and the politicians as being against them. However, as a space was created where the skateboarders could both talk about and also demonstrate the skill and the dedication required for skateboarding, the positive social implications became apparent. Skateboarding was transformed from one object to another, from a problem to a solution. Politically this has the form of the interweaving (*symploke*) of views, interests and demands into a unity; it is an hegemonic process. In research terms, the reformation of public space could be witnessed, recorded and analyzed in terms of a triangulation of observation, performance and dialogue that resulted in the emergence of a new space of exchange through which judgement could be informed, where decisions could be made and collective action undertaken.

The Dartford example shows the constitutive process whereby individuals actively create forms of social organization rather than merely reproduce them. This relates to two forms of power as distinguished by Negri (1991): 'Power' as the "centralised, mediating, transcendental force of command" and 'power' as "the local, immediate, actual force of constitution" (Hardt in Negri 1991: xiii). This distinction is critical to research methodology since contemporary forms of leadership democracy employ research to aid in the "regimentation of the public mind" (Bernays 1928). As a pioneer in public relations, Lippmann (1922) focused on the formation of habits of mind, stereotypes, and taken-for-granted values. That is to say, research expertise was employed to manufacture or engineer consent (Bernays 1928). The focus then was strictly upon the reinforcement of Power, in Negri's terms, not upon the constituting force of the power of individuals to create the terms of their everyday life.

Where Power universalizes, power particularizes. The conflict is mirrored in Mead's (1934) theorization of the self as divided between the 'I' as a creative, impulsive – indeed, constitutive – force and the 'me' as constituted by the responses of 'significant others' (for example, mother, father, friends, teachers and so on) in the lives of individuals. Where the 'I' is individual, the 'me' is formed of the general, the typical, the habitual – as it were, an internalized Power. Mead's work was developed as 'symbolic interactionism' (Blumer 1969), an approach that focused minutely upon the processes and typical structures of everyday life. The danger was well pointed out by Wrong's (1961) concern that research was focusing upon the 'me' rather than the creative, spontaneous dimensions, thus producing an 'oversocialized' conception of people. A similar argument could be applied to those versions of phenomenology stemming from Schutz's (1976) focus on the everyday world that is "taken for granted until further notice". Or, it can be seen in Goffman's 'presentation of self' in every-day life, or indeed, in the 'rational accounting' practices of ethnomethodology (Garfinkel 1967; Cicourel 1964). Although each can be said to privilege the processes through which everyday life is constructed and thereby pave the way for its deconstruction and transformation, these equally provide the materials for the shaping of behaviour by the public relations industry as advocated by Lippmann and Bernays.

Rather than skateboarding, this issue can be more critically discussed in terms of immigration. 'Immigrant' and 'illegal immigrant' are constructed categories that serve the purpose of excluding people from certain rights enjoyed by nationals (see Chapter 3). The public is reduced to those who are citizens of a particular nation state. The issue then is how does one construct and deconstruct the 'public' as a way of defining the status of those who live in a country but are not included as its 'public'? The very structures, discourses and taken-for-granted practices through which everyday life is constructed become resources for manipulation at both local and global levels. The con-cept of 'nation' becomes available for use as a block against opening public space to include the voice of 'non-nationals'. Where capital may flow largely unregulated between nations to the benefit of elites, people defined as 'labour' are strictly regulated, to the benefit of elites who can exploit the wage differ-entials that can be constructed. At one level the symbol of the 'nation' is a call to unity, a way of collectivizing a mass of people around a common interest to make a demand. At another, it divides people who have essentially the same interests but are defined as belonging to different nations. At yet another, it can become the focus of hatreds and fears in relation to what is 'ours' or what is 'pure'. In this logic, the most right belongs to those who are most 'pure' – the real 'British', for example. In Gounari's Chapter 11 we see this discussed as a politics of fear. Thus, an emancipatory politics has to be coextensive with an ethics that raises issues of 'fairness' alongside 'rights'. Emancipatory research therefore cannot disassociate itself from key political questions by claiming a position of objective indifference.

The very way in which research categorizations are formed have a constituting and confirming effect concerning what counts as the data to be processed as research-based evidence to be drawn upon in debates, the formation of public thinking, judgement(s) and action(s). Dividing the multitude of individuals who inhabit the globe into 'nationals' and 'non-nationals' has political consequences that in turn limit both evidence and the debate that ensues. Taking the issue of immigration as a particular example, research may be deployed to answer questions concerning how many immigrants should be let in per year, what kinds of immigrants in terms of their language skills, employment skills, and how immigrants should be managed in terms of length of residency and the use of identity cards containing what kinds of personal data. With the boundary erected between national and non-national, immigrants can be excluded from democratic processes regarding the use of their tax contributions by denying them the right to vote, unless, of course, they become citizens. In the UK as with many other countries this means taking a citizenship test and an oath of allegiance. Putting this together, there is an overdetermination of the processes creating and reinforcing the key categories that research inherits for its research designs.

This overdetermination can be seen in both the previous skateboarding example and the immigration debate. Both concern a notion of the 'public', both concern an included and an excluded group and in each case there is a conflict of interest and collective action expressing a demand to be treated fairly. The key difference is the role played by nationality. In the case of the skateboarders there was no need to invoke the name of nationality – it could remain latent. Each of the key organizing categories are politically determined, economically determined, legally determined and culturally determined. At the level of psychology they are also determined by the ways in which people frame their identities, the ways in which they value their sense of 'belonging' and the emotional bonds they form with people, places, territories, forms of social organization and so on. Where the interests of the young skateboarders could be legitimately included, those of the immigrants are blocked by the appeal to nationality. Research that is indifferent to the claims made by the protagonists, claiming only to be able to record and provide neutral evidence to each side, has already reinforced the political status quo and thus falls short of the principle of *égaliberté* underpinning the constitution of a 'public' from the multitude of living people in the use of reason publicly in all matters:

> Freedom, the true one, the whole one, which we love and which we live and die for, constitutes the world directly, immediately. Multiplicity is mediated not by law but by the constitutive process. And the constitution of freedom is always revolutionary.
>
> (Negri 1991: xxi)

There is a tension between the already constituted nature of nationally organized social forms and the creative free constitution of new forms. Triangulation works differently in each case. On the one hand, it draws upon the range of ready-made identities, roles and publicly legitimated voices to objectify the taken-for-granted or policy-driven organizing categories of things, processes, values, principles, structures and practices. In this sense it works imminently – that is to say, it stays inside the boundaries of a given social form or system. It does not provide an external critique because there is no recognizable valid external point. There is no external point because it does not recognize the constituting powers of individuals as members of a 'multitude' extending beyond a given concept of 'nation', or of some vast notion of 'humanity' beyond any concept of nation or other law enforcing Power, or perhaps wider still in an ecological sense of 'life' being the ultimate standpoint through which social and material forms are brought into being as a basis for the mutual organization of powers for mutual benefits. If this is so, then Nancy Fraser draws the political consequence:

> All told, then, there do not seem to be any conceptual (as opposed to empirical) barriers to the possibility of a socially egalitarian, multicultural society that is also a participatory democracy. But this will necessarily be a society with many different publics, including at least one public in which participants can deliberate as peers across lines of difference about policy that concerns them all.
>
> (Fraser 1997: 84–5)

The conceptual dimension is critical to the construction of research where research, as has been argued, has a major constitutive role to play in the formation of what counts as the public/s in which reason may be used for all matters. If research is deprived of its constitutive role in all conceptual matters then, it becomes a slave to the dominant pre-existent organization(s) of Power(s) and its manipulation of 'experts', 'expertise' and the production of expert evidence. Methodologically, there are therefore choices to be made. There is the choice between privileging one of two processes over the other, between the free acts of constitution (ground up) or the slavish reproduction (top down) of what already exists; or there is the choice of recognizing the constitutive basis to all social forms if they are to continue to exist alongside the creative play of the new. But these 'choices' resolve into a choice between the free and the unfree in social life. Thus, in making the choices, no critique, challenge, or change can be made except by engaging politically. Thus, it is argued, methodology is not politically and ethically neutral. In its challenges and political, ethical engagements is it, itself, a violent act? And, if so, does it become a violence only as a kind of counterviolence employed to redress a 'balance' or to 'right a wrong' or to overcome repressive structures by opening the spaces for the emergence of new emancipatory structures and processes? What needs to be done in order to embed emancipatory structures and processes? Such choices, issues and questions are fundamental to exploring the kinds of violence discussed by the contributors in the following sections.

References

Balibar, E. (1994) '"Rights of man" and "rights of the citizen": The modern dialectic of equality and freedom', in E. Balibar, *Masses, Classes, Ideas: Studies on politics and philosophy before and after Marx*. New York: Routledge. The original is: "La proposition de l'égaliberté", in Les Conférences du Perroquet, n° 22, Paris. novembre 1989.

Bernays, E.L. (1928) *Propaganda*. New York: Horace Liveright.

Blumer, H. (1969) *Symbolic Interactionism: Perspective and method*. Englewood Cliffs, NJ: Prentice-Hall.

Charmaz, K. (2006) *Constructing Grounded Theory: A practical guide through qualitative analysis*. Thousand Oaks, CA: Sage.

Cicourel, A.V. (1964) *Method and Measurement in Sociology*. New York: Free Press; London: Collier-Macmillan.

Fraser, N. (1997) *Justice Interruptus: Critical reflections on the "postsocialist" condition*. New York and London: Routledge.

Garfinkel, H. (1967) *Studies in Ethnomethodology*. Englewood Cliffs, NJ: Prentice-Hall.

Glaser, B.G. and Strauss, A.L. (1967) *The Discovery of Grounded Theory: Strategies for qualitative research*. Chicago: Aldine-Atherton.

Huntington, S.P. (1993) 'The clash of civilizations', *Foreign Affairs*, Summer.

Huntington, S.P. (1996) *The Clash of Civilizations and the Remaking of World Order*. London: Simon and Schuster.

Laclau, E. and Mouffe, C. (1985) *Hegemony and Socialist Strategy: Towards a radical democratic politics*. London: Verso.

Lippmann, W. (1922) *Public Opinion*. New York: Harcourt Brace and Company.

Lippmann, W. (1927) *The Phantom Public*, New York: Macmillan.

Mead, G.H. (1934) *Mind, Self and Society*. Chicago: University of Chicago Press.

MMU (2008) Barclays Spaces for Sports Final Report. Available at: http://www.barclays.com/community/spacesforsports/ (accessed August 15, 2009).

Negri, A. (1991) *The Savage Anomaly: The power of Spinoza's metaphysics and politics*, tr. M. Hardt. Minneapolis: University of Minnesota Press.

Norton, A. (2004) *Leo Strauss and the Politics of American Empire*. New Haven and London: Yale University Press.

Rancière, J. (2003) *The Philosopher and His Poor*, ed. A. Parker, tr. J. Drury, C. Oster and A. Parker. Durham and London: Duke University Press; first published 1983, Librairie Arthème Fayard.

Rancière, J. (2004) *The Politics of Aesthetics*, with an afterword by . Zizek, tr. G. Rockhill. London and New York: Continuum.

Schmitt, C. (1996) *The Concept of the Political*, tr. G. Schwab; L. Strauss's notes on Schmitt's essay tr. J. Harvey Lomax; Foreword by T.B. Strong. Chicago and London: The University of Chicago Press.

Schostak, J.F. and Schostak, J.R. (2007) 'Politics, knowledge, identity and community: Methodologist as hitchhiker, skateboarder ...', in *Knowledge Production: The work of educational research in interesting times*, ed. B. Somekh and T.A. Schwandt. London and New York: Routledge.

Schutz, A. (1976) *The Phenomenology of the Social World*, tr. G. Walsh and F. Lehnert. London: Heinemann.

Strauss, A. and Corbin, J. (1998) *Basics of Qualitative Research: Techniques and procedures for developing grounded theory*. Thousand Oaks, CA and London: Sage.

Wrong, D.H. (1961) 'The oversocialised conception of man in modern sociology', *American Sociological Review*, vol. 26, 2, 183–93.

Part B

Research accounts

Introduction to Part B

There will be two strategies to analyzing, synthesizing and discussing the implications of the research issues raised by authors for methodological purposes:

1 Following each paper there will be a short summary written by John and Jill Schostak reflecting upon issues, arguments and questions relevant to researching violence, democracy and people's rights.
2 After two or three chapters there will be a discussion section written by John and Jill Schostak that progressively draws together key strategies involved in designing emancipatory research. In all, there are four discussion sections.

The object of Part B is to provide practical insights into the development and implementation of research designs appropriate to carrying out research in complex, sensitive, controversial and potentially dangerous contexts. The resource to do this is the variety and richness of the individual authors' approaches to their topics.

Chapter 2

Rethinking justice in education and training

Jean-Louis Derouet

Is it the crisis of the democratization of education and training or the crisis of a particular model of democratization? Reflections from the French case

The inclusion of all pupils until the age of 15 or 16 in comprehensive schools and the lengthening of the compulsory schooling period are characteristic of a particular model of democratization that has been endorsed by international organizations since the end of World War II. The implementation of these policies has caused many difficulties, if not perverse effects (Duru-Bellat 2006). The reasons are hard to establish but many of the ideals embraced by left-wing supporters, especially those of equal opportunity, have been broken (Garnier 2008). The sociology of education has largely supported this political project since the 1950s and shared a part of its assumptions accordingly. A new educational project corresponding to the new spirit of capitalism (Boltanski and Chiapello 1999) is emerging: lifelong learning instead of a schooling period completely separate from professional life; no more abstract knowledge but practical skills; the contribution of local authorities and companies to the funding and governance of schools, etc. While effectiveness justifies this new model, its conception of justice is based on accountability. All these changes can therefore be considered within an overall framework – the parallel restructuring of the models of justice and of state forms.

In the field of education, the evolution dates back to the publication of *A Nation at Risk* in the USA in 1983 (NCEE 1983). This report paved the way for new standards: the main objective of education is no longer the pursuit of equality or cohesion within a society but keeping a country's rank in an international competitive environment. Its conclusions, which have since been disputed (Berliner and Biddle 1995), challenged the compensatory policies of 'democratic' presidencies. They were not only costly and ineffective but the training of competitive elites – the main objective – had been neglected. The USA was gradually falling back in world economic competition on account of these mistakes. The report advocated a complete break from the past and new foundations for educational policies. The overall objective was to develop skills reflecting the new organization of the production apparatus – in addition to professional expertise per se, the training of a new type of labour able to adapt and commit themselves to ever-changing assignments was needed. This general philosophy applied to both management and labour training. The report allowed for the reallocation of funds to the training of elites. In turn these elites were redefined. The ultimate objective was to fit future managers into international networks very early. Training standards were all reviewed in the same direction. Unlike what is sometimes suggested, this is by no means a drop in academic standards. To remain competitive in front of the 'Asian tigers', other countries are under the obligation to ever enhance the training of their labour. As stated in the report, the cultural standards that had been at the heart of social democrat policies put working-class students in difficulty and were in no way useful for the tasks they have to perform. Education should go back to basics and also develop the skills necessary to professional life. These recommendations materialized in the development of specific standards that break educational content into skills close to labour qualifications.

This report marks a probably excessive break. Indeed, although it is unattainable, people remain attached to the ideal of equality as it is part and parcel of the democratic conscience. Societies should rather stem the rise in inequalities, a threat to social cohesion. It is in this perspective that the United Kingdom developed a compromise approach – the Third Way (Giddens 1998). Unlike what is sometimes deplored, the Third Way does not reflect the retreat of the state. Admittedly, it no longer assumes some obligations as a high tax pressure brings about the relocation of businesses and jobs. Therefore governments seek to transfer some of the educational spending to local authorities and to families; however this trend is only one aspect of current evolutions. The obligation to achieve specific results entails the implementation of mechanisms that strengthen the power of the states despite a shift from ex-ante monitoring to ex-post assessment in traditionally centralized countries. This new governing approach is labelled 'the managerial state' (Clarke and Newman 1997; Clarke, Gewirtz and McLaughlin 2000).

In the USA, Congress enacted the No Child Left Behind Act (2002), a more balanced compromise. The allocation of funds for the training of elites has been completed and the instruments to monitor this policy are now in place. The three-cycle degree structure – bachelor's, master's and doctorate – is gaining ground (Charlier and Croché 2008) and quality assurance agencies assess the value of training courses to reach the best possible position in the famous Shanghai ranking. However social cohesion and economic efficiency entail attending to students in difficulty. Considerable means are accordingly allotted to schools in disadvantaged neighbourhoods in a clearly liberal orientation – the allocation of funds implies an obligation to achieve specific results. Therefore competition is fierce between schools; teacher pay varies according to student performance; schools may be shut down if poor performance continues, etc.

These orientations have been gradually endorsed by the European Union. During the Lisbon conference in 2000, Europe was set the target of "becoming the *most competitive* and dynamic, *knowledge*-based *economy* in the *world* by 2010" (Fontaine 2000). Thus member states were requested to become mutually accountable for their training performance, which implied the definition of standards for comparison. Then countries were benchmarked by the Open Method of Coordination (OMC), the poorer-performing states being invited to follow the 'good practice' of the better-faring countries (Lawn and Nóvoa 2005).

This approach both continues and departs from the principles of justice that have inspired educational policies since the eighteenth century. The best way to appreciate the shifts and assess their scope is to start from a formal, bidimensional pattern. The first bears on the relations between education and the rest of social life. Historians debate Philippe Ariès' arguments (1973). The perception of the child probably existed before the eighteenth century, but there is no doubt that the Ancien Régime experienced a guild-based educational model that included youth in ordinary social life. It applied to both young farmers or craftsmen and pages in noble homes. This system of education passed on knowledge, techniques, attitudes and values. These were of their own background and each ran the risk of being confined within their original community for life. It was to make individuals autonomous that Enlightenment philosophers opted for the separation of schooling from the social environment – and so knowledge was conceived aside from village superstitions and daily experience; funding and organization were designed to shelter teachers and schools from the pressures of the church or notables, etc. This philosophy clearly departs from what Foucault calls the great confinement (Foucault 1961). It confirms a number of conventions concerning both curricular programmes and teacher-student relationships. It is within this framework that all twentieth-century controversies about the democratization of education occurred. It is significant that the democratization of education should regularly become a topical issue as it has little hold on reality (Derouet-Besson 2004).

Several influences now converge to open this black box. First, the new organization of capitalism based on the provision of competences necessary to economic performance requires the involvement of companies. Second, several left-wing viewpoints are advanced. One explores the difficulties faced by working-class youths. While middle-class children accessed higher education in the 1960s and 1970s, now working-class children are more reluctant to launch into a long period of study. The rational anticipation of their chances of success and their resistance to paper tests may explain this phenomenon. The philosopher Alain (1932) justified the notion of exercise as follows: the student who makes a mistake in arithmetic gets a poor mark while the grocer who makes a mistake in his/her books is ruined. This disconnection from real-life experiences, once designed as a protection, has now become meaningless.

Ballion (1994) interrogated the 'new high school students', that is, those who are concerned by the target of bringing 80 per cent of an age group to baccalaureate level. They have to do odd jobs to pay for their studies and thus realize they are not on an equal footing with their better-off fellow students. At the same time they state that this contact with reality helps them give sense to academic tests.

Ivan Illich (1970) even challenges the relevance of the school institution. His assumptions are based on the experience of southern countries. In his opinion, neither a body of professionals nor the state should get involved in knowledge sharing. He suggests using only new means of communication. This utopia caused a scandal but to some extent the notions of learning companies or regions developed by the new organization of capitalism are in the same vein.

The permanent requirement for justice comes under many different forms. Since the French Revolution, the ideal of justice and the pursuit of equality have been one and the same. Critics have long exposed an abstract conception of justice and sought the means necessary to make it sound more practical. The late twentieth century marked a turning point. Societies realized how difficult it was to attain the objective of equal opportunities. Experts suggested alternatives in the same established framework – moving from equal opportunities to equal outcomes, replacing equality with equity, for example. In turn, accountability and the rising claim for the recognition of differences now set new standards (Taylor 1997; Caillé 2007). While the ideal of justice may materialize into equality, this is only one option among several. In addition, the objective of social equality should not be mistaken with what Luc Boltanski and Laurent Thévenot call the principle of common humanity (1991). The construction of a political city implies that all forms of natural inequality – racism, eugenics, etc. – should be refused. This principle represents a crucial break that does not necessarily turn into a project of social equality. Jules Ferry's speech on equal education is a case in point – he argued that his objective was to provide all men and women with the resources to exercise citizenship via the development of instruction. In no case did it mean challenging social hierarchies.

This formal pattern can give rise to countless discourses. The programme of the first modernity was based on a principle – equal opportunities – that was shared during the twentieth century. To sustain the unattainable ideal of equal conditions and face the demands of production, selection according to merit was introduced. This notion is now sharply criticized (Dubet 2004). In the project of equal opportunities, the pursuit of efficiency is considered an external constraint it is wise to abide by. The second modernity includes the obligation to achieve specific results within the definition of justice. This is one aspect of accountability: being accountable to the state and to taxpayers for the money spent, to users for the quality of the services provided, and so on.

The evolution of the programme of justice underlies that of the state. The ideal of equal opportunities had become part of the welfare state. Education was crucial to the redistribution of riches and social mobility. The managerial state rests on accountability – teachers are accountable to society for how investments in education are returned, schools are accountable to firms for how students are trained, European states are mutually accountable for the education they provide to future workers, etc.

This paper will trace the processes through which the shift from one model to another is made, study similarities and will eventually try to raise the right questions for the future. What is in crisis? Is it the definition of justice, the political project of democratization of education or the mechanisms that have been implemented since the early twentieth century?

Reasoning is based on the French example. France is probably a case in point for how seriously this country took the principle of equal opportunities and implemented systematic mechanisms – the *carte scolaire* (catchment areas), *collège unique* (all junior high school students attend the same classes irrespective of their abilities) – towards making this ideal come true. It is therefore heavily affected by the crisis of this model and the analysis of its evolution provides insight into the situation in other developed countries. The examination of American and British policies will also shed an interesting light.

We have opted for a three-step approach. We first look back on what has been overlooked in the first model of democratization. We then explore current restructuring from a sociological and political perspective and analyze the transition from the welfare state to the managerial state. We finally consider to what extent research will have to evolve to appreciate these shifts and contribute to the construction of a new model of democratization.

Why is the initial model of democratization at a standstill? A reflexive return to its origins

The difficulties of a period are often related to issues unthought of in the previous centuries. It is therefore essential to confront what sociologists notice when historians put things in perspective. François Dubet and Marie Duru-Bellat, among other sociologists, realize the obstacles the initial programme of democratization has faced. The *collège unique* is a place of suffering for all – students and teachers alike (Dubet 2002; Duru-Bellat 2006). How long will teachers remain attached to equal opportunities, an ideal they stand absolutely no chance of achieving? Working-class students themselves refuse to fit into a mould and to learn a body of knowledge that is too remote from their experience.

The works of historians interrogate this situation from several perspectives. Over a long period of time they call for an analysis that recalls Durkheim's (1938) mantra – the goal of education is to pass on a conception of the world and values to the next generation (Caspard 2008). The other objectives – social mobility, economic performance, etc. – only reflect historical contexts and are accordingly subject to change.

Over a shorter period of time, they put the 'great confinement' in perspective. It certainly was necessary to free the education of youths from the authority of the church and the influence of notables. Yet there are blind points, even perverse effects to this organization. In the early twentieth century, several approaches were in competition for the education of working-class youths. It was only gradually that the model of the *école unique* gained ground (Garnier 2008). Other approaches that rested more on working-class experience were dropped. They ranged from social Christianity to anarcho-syndicalism. The investigation into this overlooked field has only started. While it is difficult to identify the political sense of the different programmes, they all share a common point – connecting the democratization project with the world of work. We should look deeper into these different programmes and see the possible links they have with lifelong learning, today's watchword (Tanguy 2005). It is, in any case, necessary to challenge the so far undisputed discourse that presents the *école unique* as the natural translation of the democratization objective. Some left-wing supporters opposed the *école unique* until the 1930s. For instance, the communists, in their class struggle strategy, considered that the *école unique* was the means to fit academically successful working-class children into the bourgeois view of the world and make them contribute to its management. The revolutionary perspective opted for keeping them within a specific educational course and ultimately turning them into the managers of the working-class party and union. It was only when the fascist threat brought the Third International to move on to a Popular Front strategy that the *école unique* was agreed upon. A part of these alternative models remained in state or private vocational education and met success with the working classes (Thivend 2007).

In the early twentieth century, historians evidenced a complex and diverse reality. The organization of education was based on two separate orders. First, the primary order schooled working-class children. The best pupils could access higher primary education whose successful conclusion was marked by the *brevet*, around age 16. Then they occupied middle jobs. Second, the children of the *bourgeoisie* accessed the lower classes of *lycées* and were making their way up to the *baccalaureate*. No transfer from one order to the other was possible as Latin, the most prestigious subject, was not taught in the primary order. In this openly unequal system, working-class pupils could still carry on with their studies thanks to local initiatives (Briand and Chapoulie 1992). The *collèges du peuple* were set up by local authorities and guild chambers. Courses were very much in accord with local economic activity and teachers were often former professionals.

The year 1941 marked the opening of modern classes (without Latin) in *lycées* and the passage from the primary to the secondary order. Antoine Prost, in his monograph on the Orléans region (1986), found that this decision led to a rampant democratization that stopped in the early 1960s when the state took the first measures that eventually introduced the *collège unique*. How can this paradox be explained? In the face of demand for the extension of the schooling period, society and schools devised various mechanisms. When Prost examined the situation of small-town *lycées* prior to 1960, he identified various types that reflected the variety of local situations (Prost 1986). As these local tinkerings put the state in an awkward position, the state considered that it could promote the democratization project if the course offerings were rationalized. When we look back on these local mechanisms, we realize that there was something operational to them.

Confronting these analyses is both exciting and frustrating. It is exciting because they provide food for thought and raise politically incorrect questions. Didn't it backfire on the school system when the objective of equal opportunities was emphasized? As the objective of redistributing social positions holds a place of considerable importance in the welfare state and as it stands absolutely no chance of living up to its objective, it became the target of choice for criticism. This confrontation also raises questions on the perverse effects of state voluntarism. Systematization in the 1960s probably brought local mechanisms to a halt although they contributed to some democratization of education. It would, however, be unwise to claim that the democratization of secondary education would have made further progress if the state had given free rein to schools. Society may not want the redistribution of social positions after all. Many remember the clientelism that governed schools in the interwar period. Yet one may safely conclude that a strong political project does not necessarily lead to the centralization or the standardization of schools.

The transformation of justice models in postwelfare societies

The first model of democratization entered a crisis when the *Trente Glorieuses* (the 30-year boom period after World War II) came to an end. The first oil crisis (1973) marked a breaking point for all welfare state policies (Ewald 1986). International organizations became aware of these difficulties in the early 1980s and worked on several concurrent alternatives. A compromise over diversification and lifelong learning was eventually reached.

Equity and equal outcomes: a transition between the welfare state and the managerial state

The reasoning behind the transition from equal opportunities to equal outcomes is quite simple – as the objective of equal opportunities is unattainable, the situation would be less tragic if a level of minimum skills were guaranteed to all pupils. Its implementation raised controversy. This definition of equality may confine the working classes to instrumental skills without giving them the means to analyze their position objectively and criticize it. The debate dates back to 1975 when the *collège unique* (junior high schools where all pupils attend the same classes whatever their respective level) was set up. The curricular project behind the *collège unique* focused on practical knowledge and raised the fear of an *SMIC culturel*.[1] The situation changed when the *collège unique* faced a crisis. In the mid-1980s a few left-wing intellectuals gave a positive turn to this term (Baudelot and Establet 1989) and even presented it as the foundation of a new citizenship (Lelièvre 2004). This evolution, which shows some similarity to the back-to-basics Anglo-Saxon approach, is fiercely disputed by another part of the Left (Paget 2006). However, the 2005 Education Act confirmed this orientation and advanced a new definition of justice – the state would guarantee the mastery of a 'common core of knowledge and skills' at the end of compulsory schooling. This law confirms the principle of performance-based educational policies with the accompanying assessment mechanisms.

Others suggested a shift from equality to equity. This was based on the Anglo-Saxon tradition of the treatment of poverty, which does not consist of giving the same thing to everybody but each what they need. Assistance to people is not governed by impersonal national rules but is entrusted to local authorities. France long resisted this conception because it feared clientelist excesses. Moral philosophers in North America, particularly Rawls who coined the notion of 'fair inequalities' in 1971 (see Rawls 1987), provided a new insight. Meanwhile the OECD updated its indicators (Hutmacher *et al.* 2001; Groupe Européen de Recherche sur l'Équité des Systèmes Éducatifs 2003). In France, the Left seized this opportunity to reply to Bourdieu and Passeron's critique of 'indifference to differences' in the republican tradition. When the Left came to power in 1981, it implemented *Zones d'Éducation Prioritaire* (*ZEP*), a policy targeting disadvantaged neighbourhoods on the outskirts of major cities. *ZEP*s were developed on the model of educational priority areas launched in the 1970s in Great Britain. It is difficult to clearly assess its effects but public opinion saw that equality and justice were no longer synonymous.

With hindsight, the political sense of these approaches seems ambiguous. They were presented as a renewal of welfare state resources when they actually gradually introduced the concepts and instruments of the managerial state.

The fall of the redistribution project and the rise in the recognition of differences: a move towards diversification for the justice project

The mid 1990s were marked by the challenge to the redistribution project typical of welfare state policies. Compromise was found around 'diversification', a demand reflecting the segmentation of society. Several groups could then push their own interests independently, even if they agreed on the same mechanisms.

The role of the middle classes was probably crucial in this evolution. There was a turning point in 1975 when the Haby Act established the *collège unique*. The middle classes had supported this measure because they expected their children would access the schools attended by the *bourgeoisie*. When most children received upper secondary education, they feared their children might fall into oblivion (Derouet 2001). Therefore, new distinctions had to be designed in a supposedly standardized system. The most convenient instrument was school choice. The organization of state education has, since the 1960s, been based on *carte scolaire* (catchment areas) – the school pupils go to depends on where they live. Such a system assumes that all schools offer the same quality of service. School consumers (Ballion 1982) realized long ago this was a fiction. Avoidance strategies – registration in private schools in particular – have existed since the 1970s. The development of assessment at the Ministry of Education provided instruments that make it possible to fine-tune school choice. The 1989 Education Act, which puts the school project at the heart of the management of the school system, opened the door to dispensations. Agreement between a family's or a youth's project and a particular school project was necessary. Historians showed the perverse effects of standardization. Bourdieu and Passeron denounced the 'indifference to differences' of the French school system. Some degree of diversity within schools is necessary to come to grips with social and territorial differences. While the principle of catchment areas was maintained, Socialist governments gave rectors leeway to adapt them to specific cases. In 2007 the platforms of the two main candidates for presidency included the withdrawal of the *carte scolaire* system. Nicolas Sarkozy wished to put an end to what looked like Soviet-style planning. For Ségolène Royal, the Socialist front-runner, it meant the recognition of users' rights within the framework of proximity democracy. Furthermore, the sharp rise in real estate prices increased urban segregations. In these conditions the withdrawal of the *carte scolaire* could be the opportunity to avoid the spread of ghettos. Once elected, Nicolas Sarkozy announced that the *carte scolaire* would be phased out in the coming years. As of the 2008/2009 academic year, *académies* (regional education authorities) had to establish public performance indicators to enlighten parental school choice.

This evolution of the middle classes is closely related to the training of elites (Dutercq 2008). A new type of inequality is emerging between the schools that host working-class youths and those that fit future elites into international networks. Official rankings for higher education institutions now apply to upper secondary education. If high-school pupils want to register in good universities, they must attend classes in secondary schools that meet the same quality criteria.

Despite the importance of these evolutions, it is those who demand the recognition of ethnic and religious differences that are in the limelight. As memories of World War II are still very vivid, opposition to a population census with ethnic or religious indications remains fierce. ZEPs were delimited according to economic and territorial indicators, especially housing criteria in the suburbs. Yet everybody knows that most inhabitants in these neighbour-hoods are Muslim and of North African extraction. Beyond debates on the wearing of the Islamic veil, the question of inequalities was raised differently in the late twentieth century. They are inextricably linked with the question of ethnic and religious differences (Lorcerie 2003; Payet 1995).

These extremely varied interests find common cause for the time being in an 'anti-state' atmosphere. However it remains necessary to offer prospects of justice for all and thus reunify the fragmented school system. The focus is now on the issue of justice or injustice as experienced by individuals. This question has certainly not been tackled appropriately. The school system which promoted equal opportunities was sometimes quite harsh. Its moral is based on sacrifice – individuals are promised happiness, but later. Meanwhile, bodies and souls are strictly disciplined. A specific demand has been expressed since at least 1968. How can we speak of preparation for autonomy, education to citizenship, when pupils are deprived of any responsibility or even sanctioned when they do take responsibility (Merle 2005)? Dubet and Martucelli (1998) emphasized a paradoxical situation: in the lower classes, competition is fierce among pupils to represent their classmates at the different board meetings. In the upper classes, there are few candidates, if any. Does it mean that the republican school teaches not to commit oneself? The situation changed dur-ing the 1990s, when student demonstrations led to the creation of new tools for pupils – *maisons des lycéens* (premises where secondary school students can gather freely) – to voice their concerns and wishes. Yet students do not use the institutions that were created at their request (Rayou 2000).

The school system falls within the social philosophy that offers a new rela-tionship between individuals and institutions. Citizens are now less likely to be confronted with bureaucracy and state arrogance. Should it happen, they have recourse or mediation opportunities. These guarantees in some way compensate for what could be regarded as a scandal – the early training of an elite who accesses a space of international mobility denied to other categories. This combination remains fragile. A part of the working classes still demands the sharing of benefits and prospects of social mobility. Beyond that, this balance could fall apart if another part of the working classes demanded the introduction of specific rights according to the minority they belong to. This claim is equally unacceptable for the middle classes and for the state. Rancour and contradictory claims may bring about changes. In this context, how can research contribute to the emergence of a new project of democratization?

To what extent can social sciences contribute to the emergence of a new model of democratization?

Democratization policies may be entering a negative cycle after 50 years of ongoing voluntarism. Now the anti-capitalist movements that stand against the new world order know what they oppose but have difficulty designing an alternative project. This is one aspect of the crisis of criticism (van Haecht 2004). Pro-education left-wing supporters should expect a long dominance of the new spirit of capitalism, not only in the economic field but also in ideological debates. However it remains necessary to think about the construction of a new model of academic democratization.

Monitoring and assessing the implementation of social justice promoted by the managerial state

The working classes are too detached from the school system to work out a new model tailored to their interests. On the other hand, their sufferings, rancour, resistance and cunning in how they interpret and adapt official prescriptions are ferments of evolution.

The 2005 Education Act rules that all French youngsters should have a fair command of a number of knowledge and skill sets when they complete compulsory schooling. Beyond the controversies concerning this common core, the crucial test will be assessing how reliable this promise is. Don't we run the risk of having the same 20 per cent or so fail rate identified since the *collège unique* was implemented? Priority education areas had no effect on the reduction in academic failure and the objective of bringing 80 per cent of an age group shows only too clearly that it is unattainable. Can the state offer a real job and retraining opportunities to the youths who could not seize their first chance? Or will they start an endless cycle of job insecurity and live on welfare? The first studies suggest the limits of lifelong learning slogans. It is admittedly noble to claim that the fate of individuals cannot be sealed by the qualifications they gain between 15 and 25. Yet the validity of this claim depends on the mechanisms in charge of implementing alternative solutions. For instance, the accreditation of experiential learning offers prospects but the implementation of procedures is slow. As for continuous training, it is especially those who have good initial training who benefit from it.

The liberal approach makes individuals responsible for the course they take after they complete compulsory schooling. In that respect, this new definition of guidance differs much from that suggested in the wake of the Langevin-Wallon[2] plan. It no longer consists of determining the potential competencies of working-class children but in thinking how each can build and develop their skill sets in a complex and changing environment. It presupposes individuals who can assess their skills and knowledge, compare them to those in demand in the national and international job market, identify the resources they need, draw the appropriate conclusions of this analysis and make the decision to apply for a new job or move elsewhere. Even if one of the pillars of the common core is about becoming autonomous, clearly all individuals do not have the same resources. The managerial state should keep some basics of the welfare state if it is to remain within a justice framework – providing support to active guidance, securing the income and social rights of workers when they are unemployed. The supporters of the new order often point to the Danish flex security system as a successful model. This compromise is based on traditions and institutions proper to Scandinavian countries (Barbier 2008). To what conditions could it be applied generally?

Contribution to the development of a new model of democratization: Theoretical issues

The construction of a new model of democratization implies an education project set within a more global dynamic. Reflection should bear first on what is called a model of society. The projects of equal opportunities and benefit-sharing corresponded to a period when French society considered itself a large kaleidoscope of ever-changing, competing and cooperating groups. In this conception justice consisted in protecting the weaker and guaranteeing that exchanges were reciprocal. To some extent too much focus has been placed on academic failure. Therefore, the question of the training of elites was regarded as politically incorrect and was left undebated. That was probably a mistake. The political philosophy of justice should tackle together the question of education for all and that of education for the best. The core problem is to find a balance to consider these two aspects together. Nowadays, the image of the bell curve prevails (Boltanski 1999). There is a huge middle class in the middle to the point that it does not make up a class but rather a collection of individuals. However, it prescribes standards. On the two opposite sides there are minorities who do not fit into these standards – on one side a wealthy elite joins international networks that are outside state control. On the other, a poor and unqualified population is excluded, that is, it is disconnected from 'ordinary' social life. Accordingly, the main concern is the inclusion of those excluded and the question of the position occupied in social hierarchies takes only second place.

Can another model of society with a new redistributive project be designed? There are multiple constraints to take into account and this project is compounded by contradictory objectives – guaranteeing cultural transmission between generations and respecting differences in a multi-ethnic and multicultural society; providing a common core of competencies and knowledge to raise the skill standards of labour and training competitive elites; and above all, orienting learning towards real-life challenges while keeping the humanistic educational project aside from production imperatives. The approach of new capitalism, whereby a networked organization would connect the production and the education environments, may meet some of the working-class expectations. Nonetheless, pitfalls are rife. These networks are clearly governed by economic interests. If this system were to further progress, it would take the working classes to find new organizational modes to defend their interests in this framework. It implies their presence in greater numbers in governing roles but also reflection on the alternatives presented by the new means of knowledge circulation.

In search of a new model of democratization: A few elements for empirical studies

Theoretical reflections will make progress, provided they are based on empirical works that first make an inventory of the negatives to eventually further dialectical thought. It implies that teachers' strategies, suffering and moments of happiness in their daily tasks are investigated (Derouet-Besson, 2004). Ivor Goodson's research in the United Kingdom (2003) may provide inspiration. He asked teachers how they had survived the transition from the democratizing reforms in the 1970s to Thatcher's liberal policies and eventually to the application of the Third Way. The initial findings suggest a growing gap between state-driven initiatives and the sense of action experienced by field actors. While there is no organized resistance, the spirit of reforms is nonetheless not widely accepted. In an environment where points of reference are lost, field actors take few risks and avoid conflicts. Can society live in a sort of 'generalized exit' as Hirschman puts it?[3]

In this context, sociology should make a reflexive return and move away from the framework that was built when equal opportunity policies were developed. It is through an examination of the 'small things' overlooked in major surveys that research can see new perspectives emerge. A first shift took place in the 1980s when new subject matter – schools, *Zones d'Éducation Prioritaire*, territories, etc. – was the consequence of the devolution and partial decentralization of the education system. What is now necessary is to explore related realities. Such an approach is similar to the critical ethnography that was developed by American anthropologists in minority backgrounds (Gérin-Lajoie 2006).

The growing importance of major, benchmarking-regulated surveys calls for a reflexive return on the epistemology of measurement and comparative studies. Assessments are based on instruments that were designed in a specific situation and according to particular challenges. Instruments reflect the state of conventions negotiated at a particular time to determine the goals of education – a political project (reproduction of elites, democratization of education, etc.), curricula and the definition of standards and skills expected from students. Then they move across time, places and are sometimes used to serve projects very different from those initially designed. For example, the measures of intelligence designed in a eugenic perspective were used in support of equality policies (Normand 2007). There is clearly a field of research to develop for society to put the instruments underlying its management under control.

The globalization process implies a new conception of comparative studies as major surveys have become governance tools. If comparison is to restore its function as a knowledge tool, research should take an additional step towards 'exteriority' and build a larger framework that takes account of contexts (Osborn *et al.* 2003). For example, policy makers are fascinated by the excellent performance of Scandinavian countries – Finland is competitive in basic learning while the Danish flex security system commands respect for its lifelong learning policies. Policy makers ask research to identify good practices that could be easily transferred to other contexts when an in-depth analysis of each country's mechanisms, their historicity and their underlying political socialization should first be undertaken (Barbier 2008).

Reflections on education in postmodern societies: Studying the socialization processes of violence and love environments towards justice environments

The framework within which education and the democratization project are regarded tends to expand. The old model was based on a great confinement of education and the translation of the requirement for justice into the ideal of equality. These two principles are now challenged. The reticular conception of the world that establishes connections between education and production not only reflects the interests of capitalism but also partly those of the working classes. Similarly, the definition of justice was based on the ideal of equality and extended to the recognition of differences and accountability in the late twentieth century. The coming years will probably see another extension of this framework. Indeed, the educational process cannot be thought of only within the environments of reason and justice. Its overall purpose is to include children and youths in a justice-governed political context where each is given according to what they contribute to the general interest. It implicitly means recognizing that they are not part of it naturally. They come from environments – violence, love – where the relationships between individuals are not governed by a principle of equivalence (Boltanski 1990). The socio-anthropology of childhood and the sociology of developing emotions suggest the importance of these phenomena and design tools to consider them sociologically. These contributions renew the study of the socialization process. It does not mean going from love or violence to justice as the different environments are permanently intertwined (Rayou 1999). Social competence is defined by the ability to determine the right reference according to each situation. One of the goals of sociology is to pave the way for an intellectual framework that can monitor and appreciate this process.

What is the role of institutions in this process? The classic theory rests on the process of interiorization. Strong institutions (family, school, army, company) prescribe standards that individuals gradually interiorize. As evidenced by Dubet (2002), this programme is in decline as institutions are disputed. Institutions have to negotiate with individuals who mobilize the resources that suit them most. This trend entails rethinking the position of the school institution. What could be its role in this reticular organization? What also is the role of the new modes of knowledge circulation? It is in this context that learning regions should be assessed (Le Boterf 1994). Would these types of training courses give sense back to knowledge? What would be their consequences in terms of democratization?

References

Alain, E.C. (1932) *Propos sur l'Éducation*. Paris: Rieder.

Ariès, P. (1973) *L'Enfant et la Vie Familiale sous l'Ancien Régime*. Paris: Seuil.

Ballion, R. (1982) *Les Consommateurs d'École*. Paris: Stock.

Ballion R. (1994) *Les Lycéens et Leurs Petits Boulots*. Paris: Hachette.

Barbier, J-C. (2008) *La Longue Marche vers l'Europe Sociale*. Paris: PUF.

Baudelot, C. and Establet, R. (1989) *Le Niveau Monte*. Paris: Seuil.

Berliner D.C. and Biddle B.J. (1995) *The Manufactured Crisis: Myths, fraud, and the attack on America's public schools*. New York: Perseus Publishing.

Boltanski, L. (1990) 'Sociologie critique et sociologie de la critique', *Politix*, n°10–11, pp. 124–34.

Boltanski, L. (1999) 'Une sociologie sans société ?', *Le Genre Humain 1999–2000*, pp. 303–11.

Boltanski, L. and Chiapello, E. (1999) *Le Nouvel Esprit du Capitalisme*. Paris: Gallimard.

Boltanski, L. and Thévenot, L. (1991) *De la Justification: Les économies de la grandeur*. Paris: Gallimard.

Briand, J.P. and Chapoulie, J.M. (1992) *Les Collèges du Peuple: l'enseignement primaire supérieur et le développement de la scolarisation prolongée sous la Troisième République*. Paris: ENS Éditions.

Caillé, A. (2007) *La Quête de la Reconnaissance: Nouveau phénomène social total*. Paris: La Découverte.

Caspard P. (2008) "Mémoire et histoire de l'éducation", in Agnes Van Zanten (dir.) *Dictionnaire de l'Éducation*. Paris: PUF.

Charlier, J-É and Croché, S. (2008) 'The implications of competition for the future of European higher education (I)', *European Education, Journal of Issues and Studies*, vol. 39, no. 04.

Clarke, J. and Newman, J. (1997) *The Managerial State*. London: Sage.

Clarke, J., Gewirtz, S. and McLaughlin, E. (2000) *New Managerialism, New Welfare?* London: Sage.

Derouet, J.L. (2001) 'La sociologie des inégalités d'éducation à l'épreuve de la seconde explosion scolaire: déplacements des questionnements et relance de la critique', *Éducation & Sociétés, Revue Internationale de Sociologie de l'Éducation*, n°5, pp. 9–24.

Derouet-Besson, M.C. (2004) 'Les cent fruits d'un marronnier: Éléments pour l'histoire d'un lieu commun: l'ouverture de l'école', *Éducation & Sociétés, Revue Internationale de Sociologie de l'Education*, n°13, pp. 141–59.

Dubet, F. (2002) *Le Déclin de l'Institution*. Paris: Seuil.

Dubet, F. (2004) *L'école des Chances: Qu'est-ce qu'une école juste?* Paris: Seuil.

Dubet, F. and Martucelli, D. (1998) *À l'École: Sociologie de l'expérience scolaire*. Paris: Seuil.

Durkheim, E. (1938) *L'évolution Pédagogique en France*. Paris: PUF.

Duru-Bellat, M. (2006) *L'inflation Scolaire: Les désillusions de la méritocratie*. Paris: Seuil.

Dutercq, Y. (2008) 'L'implication des responsables d'établissement dans la formation scolaire des élites', *Education et Sociétés*, 21, pp. 5–16.

Ewald, F. (1986) *L'État Providence*. Paris: Grasset.

Fontaine, N (2000) 'Presidency conclusions', Lisbon European Council 23 and 24 March, Directorate for the Planning of Parlimentary Business. Available online at: www.europarl. europa.eu/summits/lis1_en.htm

Foucault, M. (1961) *Histoire de la Folie à l'Âge Classique*. Paris: Plon.

Garnier, B. (2008) *Les Combattants de l'École Unique*. Lyon: INRP.

GérinLajoie, D. (2006) L'utilisation de l'ethnographie dans l'analyse du rapport à líidentité. Special issue 'Anthropologie de l'éducation : un tour du monde', *Éducation et Sociétés*; no. 17, 1, pp. 73–87.

Giddens, A. (1998) *The Third Way: The renewal of social democracy ('La Troisième Voie Face: Le renouveau de la social-démocratie')*. London: Polity Press in association with Blackwell Publishers.

Goodson, I. (2003) *Professional Knowledge, Professional Lives: Studies in education and change*. Maidenhead and Philadelphia: Open University Press.

Groupe Européen de Recherche sur l'Équité des Systèmes Éducatifs (2003) *Rapport L'Équité des Systèmes Éducatifs Européens: Un ensemble d'indicateurs*. Liège, Belgium: Université de Liège.

Hirschman, A.O. (1970) *Exit, Voice and Loyalty*: Responses to Decline in Firms, Organisations and States. Cambridge, MA: Harvard University Press.

Hutmacher, W., Cochrane D. and Bottani, N. (eds) (2001) *In Pursuit of Equity in Education: Using international indicators to compare equity policies*. Dordrecht: Kluwer Academic Publishers.

Illich, I. (1970) *Deschooling Society*. New York: Harper & Row. Trad. fr. 1971. *Une société sans école*. Paris: Seuil.

Lawn, M. and Nóvoa, A. (2005) *L'Europe Réinventée: Regards critiques sur l'espace européen de l'éducation*. Paris: L'Harmattan.

Le Boterf, G. (1994) *De la Compétence: Essai sur un attracteur étrange*. Paris: Les Éditions d'Organisation.

Lelievre, C. (2004) *L'École Obligatoire: Pour quoi faire?* Paris: Retz.

Lorcerie, F. (2003) *L'École et le Défi Ethnique*. Paris: ESF.

Merle, P. (2005) *L'Élève Humilié : L'école, un espace de non-droit*. Paris, PUF.

National Commission on Excellence in Education (NCEE) (1983) *A Nation at Risk: The imperative for education reform*. Washington, DC: US Department of Education.

Normand, R. (2007) 'En quête d'une mesure des inégalités: genèse et développements d'une arithmétique politique en éducation'. Tome 1, Évaluations, in: Batifoulier, P., Ghirardello, A., de Larquier, G. and Remillon, D. (eds), *Approches Institutionnalistes des Inégalités en Économie Sociale*. Paris: L'Harmattan.

Osborn, M., Broadfoot, P., McNess, E., Planel, C., Ravn, B. and Triggs, P. (2003) *A World of Difference? Comparing learners across Europe*. Maidenhead: Open University Press.

Paget, D. (2006) *Aventure Commune et Savoirs Partagés*. Paris: Syllepses.

Payet, J.P. (1995) *Collèges de Banlieue : Ethnographie d'un monde scolaire*. Paris: Méridiens Klinsieck.

Prost, A. (1986) *L'Enseignement s'Est-il Démocratisé?* Paris: PUF.

Rawls, J. (1987) *A Theory of Justice ('Théorie de la Justice')*. Paris: Seuil.

Rayou, P. (1999) *La Grande École: Approche sociologique des compétences enfantines*. Paris: PUF.

Rayou, P. (2000) *La Cité des Lycéen*. Paris: L'Harmattan.

Tanguy, L. (2005) 'Examen critique de quelques idées communes sur la formation permanente en France', in *La Construction du Système Français de Formation Professionnelle Continue*, coord. E. de Lescure, GEHFA. Paris: L'Harmattan, pp. 57–74.

Taylor, C. (1997) *Multiculturalisme, Différence et Démocratie*. Paris: Flammarion.

Thivend, M. (2007) 'L'enseignement technique et la promotion scolaire et professionnel sous la Troisième République', *Revue Français de Pédagogie*, n°159, pp. 59–67, Lyon: INRP.

Tomlinson, S. (2001) *Education in a Post-welfare Society*. Buckingham: Open University Press.

van Haecht, A. (2004) (Coord.) 'La posture critique en sociologie de l'éducation', *Éducation et Sociétés, Revue Internationale de Sociologie de l'Éducation*, n°13, Paris: De Boeck-INRP.

Reflections on Derouet's chapter

If, as has been argued, there is today a 'new spirit of capitalism', then, Derouet proposes, there must also be a new educational project. This emergent project will focus on lifelong learning, practical knowledge and the involvement of companies in the funding and governance of schools. The American response of the 1980s shifted the aims of education from pursuing social equality or cohesion to assuring a high ranking in a competitive international environment. The objective was to go back to basics, fitting people for employment. The approach in the UK was more of a compromise. It involved a 'third way' between the market and the public sector. Nevertheless, the broad direction involving competitive comparisons was gradually more widely endorsed in Europe.

In this context, the key questions focus around social justice and democracy. Derouet asks, "What is in crisis? Is it the definition of justice, the political project of democratization of education or the mechanisms that have been implemented since the early twentieth century?" His answer involves exploring the nature and practice of justice and democracy. The challenge is to develop practices of democracy and justice that are able to confront the new global forces impacting upon people.

Research questions

The research questions in this chapter are all asked at a strategic programmatic level. The concepts, theories and political philosophies under discussion are universal in intent. The practical research questions concern how universal – or universalizing – categories such as 'justice', 'democracy' and the 'spirit of capitalism' play out in the institutions of everyday life. For example, questions such as the following lie at the foundation of the different chapters and discussion sections of this book:

*   What are the implicit models of education and justice in schools and other institutions that affect the lives of people?
*   What are the key political, philosophical, economic and social theories to have impacted on government policy?
*   How have changes in government policy impacted on curriculum, teaching and governance of schools?
*   What theories of justice, the 'good society', the nature of 'education', or model/s of economic behaviour have been excluded from debate?
*   What is the basis upon which a critique of different models and theories can be carried out?

Chapter 3

Between justice and pathologization

Juxtapositions of epistemic and material violence in transnational migration and domestic violence research

Erica Burman

Burman addresses the key paradox facing activist researchers of how to avoid the symbolic or representational violence that can result from researching with and about people who are subject to state and interpersonal violence. For this reason, she and her colleagues formulated three analytical principles and five interpretive strategies to support the conduct and analysis of the research. While the wider rationale and analytical approach is discussed at length in this chapter, the five principles were:

"1   *Contextual shifts in the potent intersection of asylum and domestic violence*
   A key gestalt switch that the Women Asylum Seekers from Pakistan (WASP) team had to negotiate was that the project took on different meanings within the two national contexts it researched. In the UK the project was principally about asylum and immigration issues (including access to legal representation and other forms of support, decision making etc.), while in Pakistan it was about domestic violence and associated service provision. It is worth noting that a key reason for this was that, contrary to the British popular imagination, the very possibility of escaping domestic violence by migrating to the UK was not even remotely conceivable, neither to Pakistani victims of domestic violence nor even to their service providers. Hence, in the UK the project was principally about racialization and racism, and in Pakistan it was about gendered relations. Both features therefore concerned violence, but the focus (in terms of the questions posed to interviewees) was different. The major interpretive challenge was arriving at appropriate ways of narrating these asymmetries without disproportionately emphasizing (political and domestic) violence in Pakistan. It was here that the focus on transnational trajectories and their historically overdetermined character had to be kept in mind, rather than cross-cultural comparison. In this sense the delineation of national boundaries and intra- and bi-national dynamics were being challenged.
 2   *UK vs. Pakistan: normalized absence/pathologized presence*
   In terms of the selective dynamic of problematization, it is significant to note how during the period covered by the project (2005–8), Pakistan was portrayed by the

British government as safe to invest in, but not safe to visit (according to the British Foreign and Commonwealth Office advice – a key source for political commentators as well as insurance companies). There was a similar paradox in the way Pakistan was accused of harbouring Taliban and Al Qaeda militants but 'internal flight' for women escaping domestic violence was nevertheless deemed possible. Attempts were made to address this dynamic of problematization by 'balancing' Pakistani with UK examples, and so bringing both national contexts and corresponding legal and cultural systems under critical scrutiny.

3   Legal reform vs. cultural change
There is a widespread discourse nationally and transnationally regarding the need for cultural change in perceptions of women alongside legal reform. But this kind of 'chicken and egg problem' often works rhetorically to warrant political apathy. An intervening factor in this was the further dynamic produced by international pressure (with gender mainstreaming and capacity building around the empowerment of women now a major feature within aid moneys, see Cornwall et al. 2007). Further, resistance to what might be perceived as Western meddling can be played out through a failure to implement such reforms (see also Ali 2000; Jamal 2005). While there certainly are grounds for considering gender a modern notion (Hayami et al. 2003), which can understandably acquire northern connotations, this is a spurious argument against legal and cultural changes. Both clearly are important and inform each other. In terms of this project, which was explicitly addressing provision and efficacy of legal measures of protection, these oscillations were recapitulated. Nevertheless, the position was adopted that legislation is necessary to shape and focus cultural shifts, including a more supportive cultural climate towards asylum seekers in the UK.

4   Avoiding reductionist explanations
Pakistani participants overwhelmingly discussed poverty, education, questions of custom, culture and religion, the subordinate status of women, and the three 'p's of poverty, powerlessness and pregnancy'. All of these are of course relevant factors in generating the picture of violence against women, but it is not clear which, if any, are determining (nor, indeed, whether any could such be identified). Rather, what is needed is analysis of how these work together to give rise to the complex context under investigation.

5   Political Islam vs. 'Western feminism' (and what's left out?)
There is a continuous refrain that positions feminism as antonymous to Islam; just as the law is positioned as religion's other (Sunder 2003; Mojab 1998). Both these dominant motifs colour the work of nongovernmental organizations (NGOs) working around feminism (and as feminists) and against violence against women in Pakistan. If feminism is seen as 'not Islamic', then the danger is that NGOs are seen as 'Western'. Here it is important to note how Pakistani women's movements manage to negotiate these oppositions (Jamal, 2005). Indeed this dynamic deeply inflects the ways Pakistani NGOs working around violence against women position themselves – and may indeed structure the ways they identify with, or distance themselves from, explicit affiliation with 'feminism'. This reflects wider

debates regarding the ways in which the category of gender might be thought of as 'Western', which render any clear refusal of the category unmerited; rather, the issue is the extent to which gender is a modern concept (Yoko et al. 2003). Yet, significantly, these tropes around 'Western feminism' are also both mobilized by and maintained by the British state. In the course of the fieldwork in Pakistan in 2006 it emerged that DfID (the British Department for International Development) was giving funds directly to the Pakistani government, claiming instead that it was cheaper/easier to administer their moneys this way – rather than to NGOs (which historically have been regarded as more effective partners). With the rapid political changes that are now bringing the historically non-governmental personnel into the new coalition government in Pakistan, it can only be imagined that this trend of bilateral partnerships (which has always been a feature of DfID policy) will be scaled up. The key point here is that, in paradoxical ways, the state (both UK and Pakistani) remains a key actor in the elaboration, and maintenance, of this opposition."

The complexities that these strategies addressed are discussed throughout this chapter.[1]

Introduction

This chapter addresses ethical-political dilemmas posed by and within a transnational action research project (Siddiqui *et al.* 2008) conducted (under my supervision) between Pakistan and the UK over a 30-month period ending in February 2008.[2] The project researched service provision for Pakistani women asylum seekers to and in the UK, whose questionable asylum status had arisen by virtue of domestic violence.[3] There were particularly complex challenges owing to the different meanings and foci the project came to assume in the two national contexts (domestic violence provision in Pakistan, asylum process in the UK). Moreover, there were some key *representational* dilemmas, by which I am indexing the set of debates at the confluence of social and feminist theory circulating in the 1990s concerned with: who speaks for whom, the problem of speaking or giving voice, the distinctions made between speaking and hearing or listening, between speaking and speaking for, and finally around 'representing the other' (e.g. Ahmed 2000; Hooks 1990; Wilkinson and Kitzinger 1996; Spivak 1993). In this project, these dilemmas were posed by not only the historical (and certainly actively salient) colonial relationship between Britain and Pakistan,[4] but were intensified by the current geopolitical conditions of, on the one hand, rampant transnational neoliberalism that requires flexible, mobile workers, and on the other, war and Islamophobia, feeding or producing national xenophobias portraying migrants, especially Muslim and Pakistani migrants, as possible terrorists (see Ahmed 2004; Bhattacharyya 2008). These representational dilemmas, which are inevitably recapitulated in my telling of them, illustrate the themes of this book: violence, democracy and rights. I will illustrate how violence shapes discourses of both rights and democracy in terms not only of practical responses to domestic violence, but also how these are framed by transnational and intersecting discourses of gender and racialization.

As an action research project, generated by and from a legal advocacy organization specializing in immigration cases (with my support as the academic supervisor), the practical-political context of generating documentary support to inform better (i.e. more just and supportive) decision-making around asylum claims reproduced many of the problems faced by anti-deportation and anti-immigration legislation campaigners. In particular, the ways that the demands of the practical-legal context work to pressurize appellants' accounts towards a 'victim' focus that limits conceptions of women's agency, alongside the potential for demonization of the national, cultural and religious contexts that the women are escaping. The rest of this chapter offers a rationale for and key examples of strategies for returning the problematizing gaze from those 'other' arenas to the normalized, but equally potent, cultural, national and religious context of Britain/the North.

Given the prevailing surplus of meanings that surround concepts of violence and asylum, not only via their gendered and racialized intertwinings but also as structuring the relationship between Britain and Pakistan, there was no way that the team could avoid consideration of the performative character of the research. How, in our analysis, could we *not* reproduce the very problems our research sought to redress? In particular, in attempting to draw attention to the plight of Pakistani women asylum seekers, whose asylum status arose through their efforts to escape domestic violence, how could the project avoid participation in the prevailing demonization of Pakistan? The chapter will therefore reflect upon decisions and strategies generated through the course of the research – informing its design, conduct and reporting style. While some guiding principles were arrived at through discussion and debate within the team,[5] my aim here is to attempt some further reflection upon these 'bottom line' assumptions in terms of the conceptual and ethical-political arguments they engage with and provoke.[6] Finally, I attempt some further analysis of the status of 'Pakistan' as a signifier.

Making the context visible

A key intervention of the project – in its rationale and design as well as its 'findings' – was to challenge the invisibility of state violence and, in terms of prevailing regimes of visibility, especially the British state, as a key player giving rise to and indirectly bolstering so-called 'domestic' violence (for Pakistan's collusion and contributions in this regard are certainly not invisible). Borrowing from feminist whiteness studies, this could be called 'colouring in' the dominant culture (cf. Charles 1992). Culture here includes matters not usually identified as being 'cultural', such as organizational, professional and political norms and practices. Yet cultural they are – in their form and effects.

Hence its relevance in highlighting wider political agendas fulfilled by the prevailing terms of the debate (including: poor Pakistani women victims/lawless Pakistan or bogus asylum seekers/modernizing-democratizing Pakistan) in order to bring into the picture British imperial legacies and current interests. Furthermore, it is relevant to attend to the representation of Pakistan as a 'history of the present' with its narrative features consistent with Euro-US (and especially Anglo-US) Middle East agendas.

Pakistan's strategic position, first with Russia and then more recently with Afghanistan, has long been a source of political (and literal) capital. Brown (2006) recently noted that Pakistan was the world's third largest recipient of official development aid from 1960–98, after India and Egypt (Brown 2006: 119). In general, accounts also emphasize the heavy toll militarization and multiple political stakeholders take on the natural wealth of the country (a footnote in Brown (2006: 133) addresses the discrepancy between the Human Development Index and the Gross Domestic Product). In the context of the so-called 'war against terror', it is significant to note that Pakistan's proximity to major world theatres of war (especially Afghanistan and Iraq) has also meant that it has received the largest number of refugees, more than any other country (Chantler, in press). Pakistan's slowing economy [with four fifths of state spending going on army and state bureaucracy and debt repayments (Brown 2006; Siddiqui 2007)] has warranted the introduction of neoliberal economic reforms that disproportionately target the poor in ways that intensify the pressure upon women's (and children's) labour. Khan (2003) takes this analysis further highlighting how such reforms enter in ideological as well as material ways to further, women's vulnerability, in making women carry the impossible burden of morality within a corrupt state.

What is important to keep on the representational agenda is how (what we inadequately call) the West carries a major historical and contemporary responsibility for current events in Pakistan. The West's interests are clearly at issue in the vicissitudes of political interest generated by violence against Pakistani women in Pakistan, just as much as national political interests and 'pandering to the tabloids' structure immigration agendas that return such women to Pakistan. The UK Conservative electoral slogan of 2003 – 'Are you thinking what we're thinking?' – may have marked a particular political nadir in explicitly soliciting, or at least warranting, the expression of racism at the same time as performing the very exclusion it justifies (so 'you' and 'we' are all interpolated as being in agreement by virtue of not being one of 'them'), but it is of a piece with many current (New Labour) measures. As recent Home Office-funded consultations around forced marriage amply illustrate (Hester et al. 2008), the doublethink surrounding the call to protect women (both women 'abroad' and minority women at 'home') always threatens to covertly enforce more stringent immigration policies.

Objective and subjective violence

Many authors, including Žižek (2008), have critiqued the increasingly prevalent left-liberal humanitarian discourse that urges the need to help and rescue (see also Gronemeyer 1993; Rahnema 1997). Žižek adds to these arguments an analysis of this 'fake urgency' (Žižek 2008: 6) by distinguishing between objective and subjective violence, with language as a primary example of the former. In particular, a key feature of this distinction is that attending to one form of violence can preclude recognition of the other:

> The catch is that subjective violence is experienced as such against the background of a non-violent zero level. It is seen as a perturbation of the 'normal', peaceful state of things. However, objective violence is precisely the violence inherent to this 'normal' state of things. Objective violence is invisible since it sustains the very zero-level standard against which we perceive something as subjectively violent.
>
> (Žižek 2008: 2)

In terms of its relevance to *domestic* violence, it is worth recalling how the discourse of 'home', connecting family to the state, already presumes precisely the elision that is thrown into question by immigration cases generated through the break-up of households due to domestic violence. Hence it is this objective violence – the normalized, everyday, 'rational' and bureaucratized violence of state and transnational apparatuses – that forms the background to the very visible, supposedly subjective, violences meted out to Pakistani women (see also Burman, in press, for an analysis of the tactics of banal racism enacted by the British Home Office bureaucracy). This objective violence also gives rise to the particular ways women tell, and have to tell, their stories in attempting to access justice and protection (Bögner *et al.* 2007). These are the material and epistemic violences I refer to in my title.

I am therefore invoking an analytic concerned with state violence at a number of levels: the violence of military (and economic) conquest which forms the geopolitical context for this study, the violence of immigration control, legislating against free movement and often returning people to national contexts where they face major discrimination and even threat to life. Further, as I discuss below, there is also the systemic violence of the structures of the state, the agencies, even so-called welfare agencies that fail to provide and – worse still – sometimes do not even acknowledge that they are implicated in these exclusions. All these frame the very material (or what Žižek would call 'subjective') forms of domestic violence prompting the journeys of Pakistani women to or within the UK. But principally, in terms of research practice, I will be concerned with questions of epistemic or symbolic violence: the violence of representation, or rather the challenges of mediating the competing pressures to claim justice but avoid inflicting further representational, or epistemic, violence.

While Žižek argues for the need to resist the rush to action, to help, and instead to reflect – rather than become implicated in various regimes of symbolic violence, in this chapter I reflect on the interpretive processes undertaken within our action research with the aim of motivating for more critical and reflective action. As an action research project, the Women Asylum Seekers from Pakistan (or WASP) project was (as reflected also in its name – as the sting in the tail of the usual acronym for White Anglo-Saxon Protestant) already formulated to interrogate and critique dominant practice. Within the constraints and pressures of funded research, the nature of its topic and rationale meant that the research team had to navigate dangerous symbolic territory in terms of how it framed and presented the research.[7]

Gender, rights and democracy

While discussions of women's rights are high on the global political agenda (although insufficiently addressed in the UN's Millennium Development Goals), the allocation of such rights is increasingly predicated on nationality and citizenship. The position of minoritized[8] women in the UK seeking justice (in the reduced form of freedom from violence and persecution) interacts with other agendas around immigration control and claims to national security and resource allocation. The widespread claims made by the 'allied' forces for the invasion of Afghanistan on the basis of freeing women from Taliban oppression revealed how opportunistic subscription to discourses of women's empowerment could cover more insidious political agendas.

Many feminists have attacked the trope of 'white men saving brown women from brown men' (Mohanty 1991, 2006; Spivak 1993; Thobani 2007; Bhattacharyya 2008) as a contemporary (as well as longstanding) warrant for neocolonial and imperial intervention. Others have addressed how changes in the structures of national and international governance as exemplified by, but not exclusive to, the 'war against terror' waged in Iraq and Afghanistan (and with Pakistan positioned as a key player), has given rise to a proliferation of private armies and security forces that render clear-cut distinctions between peace and war impossible (Duffield 2001). These so-called 'new wars' increasingly involve civilian populations (both as protagonists and as 'collateral damage'), and rely on varieties of informal economies for funding. The undermining of traditional state structures and the blurring of boundaries between the governmental and non-governmental (and even international non-governmental) sectors also has particular gendered effects. Spike Peterson's (2008) discussion of such effects in relation to the new 'coping, combat and criminal' economies is relevant here in terms of how these wars dynamically shape the relationship between the UK and Pakistan (with Pakistan both a key partner for the UK/US and a key suspect in the search for 'terrorists'). While she also indicates how this condition inflects gender relations between and within both countries, Shepherd (2008) highlights how discourses of national and international security are also implicitly gendered, with implications for the understanding of, and corresponding responses to, gender-based violence: "Violence, in this view, performs an ordering function – not only in the theory/practice of security and the reproduction of the international, but also in the reproduction of gendered subjects" (Shepherd 2008: 172).

Feminist critiques of liberal multiculturalist policies show how they privilege discourses of 'culture' and 'cultural respect' over gender. Typically, in the UK, cultural rights appear to trump women's rights, except in certain contexts where transnational, imperial wars demand justification. As both precondition and effect of this, the public-private split that has traditionally secured women's oppression is maintained (Gupta 2003; Burman and Chantler 2005; Patel 2008). Such critiques have also built on feminist analyses (e.g. Yuval-Davis 1997) which illuminate how women's traditional roles within social reproduction have come to warrant the elision between moral responsibility for the care of children and nation building. From this perspective two things become clear: first, that pretty well all cultures and religions have focused on the regulation of women's behaviour and sexuality so that, in contrast to prevailing Islamophobic discourses of the North, there is nothing specific to Muslim communities or nation states in this preoccupation; second, that the apparently private domain of familial roles and responsibilities is in fact deeply implicated within discourses of citizenship and national identity. McClintock's (1995) historical analysis illustrates how this practice was central to the colonial project from its inception: the supposedly natural order of the family. Thus the double meaning of domestic as household and as nation/national is no coincidence and worked to justify the colonial project through the Social Darwinian motif of 'unity through hierarchy'. More recently this has extended from the nation state to the new regional power bloc of 'Fortress Europe'.

> The claim to European specificity is an idea that translated into a claim of socio-political advancement and superiority that rests upon an image of women's freedom and a particular kind of gender order between women and men. It is a symbolism that positions Europe and the European as the standard of humanity and closes down questions as to whose identity, autonomy, family and privacy are to be respected, at whose cost and with what consequences for Europe's potential for an economy of gender equality. In so doing, it throws back the issue of visibility, not only to ask who and what is visible but who sees what.
>
> (Lewis 2006: 92–3)

A/symmetries of the transnationally gendered gaze

Ironically, as documented amply in our research, Pakistani women are subject to two distinct pathologizing gazes within the two national contexts. In

Pakistan the trope of 'woman-nation-state' (Yuval, Davis and Anthias 1989) renders any transgression of traditional gendered positions (of wife and mother) particularly problematic. This is in the context of a rather (territorially and politically) fragile nation state, with deep regional tensions and divisions, such that the US moneys given to quell Taliban activity in the North West Frontier Province over the past decades have funded state military crackdowns on insurgents to the Pakistani state's national authority. Such instability and insecurity has also bolstered the power of the traditional community authorities, including the *jirgas* (tribal courts) who (by virtue of power-sharing agreements enabling Musharraf to stay in power so long) operate according to customary law and maintain (among many other misogynist practices) the exchange of women to settle disputes (news of the latest of which reached the UK in early June 2008). But even at the level of the state there remains legislation, including the infamous Hudood Ordinances (much campaigned against but still not repealed), introduced by General Zia ul Haq in 1979 as a concession to the Islamists, that makes adultery punishable by imprisonment (and even death, although the death penalty has so far not been applied) but also renders any woman who seeks to leave a violent relationship (and potentially any individuals or agencies that help to support her) vulnerable to the counter claim of kidnapping or adultery under this legislation (see Siddiqui *et al.* 2008).

In the UK, Pakistani women are subject to a differently framed, but arguably just as exclusionary and punitive, gaze. For if their residency relied upon the spouse (and his household – since perpetrators regularly also include other family members)[9] that they are seeking refuge from, and the woman leaves the marriage within the minimum period designated by the British Government (currently two years, but under discussion to be raised to five – in the name of harmonization of European law, since Denmark and the Netherlands specify even longer), then her legal entitlement to stay in the country is in question. She faces possible deportation and she is unable to call upon support services that rely on public resources. This status of 'no recourse to public funds' affects many asylum seekers, especially 'failed' asylum seekers in the UK, and limits statutory provision of support to those who are surely the most marginalized and vulnerable. Thus, once outside the regulatory remit of citizenship which prescribes certain normative positions for women, minoritized woman in the UK have even fewer rights or entitlements. In fact, currently Pakistani women are possibly in a slightly better position than women from other countries, owing to a key test case (Shah vs. Islam, 2000) by which a House of Lords judgement determined Pakistani women to be a 'PSG' or 'particular social group' persecuted on the basis of their gender. This was on the rather politically ambiguous basis of considering women in Pakistan to be treated as second-class citizens.[10] As a result of this judgement, returning (i.e. deporting) women to Pakistan can be challenged, so resisting the so-called 'internal flight alternative' (IFA). This is the argument put forward by the British Home Office that the woman would be safe to live in another part of the country from which she is seeking asylum, rather than staying in the UK (see Bennett 2008; Ismail 2008).

Hence a key rationale for the project was to formulate arguments and strategies that would help the legal position not only of Pakistani women asylum seekers, but of women of other nationalities. The current picture for asylum cases (amply demonstrated by our UK-based work) is that (even for Pakistani women) nearly all asylum applications are turned down initially, and it is only on the basis of appeal or the presentation of 'fresh evidence' that they are won. (The project also traced through several such cases which document the arbitrary character of decision making and the role of minor bureaucratic technicalities in arriving at such crucial decisions.) As Steve Cohen (2001, 2006) and the 'No One Is Illegal' campaign have pointed out, the asylum system requires applicants to be presented as desperate, abject and powerless victims – producing a kind of orgy of what in other contexts has been called 'disaster pornography', and a hierarchy of victimhood (see also Palmary 2006).[11] Certainly, in our project, the contrast between research interviewing of applicants and interviews for the purposes of an asylum application was revealing. As Cohen (2006) has argued, fighting asylum/deportation claims using 'compassionate grounds' not only works to accord a spurious legitimacy to immigration controls (by portraying the possibility of 'fair' decisions) but it also works both to dehumanize and pathologize the appellant, and produces a competition between cases that is divisive.

Domestic and structural violence: privatizing the social

Within the broader problematic of domestic violence discourse, previous work around domestic violence and minoritization has highlighted specific ways in which liberal individualism inflects the representation of (and intervention on behalf of) minoritized women experiencing violent relationships in the UK (Batsleer et al. 2002; Burman and Chantler 2004, 2005; Burman et al. 2006; Burman 2005). Not only does the 'domestic' frame warrant non-intervention but prevailing discourses of 'cultural respect' extend notions of individual privacy to promote a strategy of non-intervention within supposedly autonomous and homogeneous communities who are perceived to 'look after their own'. Recent UK government pronouncements on promoting 'strong and stable communities' illustrate this, by calling for communities to be 'cohesive' and self-regulating (alongside the implicit threat that this status is provisional, or conditional).

Even more hidden in this set of representations is the way the state creates the conditions for some women's abuse and distress because their abusers can coerce them to stay by mobilizing the threat of deportation. Here state and structural violence collude with familial abuse but, within prevailing discourses of 'culture', this remains invisible. Thus a key analytical-political intervention has been to highlight the constitutive role of the dominant culture. This attention to the dominant culture works to explore what counts as 'cultural' (as where only the cultural *minority* is perceived to possess ethnicity or 'culture', with everything else normalized into a 'naturalized' invisibility and hence legitimacy). Furthermore, this strategy can also be used to 'colour in' the cultural, and culturally normative, character of state practices. This includes organizational cultures (e.g. of health and social service interventions, where the delineation of regional 'patches' for service responsibility or professional 'roles' both structures and limits the scope of intervention), and of course of the British state itself. Similarly, a key intervention can be made in relation to the 'why does she stay?/why doesn't she leave?' debate that surrounds women of all backgrounds experiencing domestic violence, but differentially structures the representation of minoritized women experiencing domestic violence. This can be seen as a particular version of the 'ordinary/mundane plus extraordinary' dynamic that can lead to one feature being emphasized at the expense of the other (Burman and Chantler 2005). One key issue arising from our previous work in the area was how (apart from workers from Black or Asian refuges) service providers' explanations for why minoritized women might attempt suicide or self harm, or might not leave violent relationships, almost never made reference to vulnerability on the basis of state and structural issues such as immigration status or 'no recourse to public funds'. This was in stark contrast to the ways 'no recourse' emerged from our survivor accounts as a material disincentive, and also as a psychological tactic of harassment that was often mobilized by perpetrators to prevent a woman from leaving (Chantler *et al.* 2003; Chantler 2006).

Dilemmatic navigations

Three analytical principles informed the political-rhetorical trajectory of the WASP project. These were arrived at through lengthy discussion among the project advisory group. Significantly, these were as much concerned with warding off spurious interpretations of the project's claims and remit, as with clarifying what its claims and concerns actually were.

A first key intervention was to reiterate that the project was *not a comparative study*. That is, we were not comparing legal protection of women or domestic violence service provision in Pakistan with that of Britain. It would in any case have been hard to sustain this, given that – as a UK team – our expectations were framed by what we knew of our own context, and even team members with longstanding knowledge of Pakistan had some of their assumptions challenged through the fieldwork process (as, for example, where certain features of provision or practice in Pakistan are actually better than in the UK).[12] It was also a particularly difficult position to maintain when the broader agenda of the project in relation to immigration issues was largely to counter Home Office claims that it is safe to send women back to Pakistan, or that Pakistani women can remain safe in Pakistan by 'internal flight' to another area within Pakistan and so have no need to seek asylum in the UK.

It was important to keep this principle in mind, at least formally, in the same way that it was necessary to continuously thwart media and policy makers' expectations of our previous projects, which had always posed their questions in terms of comparative rates of violence across the various minority cultural communities.[13] Obviously major representational and material factors enter into how domestic violence is recognized, disclosed and services sought out (not least class or economic position) (see also Bögner et al. 2007). As in previous work where we argued that we were not addressing questions of cultural comparison or cross-community prevalence, so in this project we made efforts to limit the assumption of Western cultural superiority that historically and, largely, currently continues to structure claims of cross-cultural comparison (Burman 2007). Indeed this claim also functioned alongside and bolstered another erroneous presumption: that such comparisons are only made one way. For, contrary to being passive objects of the gaze of researchers and service providers, Pakistani survivors and workers interviewed in our study were clearly evaluating and navigating strategic ways within the British context just as much as we were in theirs.

Avoiding the homogenization of 'Pakistan' (and 'Pakistani women')

A second analytical principle intra-country comparison emerged from our discussions. So, rather than privileging contrasts between the UK and Pakistan, the study was designed to attend to variations of practice within each country. Thus, we aimed to ward off essentialist, culture-blaming explanations (although the reception of such work often hammers home how authorial intention matters little in how such work is taken up and interpreted). This principle entered into the selection of the research sample, including who was interviewed, and where.

A first key contrast to attend to in conducting the fieldwork was between cities and rural areas, since most services and support around domestic violence are in cities (in both national contexts). The status accorded women, and corresponding patterns of violence, vary considerably between urban and rural contexts (with many of the most severe cases in Pakistan happening in Sindh or on the North West Frontier, both regions where customary law flourishes). Geographical and cultural diversity in so large a country meant that it was important to research across different regions, and to attend to the differences between rural and urban contexts.

Typically, as we documented, women escaping violence make their way to cities to find shelter and support, although their journeys can be long and arduous. Our focus on women's accounts of their trajectories to safety traced itineraries of often many thousands of miles in circumstances of great danger, which was also thematized in the title of our initial project report: *Safe to Return?* (Siddiqui et al. 2008). This attention to women's journeys not only enabled a focus for the interviews that did not require the women to describe the details of their abuse (which frequently elicited much distress) but also documented their resilience, resistance and resourcefulness in accessing networks of support (for example, when arriving in a city to find the shrine where poor and hungry people congregate, which also guides women to shelters). Many women had stories to tell of living in hiding and evading pursuit, with elaborate subterfuge to enable their survival.

A second analytic focus was to attend to and evaluate the significance of class position. Totalizing accounts of practices in Pakistan too easily neglect the role of class and how domestic violence is structured by class considerations that themselves are intensified by current global economic relations. Pakistan's economic recession has attracted international aid that is increasingly tied to neoliberal agendas. These differentially target the poor. In her analysis of charges on grounds of *zinah* (adultery) within the Hudood ordinances, Khan (2003) has highlighted how poor women carry the burden of moral respectability within what was understood to be an increasingly immoral state.

In terms of UK asylum decision making, class status appeared to interact in apparently arbitrary and unpredictable ways with other features of a woman's situation. If she was educated and English-speaking then the judge might consider her sufficiently advantaged to be able to make a new life in Pakistan and so order for her to be returned, while an uneducated, non-English-speaking woman from a rural area with small children might elicit pity or sympathy. Alternatively the latter's abject status (in being unable to communicate directly, for example) might limit identification and so her claim might be more likely to be dismissed.[14]

What emerged from our study was that while class and economic status might enter into the strategies by which a woman might seek to escape abuse, it was less clear in what ways class position might advantage her (especially as her access to resources is likely to rely upon the husband or family she was seeking to escape – a reminder of how class and patriarchy intersect). Further, while more middle-class women might have access to more resources to help them leave, such women would still be unable to rent accommodation within Pakistan without a male guarantor, and their single status would not only attract attention [which might result in being found by the domestic abuser(s)], but would also position them as women of 'bad character' and so generate harassment.

Thus, counter-intuitively, it was not clear that higher-class status was a protective factor in terms of maintaining safety within the country. Furthermore, UK asylum judges seemed to fail to appreciate how perpetrators from middle-class and elite families had more resources at their disposal to track a woman down (both within and across countries) and to procure false documents (including marriage certificates). Khan's (2003) study of women detained under charges of *zinah* similarly suggested that middle-class and elite women may be in a more vulnerable position than poorer women, precisely because of the greater economic resources at their husband's disposal, although she also notes that poorer women may languish in prisons longer because they cannot pay for legal representation to bring their cases to court.

A third key issue is the question of religious minorities. A dominant discourse about Pakistan emphasizes urban-rural regional differences; but religious minorities are differentially impacted on by domestic violence too, illustrating the impossibility of seeing violence as only 'domestic'. Obvious examples emerging from our study included the position of Christian women in Pakistan who as women from a religious minority were targets for violence, and were subject to forced conversion as well as violence within forced marriages (thus showing the impossibility of disconnecting public from private, or cultural/political from familial/interpersonal, violences). There are also several forms of Islam that are not recognized in Pakistan and whose adherents suffer similar oppression.

All these factors made any generalization about the situation of women in Pakistan even at the specific historical moment of the study (2005–8) very difficult. In terms of resisting other representations about Pakistan, it is worth noting as a final example the widespread discourse about corruption. This was widespread both in the sense of being documented again and again in our material, and being associated with Pakistan in general; and in particular concerned with the corruption of the police and lower levels of the legal system. Within our own material, as elsewhere, we documented many examples where women who had sought to register charges of domestic violence against their husbands found themselves accused of adultery and imprisoned under the Hudood Ordinances because the police had been bribed by the husband. In some cases service providers from shelters and other support organizations were also imprisoned.

It may be indisputable that corruption has been a key political strategy in the buying of, and vying for, power within Pakistan's turbulent 60-year post-independence history (but, significantly and equally indisputably, continuing a set of strategies initiated by British colonial occupation). Yet finding a within-country counterexample proved to be very illuminating. So, to take an example provided by one of our Pakistani participants (interviewed in June 2006), it was reported that once traffic wardens had been given an adequate salary they were no longer corrupt; whereas it seemed the police in effect continued to rely on bribery and extortion in order to gain a regular and adequate income. Such counterexamples and explanations of the contingent and provisional character of these practices not only challenged homogenizing and essentialist explanations for Pakistani practices, but they also indicated clear strategies for changing them.

From differences to commonalities

Alongside the strategy of playing up differences, we formulated one of *high-lighting covert similarities*. This resists polarization by playing up sometimes surprising commonalities. This is the other response to the cultural relativism of cross-cultural comparison. Clearly there are risks here of ignoring local, contextual conditions for longstanding problems, yet it is useful to consider claims that, for example, violence against women in India has increased as a result of women's *enhanced* social status. This appeared to challenge one kind of argument, regularly expressed by our (UK and Pakistani) research participants, that violence against women arose because of women's subordinate social position, but by seemingly asserting its contrast. Yet there was no reason why both positions should not be true, that is, that destabilizations to women's traditional social status generate resistance. Talk of patriarchy has an old-fashioned ring about it, and its sweeping invocation has often substituted for, rather than informed, explanation – crucially in ways that reinforce racisms. Yet obviously feminists have always had a cautious and often disputed claim on universality – in asserting some kind of common cause, notwithstanding the elusive character of (or rather perhaps precisely to interrogate the conditions of possibility for) sisterhood.

Rather than asserting global equivalence, it was useful to remind ourselves of local UK correlates for some of the issues emerging from our Pakistan material. So, regarding charges of corruption and lawlessness in Pakistan, which can seem so devastating, totalizing and difficult to address, it is worth recalling recent revelations about UK parliamentary and political processes involving not only 'cash for questions' but also 'loans for honours', and inquiries into the use of parliamentary expenses used to employ family members and support second homes, while the (New Labour) British government has continuously quashed investigations of its collusion and support for the (ex-government but now private) arms trader BAE (British Aerospace Engineering) Systems so that this case is now being taken up only in the US.

A second example related to the refrain from the whole spectrum of service providers we interviewed in Pakistan (and confirmed by the accounts of survivors) that it was not safe for women to go to police stations, because they would be harassed or even raped. Yet it could be argued that the situation is little better in Britain. So, along with the appalling *and (until very recently) declining* conviction rates for rape in Britain, our previous research documented examples of women, especially Black and Asian women, being subject to appalling treatment at the hands of the British police and other state authorities. Indeed the research team noted that, during the period of our study, a journalist (Julie Bindel) opened her article on the 'women's page' of the *Guardian* with the 'confession' that if she were raped she would not go to the police (27 October 2006).

To take a third example, where our Pakistan participants talked of the longstanding, and early, structuring of women's lives according to gender discrimination – citing examples not only of being provided with less access to education but also, from an early age, less food – within the personal experience of the (culturally diverse) research team we could generate equivalent examples from a UK context. Obviously there are matters of scale here (i.e. neither claiming that the situation for women in the UK is the same as in Pakistan, nor that it is absolutely different), and hence the first principle I outlined – that of avoiding cross-cultural comparison – remains central. Rather, these principles worked in relation to each other, cross-cutting and to some extent mitigating the inevitable representational problems posed by each.

Between justice and pathologization

This chapter has discussed the central dilemma for the WASP project: how to acknowledge, and indeed offer resources to support campaigns against, the injustices and 'barbarities' occurring within the Pakistani state, whilst attempting to mitigate its further pathologization. It did so by also exposing injustices within the British legal system. This strategy of disrupting homogenization could be seen as opening up for interrogation the wider problem of racialization. In all too practical ways, this work highlights the dangers of producing new orthodoxies about how women who have experienced terrible interpersonal (including sexual) violence should react, in ways that presume culture and context-free normalized responses. Thus, if a Pakistani woman could in fact provide a coherent and factual account of her journey and the abuse that precipitated it, then she may not be deemed credible since she then fails to exhibit the behaviour deemed appropriate for the level of trauma associated with the violence she is claiming. She is thus caught in a double-bind wrought from the fateful intersection of dominant cultural representations of her homeland and the status she is accorded there as a woman, alongside – equally cultural but naturalized through their professional status – representations of knowledge about responses to abuse. This is the work of symbolic and systemic violence, together with structural violence. These intersections – that are simultaneously political, cultural and gendered – have clear implications for a range of decision makers and providers across the spectrum of advocacy and support services in both the UK and Pakistan. Even as I finish this chapter Pakistan remains on the frontline of the 'war against terror', with violence, justice and democratic rights at the forefront of daily practical-political struggles. Yet once again, at this moment of profound possibility for change, the agenda for women's advocacy and empowerment – of which domestic violence is surely a symptom – appears even further off the national-political agenda than before. It thus remains as urgent as ever to clarify the responsibilities and possibilities of transnational partnerships.

References

Ahmed, S. (2000) *Strange Encounters: Embodied others in postcolonialism.* London: Routledge.
Ahmed, S. (2004) *The Cultural Politics of Emotion.* Edinburgh: Edinburgh University Press.

Ali, S. (2000) 'Law, Islam and the women's movement in Pakistan', in S. Rai (ed.), *International Perspectives on Gender and Democratisation*. Basingstoke: Macmillan, pp. 41–63.

Batsleer, J., Burman, E., Chantler, K., Pantling, K., Smailes, S., McIntosh, S. and Warner, S. (2002) *Domestic Violence and Minoritisation: Supporting women towards independence*. Manchester: Women's Studies Research Centre, MMU.

Bennett, C. (2008) 'Is internal flight a real alternative? – An exploration of the legal principle and the impact on women asylum seekers who have experienced gender-based persecution', paper presented at British Psychological Society Psychology of Women Section Conference, Windsor, July.

Bhattacharyya, G. (2008) *Dangerous Brown Men*. London: Zed Press.

Bindel, J. (2006) 'If I were raped today, I would not report it', *The Guardian*, 25th October. Available online at www.guardian.co.uk/society/2006/oct/25/penal.crime

Bögner, D., Herlihy, J. and Brewin, C. (2007) 'Impact of sexual violence on disclosure during Home Office interviews', *British Journal of Psychiatry*, 191, 75–81.

Brown, G. (2006) 'Pakistan: On the edge of instability', *International Socialism*, 110 (Spring), 113–34.

Burman, E. (2005) 'Engendering culture in psychology', *Theory & Psychology*, 15, 4, 527–48.

Burman, E. (2007) 'Between orientalism and normalisation: Cross-cultural lessons from "Japan" for critical psychology', *History of Psychology*, 10, 2, 179–198.

Burman, E., (in press) 'Explicating the tactics of banal exclusion: a British example', in Palmary, I., Burman, E., Chantler, K. and Kiguwe, P. (eds) *Gender and Migration*. London: Zed Press.

Burman, E. and Chantler, K. (2004) 'There's "no place" like home: Researching, "race" and refuge provision', *Gender, Place and Culture*, 11, 3, 375–97.

Burman, E. and Chantler, K. (2005) 'Domestic violence and minoritisation: Legal and policy barriers facing minoritised women leaving violent relationships', *International Journal of Law and Psychiatry*, 28, 1, 59–74.

Burman, E., Ismail, S., Siddiqui, N., Martins, V., Prendergast, Y., Grogan, A. and Allen, M. (2006) 'Trans/National topologies: Power gradients of multiculturalisms', paper for Conference on 'Beyond "Feminism vs. Multiculturalism": Revisiting the relationship between power, beliefs, identity and values, London School of Economics', 17 November.

Chantler, K. (2006) 'Independence, dependency and interdependence: Struggles and resistances of minoritized women within and on leaving violent relationships', *Feminist Review*, 82, 27–49.

Chantler, K. (in press), in I. Palmary, E. Burman, K. Chantler and P. Kiguwe (eds), *Gender and Migration*.

Chantler, K., Burman, E. and Batsleer, J. (2003) 'South Asian women: Systematic inequalities in services around attempted suicide and self harm', *European Journal of Social Work*, 6, 2, 34–48.

Charles, H. (1992) 'Whiteness – the relevance of politically colouring the "non"', in H. Hinds, A. Phoenix and J. Stacey (eds), *Working Out: New directions in women's studies*. Lewes: Falmer Press, pp. 29–35.

Cohen, S. (2001) *Immigration Control, the Family and the Welfare State*. London: Jessica Kingsley Publishers.

Cohen, S. (2006) *Standing on the Shoulders of Fascism: From immigration control to the strong state*. Stoke: Trentham Books.

Cornwall, A., Harrison, E. and Whitehead, A. (Eds) (2007) *Feminisms in Development: Contradictions, contestations and challenges*. London: Zed Press.

Duffield, M. (2001) *Global Governance and the New Wars*. London: Zed Press.

Gronemeyer, M. (1993) 'Helping', in W. Sachs (ed.), *The Development Dictionary*. London: Verso, pp. 53–69.

Gupta, R. (2003) 'Some recurring themes: Southall Black Sisters 1979–2003 – and still going strong', in R. Gupta (ed.), *From Homebreakers to Jailbreakers: Southall black sisters*. London: Zed Press. pp. 1–27.

Hayami, Y., Tanabe, A. and Tokita-Tanabe, Y. (eds) (2003) *Gender and Modernity: Perspectives from Asia and the Pacific*. Kyoto and Melbourne: Kyoto University Press/Trans Pacific Press.

Hester, M., Chantler, K., Gangoli, G., Devgon, J., Sharma, S. and Singleton, A. (2008) *Forced Marriage: The risk factors and the effect of raising the minimum age for a sponsor, and of leave to enter the UK as a spouse or fiancé(e)*. London: The Home Office.

Hooks, B. (1990) *Yearning: Race, gender and cultural politics*. Boston: South End Press.

Ismail, S. (2008) 'Fright or flight? The implications of the concept of "internal relocation" as an alternative response to granting refugee protection to Pakistani women fleeing domestic violence', paper presented at British Psychological Society Psychology of Women Section Conference, Windsor, July.

Jamal, A. (2005) 'Feminist "selves" and feminist "others": Feminist representations of Jamaat-e-Islami women in Pakistan', *Feminist Review*, 81, 52–73.

Khan, S. (2003) 'Zina and the moral regulation of Pakistani women', *Feminist Review*, 75, 75–100.

Lewis, G. (2006) 'Imaginaries of Europe: Technologies of gender, economies of power', *European Journal of Women's Studies*, 13, 2, 87–102.

McClintock, A. (1995). *Imperial Leather*. New York and London: Routledge.

Mohanty, C. (1991) 'Under western eyes: Feminist scholarship and colonial discourses', pp. 51–8, in C.T. Mohanty, A. Russo and L. Torres (eds), *Third World Women and the Politics of Feminism*. Bloomington: Indiana University Press.

Mohanty, C. (2006) 'US Empire and the project of women's studies: Stories of citizenship, complicity and dissent', *Gender, Place and Culture*, 13, 1, 7–20.

Mojab, S. (1998) '"Muslim" women and "Western" feminists: The debate on particulars and universals', *Monthly Review*, 50 7: 19–30.

Palmary, I. (2006) 'Gender, nationalism and ethnic difference: Feminist politics and feminist psychology', *Feminism & Psychology*, 16, 1, 44–51.

Patel, P. (2008) 'Faith in the state? Asian women's struggles for human rights in the UK', *Feminist Legal Studies*, 16, 9–36.

Rahnema, M. (1997) 'Towards post-development: Searching for signposts, a new language and new paradigms', pp. 377–404 in M. Rahnema with V. Bawtree (eds). *The Post-Development Reader*. London: Zed Books.

Shepherd, L. (2008) *Gender, Violence and Security*. London: Zed Books.

Siddiqui, A. (2007) *Military, Inc: Inside Pakistan's military economy*. London: Pluto Press.

Siddiqui, N., Ismail, S. and Allen, M. (2008) *Safe to Return? Report of a transnational research project investigating Pakistani women's access to domestic violence and asylum support services in the UK and Pakistan*. Manchester: Women's Studies Research Centre, MMU/South Manchester Law Centre.

Spike Peterson, V. (2008) '"New wars" and gendered economies', *Feminist Review*, 88, 7–20.

Spivak, G.S. (1993) 'Can the subaltern speak?', in P. Williams and L. Chrisman (eds), *Colonial Discourse and Post-colonial Theory*. London: Harvester Wheatsheaf, pp. 66–112.

Sunder, M. (2003) 'Piercing the veil', *Yale Law Journal*, 112, 1399–1472.

Thobani, S. (2007) 'White wars: Western feminisms and the "War on Terror"', *Feminist Theory*, 8, 2, 168–85.

Wilkinson, S. and Kitzinger, C. (Eds) (1996) *Representing the Other*. London: Sage.
Yoko, H., Akio, T. and Tokita-Tanabe, Y. (eds) (2003) *Gender and Modernity*. Melbourne: Transpacific Press.
Yuval-Davis, N. (1997) *Gender and Nation*. London: Sage.
Yuval-Davis, N. and Anthias, F. (1989) *Woman-Nation-State*. London: Macmillan.
Žižek, S. (2008) *Violence*. London: Profile Books.

Reflections on Burman's chapter

Burman addresses the political, social, cultural, ethical and research dilemmas raised by the experience of working with Pakistani women in the UK who have been abused and whose asylum status has been placed into question as a consequence. The context includes not only the colonial relationship between Britain and Pakistan but also the current climate of Islamophobia. The chapter draws upon feminist critiques of liberal multiculturalism which show how this privileges discourses of 'culture' and 'cultural respect' over gender and so reinstates the public-private split that secures women's oppression. Burman explores how the practical-political context of generating documentary support to inform better decision making around asylum claims pressurizes accounts towards a 'victim' focus that limits conceptions of women's agency, alongside the potential for demonization of the national, cultural and religious contexts that the women are escaping. In brief, she offers a rationale and key examples of strategies for returning the problematizing gaze from those 'other' arenas to the normalized but equally potent cultural, national and religious context of Britain/the North.

Research questions

Of critical importance in this chapter are the ethical principles of procedure that were developed to underpin participation and address the potential for the research process itself to unwittingly produce or be experienced as a form of violence on vulnerable people. Research as a practice is thus opened up to critical debate concerning its products and processes. What are the possibilities of including such principles and practices in the processes of creating, organizing, designing and undertaking projects? Should such an approach become embedded in all kinds of research projects? If so:

- How can such an approach become embedded in all kinds of research projects?
- How, in particular, can the powerful be drawn into democratic procedures in ways that inscribe democratic operational principles into their working practices?
- What are the implications for other marginalized, vulnerable subjects of research?

- How are boundaries between public and private constructed and deconstructed in order to generate genuine public debate, decision making and action?

Methodological discussion section *i*

Values, justice, knowledge and identity

Jill Schostak and John F. Schostak

What does making a critique depend on? How can it be claimed that one form of social organization or practice is better than another? No research will ever be able to answer these questions unless there is some criterion or criteria by which judgements can be made. Do such criteria exist? In the real contexts of social action there are multiple perspectives and differences in beliefs, values, faiths and what counts as 'truth' and the nature of 'reality'. Different cultures, different faiths, different ways of perceiving the world lead to disputes and disagreements. A common law, perhaps, can settle such conflicts. But in terms of research, how are laws themselves evaluated? The law in one place and one historical period may bear little relation to the law in another time and territory. Yet, in making their justifications, in calling one thing unfair or another 'good', the strategy employed makes claims that go beyond immediate contexts and circumstances. Critical research begins with the multiplicities of claims that are made. But if it is to provide more than conceptual analysis of the accounts made by different protagonists, it too must appeal to some 'transcendental', that is, some criterion that is capable of calling the difference between the just and the unjust regardless of circumstances and contexts.

Derouet's Chapter 2 leads us to ask in what public space can the meaning of justice be elaborated? The education of a given group or population provides a way of thinking about a concept of the public. Following the 1867 Reform Act in the UK extending the vote, Robert Lowe is claimed to have remarked "we must educate our masters". The masters' as the new public could – in theory at least – vote for radical changes within the government and thus against elites. Hence 'educating the masters' was an urgent proposition that led very quickly to the Education Act of 1870. This theme was at the back of the very influential work of Lippmann and Bernays in public relations discussed in Chapter 1. Education, in this sense, is very much about social control. Its pedagogy seeks to embed a given political and economic order as a universal good.

Following the Second World War in the UK, there was a political mood to extend opportunities through education, provide universal healthcare and ensure basic benefits for people, thus developing a concept of the state as a welfare state. In effect this meant that the power of the state – or the public sector – was growing at the expense of the private sector. Where the broad purpose of the public sector was to redistribute wealth – generated through profit – to the poor, the purpose of the private sector was to enable entrepreneurs to construct wealth by keeping costs – principally wages – as low as possible in order to generate profit that could be distributed to shareholders. The more the state demanded for government and the provision of social goods such as education, health and welfare, the less profit. Where from a social or public point of view profit can be seen as a tax on the hard work and risk-taking of employees, it is seen in the private sector as a sign of business efficiency by shareholders, the reward for risk-taking and hard work and justifiable in terms of an ethic of competition and the survival of the fittest. The global countercultures of the 1960s, the protests against wars, racism, sexism and exploitation, and the power of organized labour became the focus for a conservative – or neoliberal – backlash that desired a return to the political, cultural and social conditions conducive to the peaceful accumulation of wealth in private hands. Education was seen to have promoted 'permissive values', young people did not have the appropriate skills and attitudes that employers needed, and, indeed, through 'trendy' teaching methods and philosophies were seen as subversive of social order and market capitalism (cf. Schostak 1986, 1993). Thus, in the view of a senior civil servant in the Department for Education and Science: "people must be educated once more to know their place" Simon (1985: 223). In this sense then, where schools, as key institutions for the development of the powers of the future citizens, are maladjusted to the needs, demands and interests of individuals (Schostak 1983), the theme of 'justice' provides a way of challenging prevailing structures of Power and taken-for-granted beliefs, values and practices.

As described in Chapter 1, Balibar's concept of *égaliberté* (1994) – where equality and freedom are coextensive – provides a criterion by which the justice of an act or state of affairs can be assessed. For Fraser (2007):

> Justice requires social arrangements that permit all members to participate in social interaction on a par with one another. So that means they must be able to participate as peers in all the major forms of social interaction: whether it's politics, whether it's the labour market, whether it's family life and so on.

To embed such a concept of justice requires a very different kind of education and pedagogy. Derouet approaches this question by tracing the trajectory of various historical models of education. In so doing, he draws upon the work of Thévenot and Boltanski. The background to this approach lies in the work of the American political philosopher Michael Walzer who draws upon the tradition of 'pragmatism'. As described in Chapter 1, Walzer formulates a concept of 'complex equality' where justice, eminence and Power in one sphere of life – e.g. business – does not leak into that of another – e.g. politics. Each 'sphere' is equal to every other sphere. Individuals may be leaders in one sphere but not in another.

This concept of different spheres is developed by Boltanski and Thévenot (1999) and Thévenot and Boltanski (2006) through a concept of the *'cité'*. The model of the city has provided a focus for philosophical and political discussions since Plato's *Republic*. Each such 'city' can be defined in terms of its governing regime of justice or how individuals are defined in terms of their 'worth' (or worthiness) – the city of inspiration based upon St Augustine's *City of God*, the world of the market developed from Adam Smith, the industrial city derived from St Simon, the 'domestic world' based on Bossuet's *La Politique Tirée des Propres Paroles de l'Écriture Sainte*, the city of renown from Hobbes' *Leviathan* and the civic city from Rousseau's *Contrat Social*. More recently, what can be called the postmodern concept of city has been explored where individuals engage in time-limited projects, pick up project-related skills and experience then move on to the next project (Boltanski and Chiapello 2002). All of these cities or domains for developing 'worth' coexist. Individuals negotiate their way through this pluralistic social space, perhaps excelling in one or more. Boltanski and Chiapello used their approach to explore the changing nature of capitalism, echoing Weber's (2001) classic study of Protestantism as the spirit of capitalism, in their studies of the 'new spirit of capitalism'.

Drawing upon this, Derouet's analytical framework focuses on the different models of education appropriate to the changing spirit of capitalism. The historical perspective traces schooling from its guild-based origins through to the lifelong learning model currently appropriate to the contemporary spirit of capitalism. This provides therefore a global picture of the generalized model that operates in the Westernized world. Then a more specific account is provided of how the models of education are acted out in real schools in France. The analytic and critical strategy therefore involves formulating a global framework – 'spheres of justice', 'economies of worth' – in the context of which, particular historical social forms such as schools and the everyday practices of particular teachers and pupils can be studied. The methodological approach is to relate the general or indeed the universal such as justice, equality, freedom and so on in relation to the particular articulations of these universals in practice.

The particular focuses in on the detail, on the action, on the interactions and relationships when a teacher confronts the 'real' where, for example, in France, the lesson content needs to articulate across a wide range of abilities since, in the *collège unique*, all pupils attend the same classes no matter their level. This is the 'real' where the impact of the logistics, the rhetoric, the conceptualizations of doing and acting out the specifics of the curriculum for all pupils, acts itself out and makes itself felt. That felt-ness is mediated through multiple notions of 'justice' held by people, which, since the time of the French Revolution, has been synonymous with equality. While, on the one hand, this elision of justice and equality occurs in the register of the symbolic or the conceptual, it plays a major role in the struggle for the real at the level of everyday practice.

By focusing on historical models of education, Derouet clearly indicates that justice and equality have not in practice been synonymous at the level of the real. Are notions of equal outcomes, equity, merit and efficiency any more practicable? Interrogating each model in turn, Derouet systematically shows the problems of each, and then proposes the case for an emergent new project of the democratization of education, better able to incorporate the plurality of spheres of justice and the complexities of equality.

Complexity is again found in Burman's Chapter 3 but this time in relation to the UK and Pakistan and the complex dynamics involved in issues of domestic violence against Pakistani women who desperately need to seek asylum. Their vulnerabilities are compounded by neoliberal attitudes to labour and the fear composed of terrorism, Islamophobia, and xenophobic nationalism. Critical analysis is brought to bear on the split between the public and the private. This is done in the context of neoliberal political and economic globalization impacting on the flow of labour from country to country. People's rights and the nature of democracy are shaped by the multiple ways in which 'gender' and 'race' are culturally produced linguistically to describe and differentially ascribe values, characteristics, duties and identities to people, as well as, under particular conditions, to proscribe entitlements to residency and citizenship to certain classes of people. In general terms, the methodological problems focus on voice, representation and rendering the organization of Power as violence visible at every level from the local to the global. Furthermore, Chapter 3 helps us think about what counts as 'normal' or 'problematic' about 'others' and the processes through which others are marginalized, repressed, excluded or demonized. What's at stake in designing projects sensitive to these kinds of issues as a first, crude way of thinking about the methodological issues can be visualized in Figure 1.

The diagram maps some of the key politically significant boundaries to be addressed when researching powers, rights, violence and the construction of democratic practices. Starting from the outer concentric ring, there is the 'Multitude' as the totality of all living individuals. Inside that is a smaller group that can be defined as the 'People'. The People may be delimited by such terms as 'race', 'culture' and/or 'faith', and/or 'shared history'. However, not all individuals composing the People may be considered as the 'Public' as discussed in the Introduction and Chapter 1, that is, as individuals able to take part in policy decision making, or governance. In addition, not all who may be thought of as the People may be citizens of a given nation. In particular, as Burman comments, rights are predicated on nationality and citizenship. Hence, the boundary between nationals and non-nationals is jealously guarded. It is the place where distinctions are made between those who are acceptable and those who are to be rejected. Burman describes the ways in which language is used to render others as 'other', that is, as 'other than us', or 'not like us', or 'different'. A people, a nation, a citizen is defined by what they are not, as

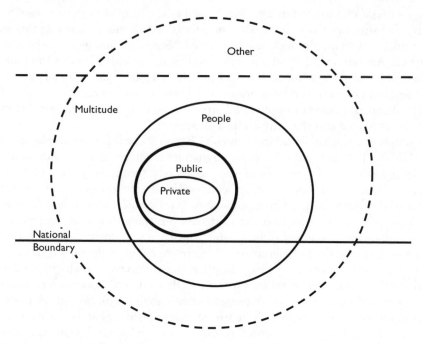

Figure 1 Mapping boundaries.

much as by identifying similarities. When the 'other' is demonized, it defines the 'enemy' as the focus of fear and terror (see Chapters 7, 10, 11 and 12).

When a given 'People', with a given political and faith perspective, rigidly designates others as 'evil' – say, as defined by Bush's 'Axis of Evil' (State of the Union Address 29 January 2002)[1] – how may it be challenged? It can only change when the rigidity of names, categories and boundaries fall away. This cannot happen at the level of the state, the people or the public, where 'public' defines the citizen as a bearer of rights for a given territory. Rather it can only happen at the level of the multitude where this signifies only the total collection of living people at a given time. The multitude is rendered visible only when all hierarchies collapse and in Balibar's (1994) sense there is *égaliberté* – that is, where liberty and equality are co-extensive – as discussed in Chapter 1. The state exists only through the borrowed powers – or the manufactured consent – of those who compose the multitude. If this is so, then they are dangerous to Power and need to be managed, shaped, regimented and, of course, subjected to surveillance. Public space that is available for the constitutive powers of individuals to engage in the creation of social forms, cultural productivity, discussion, decision making and action would thus have to be strictly limited to the elites who 'represent' the voting public, or citizens of a country.

Private space further restricts democratic practice amongst the mass of the population. In the private sector of the economy, global corporations can create wealth that is the equivalent of small states. Since this wealth is in private hands it can be utilized in any legal manner according to the desires of the owner. As a legal 'person' having 'rights' of ownership independent of the investors, the directors of the corporation are able to act in the name of the corporation. The risks directors take can be subsumed under the protection of limited liability accorded to the corporation. The question for research, that is, radical research, necessarily becomes: How can methodology be designed to promote the constitutive powers of individuals for the creation of public space, democratic decision making and action? One approach can be seen in the work of Laclau and Mouffe (2001) in terms of their concept of hegemony that is created out of a logic of difference and a logic of equivalence. The notion so far employed in this book of the 'multitude' effectively privileges difference and at the limit sees an equivalence only in terms of each member as living intelligent beings who are able to constitute social organization. Given a plurality of values, perspectives, demands and limitations in terms of resources, antagonisms and conflicts, any creation of social organization will create boundaries of various kinds. Individuals can form relationships with each other to oppose or contest the actions of others. In that sense, while maintaining their difference from each other, people find an 'equivalence' with each other in terms of their opposition to an other. Those who join together to oppose another logically form a 'chain of equivalence' – each hand in hand in their opposition to a mutually identified other. This chain of equivalence provides a basis for a generalization of views and actions. It is valid and objective to the extent that the chain holds, or resists being broken. A triangulation of perspectives can be organized to explore the extent to which it achieves objectivity, validity, and generalizability over time and space. However, as a chain of equivalence it does not imply homogeneity, nor consensus amongst its members; it produces a triangulation that includes disagreements between members and the production of fault lines along which any chain of equivalence can splinter and collapse. The task, as Rancière (1995) puts it, is to remain faithful to the disagreements. This refers to the essential principle of the construction of public space as a forum where it is safe to disagree and where each member respects the right to disagree and to take those disagreements into account in democratic debate, decision making and action. In a public space constituted by disagreements, chains of equivalence will form, transform, dissolve and reform. The objectivity of any fault line constituted by disagreements is determined by their resistance to dissolution. Similarly, the objectivity and the reality of Power is constituted by the force that can be brought to bear in resisting the erosion and deconstruction of boundaries. In this sense, in the battle for power the private and the public generate key global and opposing chains of equivalence that leave little room for individuals to combine their powers in the form of the multitude. It is the multitude that is the basis of all organizations of power through which alternative futures can be created. Figure 1 can be re-read as:

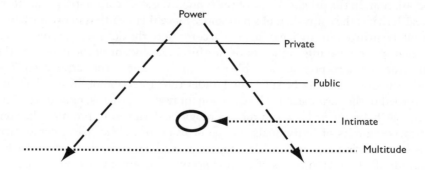

Figure 2 Power and the multitude.

In terms of hierarchy, elite Power in market-driven neoliberal leadership democracies privileges the private over the public. Indeed, it seeks to limit the function of the government (of the people for the people) to a supplementary role of operating the market where private individuals compete with each other in the accumulation of wealth (see for example Harvey 2005). The market is assumed to reflect the will of the people as owners, workers and consumers. If this is so, then the government exists only to ensure the smooth functioning of the market and to ensure basic needs like defence, education and a basic level of social security for those unable, due to unfortunate circumstances, to compete in the marketplace. The market can be read as a means of registering and coordinating the demands of the multitude, triangulating them in terms of 'objectively' and 'validly' allocating resources according to the ability to pay. Both objectivity and validity are then constructions of the operation of the mechanisms through which demand and supply operate. For Hayek the market is the foundation for human cooperation and freedom. With Freidman's free-market, monetarist economics, this view became fundamental to the governments of Thatcher and Reagan in the 1980s which broadly set the framework of the deregulated markets of the next decades leading to the 'credit crunch' in 2008. In this view, the market is broadly speaking a mechanism for social justice in terms of allocating socially produced goods to people according to their means to pay for them. Their means to pay for them would, of course, be dependent on their ability to compete fairly with others in the marketplace. However, in Walzer's (1985) terms, the market is only one sphere of justice and thus cannot be the fundamental guarantor of freedom and justice. It could be argued that the 'third way' politics of Giddens and of Blair's New Labour government from 1999 was merely a modification of the market as the basic framework for underpinning freedom and justice. What has been removed from the equation is 'equality' in order to justify inequalities whether resulting from 'talent', 'hard work', the capacity to work, intelligence and so forth, and that thus lead to unequal distributions of economic reward within societies that are essentially structured according to the preservation of elites in all domains of activity. Methodologically, without something like Balibar's notion of the co-extensiveness of equality and liberty or Fraser's definition of social justice requiring that individuals be able to interact on a par with each other in all the key institutions of life, there will be the production of bias, invalidity and distortion in the representation of people's voices, their demands, their interests, their needs, their values, their beliefs and their knowledge. Research methodology can be said to be co-extensive with the creation of the conditions for an effective 'public' with respect to the multitude and in this matter, the co-extensiveness of freedom and liberty is an essential precondition for the production of valid, objective, generalizable and reliable representations of the social, and more specifically, the articulation of the powers of individuals for the creation of the social, the public, the private and the intimate.

Currently, the forms of social organization in the private and the public domains are fundamentally conditioned by the market. The market provides the key mechanisms for assuring a sense of existence in terms of having a valid place in the system as owner, consumer, employer or employee. Through its mechanisms it attributes a value (as price/income/worth) to the individual in terms of their market-valued qualities (such as intelligence, skills, knowledge, talent, strength, character, beauty, gender, race, class, ethnicity and level of education). It thus recognizes the individual only as a competitive agent in the market processes of selling, demanding, possessing and consuming. In short, it solves the issue of how to allocate resources by resolving the conflicts of individuals through the processes of supply and demand. It also generates the social organizations necessary to run and regulate the economic system, provides a means of security for most, provides a framework for individuals to engage in business and social projects and more generally organizes the time and behaviour of the masses. Hence, the prevailing 'spirit of capitalism' becomes the fundamental frame for understanding the conditions in which education and democracy operate, identities are formed, values ascribed – whether to people or things – and resources allocated. There is thus a promise implicit in the spirit of capitalism – to provide the basis for self-enrichment. Some will be satisfied and others disappointed and yet others systematically deprived and excluded. Disappointment alongside deprivation and exclusion generates the conditions for change, for resignation, for indifference or for violence (see, for example, Critchley 2006).

The new spirit of capitalism is not confined, as it was in older formulations, to the nation state but is transnational, able to incorporate and appropriate differences. Rather than global, it is globalizing, it is generative of global power(s) to create the conditions for continuous expansion, appropriation and accumulation. Drawing on Boltanski and Chiapello's (2002) argument concerning the 'new spirit of capitalism', Fraser (2009: 110) recognizes that "that spirit includes a masculinist romance of the free, unencumbered, self fashioning individual" but also that:

... neoliberal capitalism has as much to do with Walmart, *maquiladoras* and microcredit as with Silicon Valley and Google. And its indispensable workers are disproportionately women, not only young single women with children; but also married women with children; not only racialized women, but women of virtually all nationalities and ethnicities. As such, women have poured into labour markets around the globe; the effect has been to undercut once and for all state organized capitalism's ideal of the family wage.

(Fraser 2009: 110)

In her view, second-wave feminism has "unwittingly provided a key ingredient of the new spirit of neoliberalism". It is an example of the ability of market capitalism to hijack and appropriate demands and protests for its own purposes.

Burman and her colleagues, for example, were clearly aware of the issue of unwittingly serving, reproducing and reinforcing prevailing neoliberal forms of violence. In the public domain there is geopolitical military and economic violence; the violence of immigration control; the violence of agencies, such as so-called welfare agencies; the violence of representation resulting in the demonization of victims, or pathologizing gazes, indeed a 'disaster pornography'; more generally of state and structural violence colluding with familial abuse out of 'cultural respect'; and of course forms of corruption where the vulnerable can be exploited to the benefit of the rich. There is the catch-22 violence produced where Pakistani women escaping domestic violence in the UK find that they have inadvertently changed their asylum status and thus face immigration control. By leaving 'home' and by engaging in a simple act of self-preservation in the hope of escaping one form of violence, they find themselves facing another.

There is then an overdetermination of violence. That is to say, the behaviours, values and identities of the individual are conditioned by multiple social forms of organization and their mechanisms: schools, the marketplace, the workplace, the construction of public and private, the laws, the courts and the various systems of surveillance pervasive in everyday life but more noticeable and officious at every boundary, whether they are those that protect private corporate property or regulate entry and exit between nation states. In her chapter Burman has made those spaces of power wielded by public infrastructures visible in the context of domestic abuse and the seeking of asylum. She and her fellow researchers consciously adopted a strategy to counter the possibility of methodology becoming a form of symbolic violence by contributing to this overdetermination, whether by reinforcing the status quo in the guise of emancipation or by appropriating the voices of others for theory development. Bourdieu (1993) thought such violence inescapable and sought only to minimize it. Rather than see methodology and theory as violence, it is more appropriate to use it to create the conditions for the inclusion (rather than simply their representation or appropriation by the researcher) of voices and thus the constitution of a public. This, as discussed in Burman's chapter, was accomplished through principled, participatory strategies. Derouet's chapter, by focusing upon models of education, has argued for the necessity of an emerging model that is capable of assuring democratic practice. The neoliberal fallacy is to confound the market with democracy and thus to believe that freedom is equivalent to the free market, thus contributing to the overdetermination of exploitative hierarchies. In doing so, it restricts the public sector and regiments the minds of the young through the mechanisms of schooling, and more generally the consuming public through the mechanisms of media-based public relations working in the interests of elites.

The chapters of the next section explore more closely the spaces that open up in which identities are constituted and resistance made possible or repressed. In Figure 2 (p. 68), such a space is the intimate which appears like a 'hole', the strange place that is both desired and guarded against, an 'outside' that is also an 'inside'. That is, it is neither private (in terms of private property, private wealth, private opinion, private identity) as understood in market democracies, nor is it public in the sense of having an identity able to have a voice that can be heard by others and taken into account. As in the domestic spaces of Burman's chapter, it is a place of vulnerabilities, a place where the violence committed will not be addressed, or cannot be seen or heard within the private and public spaces of social interaction. However, it is also a source of the powers that make the individual both unique and demanding and when recognizing and universalizing itself in terms of being a member of the 'multitude', it is a force to be feared and thus controlled, repressed and excluded.

References

Balibar, E. (1994) '"Rights of man" and "rights of the citizen": The modern dialectic of equality and freedom', in Etienne Balibar, *Masses, Classes, Ideas: Studies on politics and philosophy before and after Marx*. New York: Routledge. The original is: "La proposition de l'égaliberté", in Les Conférences du Perroquet, n° 22, Paris. novembre 1989.

Boltanski, L. and Thévenot, L. (1999) 'The sociology of critical capacity', *European Journal of Social Theory*, 2, 3, 359–77.

Boltanski, L. and Chiapello, E. (2002) 'The new spirit of capitalism', paper presented to the Conference of Europeanists, March, 14–16, 2002, Chicago.

Bourdieu, P. (1993) *La Misère du Monde*, Éditions du Seuil. It was published in English as *The Weight of the World: Social suffering in contemporary society* (trans. Priscilla Parkhurst Ferguson *et al.*), 1999, Oxford: Polity.

Critchley, S. (2006) *Infinitely Demanding: Ethics of commitment, politics of resistance*. London: Verso.

Fraser, N. (2007) 'Emancipation is not an all or nothing affair', interview by Marina Liakova, available at http://www.eurozine.com/articles/2008–08-01-fraser-en.html (accessed August 15, 2009).

Fraser, N. (2009) 'Feminism, capitalism and the cunning of history', *New Left Review*, 56, 97–117.

Harvey, D. (2005) *A Brief History of Neoliberalism*, Oxford: Oxford University Press.

Laclau, E. and Mouffe, C. (2001) *Hegemony and Socialist Strategy: Towards a radical democratic politics*. 2nd edition; first published 1985. London: Verso.

Rancière, J. (1995) *La Mésentente: Politique et philosophie*, Paris: Galilée.

Schostak, J.F. (1983) *Maladjusted Schooling: Deviance, social control and individuality in secondary schooling*. London, Philadelphia: Falmer.

Schostak, J.F. (1986) *Schooling the Violent Imagination*. London, New York: Routledge and Kegan Paul.

Schostak, J.F. (1993) *Dirty Marks: The education of self, media and popular culture*. London: Pluto Press.

Simon, B. (1985) *Does Education Matter?* London: Lawrence & Wishart.

Thévenot, L. and Boltanski, L. (2006) *On Justification: Economies of worth* (trans. Catherine Porter). Princeton NJ: Princeton University Press.

Walzer, M. (1985) *Spheres of Justice: A defence of pluralism and equality*. Oxford: Blackwell.

Weber, M. (2001) *The Protestant Ethic and the Spirit of Capitalism*. London and New York: Routledge; first published 1930, Allen and Unwin.

Chapter 4

The scarf unveiled

Proximity to the test of law in a French school

Romuald Normand

Normand discusses the case of "a young minority girl who decided one day to enlarge the headscarf or 'bandana' she had been wearing in a French secondary school since the beginning of the school year". As Arendt (1981) states, "Appearing always means seeming to others, and this appearance varies according to the point where the spectator is situated and the perspective chosen". Thus, "making the event public is not self-evident (Derouet 2003; Dutercq 2004)" since "many teachers do not dare voice their sentiments outside classrooms: so on a daily basis they often prefer loyalty or to step back (Payet 1997; Hirschman 1970; Van Zanten 2001)." The event occurred in a school "located in a disadvantaged area in a large regional town where many French citizens of North African descent live. Many young girls wear a veil but they take it off at the entrance of the school. It is a popular vocational school which has however seen its reputation decline for a few years. Because of a tradition of excellence and because of the commitment of the successive principals to maintain it at the best level, hierarchical links constitute a strong component of the relationships between agents in the school (Derouet 1992; Boltanski and Thévenot 1991)."

> *Before reporting on the story, we have to consider what legal power each individual has to settle disputes and to arrange the thing publicly, particularly in schools. Indeed, in this school as elsewhere, a rather strict legal framework sets the modalities of institutional representation for teachers and pupils, the limits of their autonomy, the responsibilities and sanctions applied in case the law is breached. Where, in the case of a dispute, charges are often brought to justice and sometimes to courts, this case allowed us to consider how law is interpreted and how it supported the skills of human beings and events in passing judgments according to convention (Thévenot 1992). The law, whose effectiveness is important both for the administrator and the jurist, provides different modalities to close disputes and forces individuals to face several tests of tangibility and topics of evidence (Chateauraynaud 2004). Therefore, on the occasion of the 'headscarf-related trouble' we have sought to show the various modes of commitment, whether they are tolerated or not by the procedures typical of the statutory and legal formalities within French republican schools.*
>
> *(Thévenot 2000)*

In brief, the story is of a 16-year-old girl, Samira, who had been:

> ... *wearing a discreet bandana as proof of smartness and elegance in her eyes. This rather good pupil would change clothes and colours regularly in an aesthetic quest widely shared among teenagers. During the first term, the young girl gradually decided to lengthen her bandana until the day when it covered her whole hair and before she replaced it by a mantilla (a three-tip silk or nylon scarf). The few and flimsy clues left by Samira and her behaviour which was very different from one teacher to another, in an attitude of ruse and challenge, sowed confusion as the teachers of the class had difficulty assessing the situation and were embarrassed and irritated by her behaviour.*

Eventually, a class teacher:

> ... *tried to find the right moment to remind Samira of the school rules as long as her move was not taken as a personal accusation or as stigmatization in front of the class. She was offered the opportunity when Samira entered the math lesson with a class representative, a minority girl of North African extraction who was wearing a cap as well. The teacher immediately asked them to take their hats off and reminded them they were not allowed to wear anything on their heads in the school. The class representative obeyed but Samira refused to comply and take her bandana off. She justified her act stating that it was a religious choice and that she was allowed to wear it. Her refusal to comply pushed the teacher, outside the classroom, to report the incident to her colleagues.*

Normand now presents the story and analysis below:

Once she overcame her doubts about asking her colleagues' advice and once it was clear that the young girl had broken the school rules, the class teacher had sufficient support to report the incident to the school-life officers. But the fear of public exposure and of calling out the school management with its potential effects, led her to seek guidance once again from a close friend, the maths coordinator in the school with whom she often worked. At that time, her colleague was preparing for the competitive exam to become a principal and was interested in regulations on school management. He advised his colleague to let the principal know the situation because she was the only person who could legally remind the young girl about the school rules from the moment that she had invoked her religous convictions. The class teacher heeded his advice and during a break decided to report the event to the principal. The latter was obviously furious and replied that "it is unacceptable in the school, she is not allowed to wear a veil", and soon alerted the other principals and asked the class teacher to immediately summon the girl to an interview. Meanwhile, the principal rushed into the staffroom, as usual, to demand that teachers enforce the school rules against hats. Then, she kept Samira with her during a part of the morning to talk and asked her about her motives for wearing an Islamic veil. As this episode took place at the end of the week, the pupil did not go back into her classroom.

The following Monday, the English teacher, who was willing to enforce school rules, again saw this girl wearing a bandana and asked the representative of pupils to take Samira to the school-life officers. On their way, the two pupils met the principal with her deputies. In the meantime, the principal had sought advice from the legal department of the local education authority which was against the exclusion of the girl. She rushed into the classroom and informed the teacher vehemently in front of the whole class that Samira had to be accepted back into the classroom. The teacher, who felt deeply offended, complained to the staff and school board representatives. The offence was all the more acute as the teachers felt indignant at the principal who blamed them for not having applied the school rules from the first day. According to her, this delay and their incompetence contributed to the emergence of this trouble in the school. From then on, in the face of 'hysterical' behaviour, and while the principal was labelled a 'fury', teachers, who felt profoundly humiliated and scorned, decided not to accept the young girl into the classroom anymore. Not only did this moral abuse not ensure a closure of the protagonists' opinions on the settlement of this problem but it also contributed to making the dispute increasingly antagonistic.

Making a thing public and inventing legal procedures

The work and communication process which followed the interpretation of the school rules, although it came in reaction to the decision of the principal, as the event was so contrary to proprieties, also contributed to the emergence of the bandana as a public issue. Indeed, until then, the modalities of association were limited to a small community formed by teachers whose comfort was affected by the irruption of an intentional act outside typical school sanctions. But in raising the question of inadequate school rules to settle the trouble and in delegating the authority of the class teacher to the principal, the association extended beyond the links of proximity to other forms of life together inside or outside the *lycée* around different grammars of civic good (Thévenot 2004). In that sense, the republican state constitutes the first form of public organization, in the person of its representatives, such as the principal or the chief education officer in charge of seeing to respect for the public interest and of assuring separation from vested interests and the values defended by a smaller community. The rule of law then gives authority to the state to normalize activities and equalize treatment within schools. It is the reason why, as a reminder of the Council of the State's opinion, the chief education officer saw fit, in a memo addressed directly to the teachers and posted in the staffroom, to ban the exclusion of Samira for wearing a clothing accessory.[2] But in public schools, besides the state, other forms of voluntary associations exist which represent their members' interests, support teachers, pay attention to the respect of rules and are committed to working for the common good: these are the subject associations and trade unions.

In the school, there was a well-known nationwide trade union which had the majority in the school board even if it was in competition with an 'independent' list during the elections. However the positions of unionists drew closer together in the revolt against the principal and they turned into a 'big family'. The female representative of the main trade union, who assumes national responsibilities, was called for by the teachers of the class. Although she regarded the event as the 'sign of a serious situation', she wished to settle the trouble through discussion and negotiation, and for the incident not to be given too much publicity by the media at the risk of 'increased confrontation', 'uproar' or 'distortions'. This prudence towards public opinion can be explained by the fact that the trade union did not really know then what position to take at national level while a bill on secularism was going through the French parliament. In the school, the school board representatives and trade union members also wished, in the name of secularism, to see the values of integration prevail.

To stop rumours and share accounts, trade unions organized a meeting one day at noon. To everyone's amazement, the strong presence of teachers in the staffroom (about 70 per cent of them) transformed the meeting into a collective. From then, a general meeting was arranged which became the main decision-making and regulation authority for collective action in the school. It is another form of public organization, which is more liberal than the state or a voluntary association, because individuals can speak freely on an equal footing and not in virtue of a mandate, and also because individuals can join and leave the general meeting as they wish. Extending the circle of people involved and making the protest more overt in a public arena entails necessary publicity for the general meeting. As in other similar cases, it is up to representatives to address their complaint against the breach of school rules and the principles of secularism (Gautherin 2000).

Giving the complaint publicity: From protest to accusation

The general meeting gave rise to a public scene which, despite its dramatic dimension, made it easier to define the scope of interpretations by helping to list the justifications in support of the teachers' claims (Cefaï 2001). But the definition of common good and the qualification of the event raised questions of evaluation and made it necessary for protagonists to share the same views according to a process based on civic principles. The motives put forward aimed to structure the complaint in the list of public problems available, rather than express values or interests, and were to be used as a framework of interpretations and support for commitments (Tromm 2001). If some teachers made racist and xenophobic remarks, as did the maths teacher who was convinced that "these people with a dozen kids who are educated in the same spirit are going to invade us for good", others – who were often female teachers – defended women's dignity and the recognition of their rights to emancipation. While claims sometimes expressed a reaction of fear in the face of what was felt by many as a menace, two teachers belonging to minorities argued that the young girls were manipulated by fundamentalist networks. The defenders of secularism were divided: some thought that wearing a veil was unacceptable and was an act of proselytism expressing religious fundamentalism; others were calling for the application of firm principles and of school rules but also for sustained dialogue with the pupil.

Most of Samira's teachers found her behaviour unacceptable and felt embarrassed by conspicuous signs which were intolerable in their eyes. However, the French teacher, who was against possible anti-Muslim words, warned his colleagues about the risk of potential discrimination against the young girl. Nevertheless, only a minority of the teachers of the class considered that it was possible to welcome the pupil and trust educational work to liberate the pupil from her 'mental jail'. Again, there was the conviction of the history teacher, who was hostile to the action of his colleagues and who, during the meeting, pointed out one teacher who was wearing a headband and argued that it was absolutely not the expression of religious beliefs. His demonstration immediately met strong opposition from his colleagues. Other teachers hesitated to sanction the pupil for wearing a veil because she was a trouble-free pupil in her schoolwork and was very discrete. An agreement was finally reached about the need for the pupil to respect school rules. A delegation of representatives asked for a meeting with the principal to discuss the proposal. They were satisfied with this meeting and felt they had been listened to and understood. They were also aware of the difficulties faced by the principal towards her hierarchy and the neighbourhood; indeed, police officers and city hall officials had voiced their concern about the possible repercussions of the incident.

The teachers and the principal decided to meet Samira and her parents to find common ground. Her parents, of modest extraction, who were tolerant Islamists concerned about the academic achievement of their daughter, seemed overtaken by the event and surprised by her position. But beside her parents who spoke little French, Samira's sister and her lawyer soon took centre stage during discussions. Samira's sister had been excluded from school for absenteeism, had failed her *baccalaureate*, was married to a Muslim and was wearing the veil. Her lawyer, of Algerian extraction, did not wear any veil but defended the Council of the State's opinion and argued that the absence of any act of proselytism justified Samira keeping her headscarf. Samira's firm position and the support of her lawyer convinced teachers, even the most reticent ones, that the young girl was not a 'teenage drop-out' but was 'determined and target-driven' and benefited from the support of 'active minorities' or 'fundamentalist networks'. Consequently, as Samira's act proved intentional, the most reticent teachers changed interpretations and were persuaded that they were the victims of a plot and that the young girl belonged to a 'Salafist group'. It was not an 'isolated case' but a 'tangible fact' upon which they could intervene. During the second general meeting, the different positions hardened while similar testimonies pointed to the 'premeditation' of her act and to the fact that the school was 'infiltrated'. Therefore, as it was impossible to settle the incident through conciliation, the collective protest continued in an attempt to gather evidence to make the girl liable for her act and charge her with breaking the school rules.

The launch of an alert, the process of accusation and trials of confession

Entering the trial required a political work of delegation which, apart from recording the complaints and worries, could be supported by a socially known and qualified agent to convey the message (Chateauraynaud and Torny 1999). Within the general meeting, the school board members largely assumed this role of representation, but light was soon thrown on an economics teacher who, in assuming the role of 'prophet of doom', contributed to reshaping the report of the event. He soon became influential enough among his colleagues to alert them about the threat that wearing a bandana makes against the principles of secularism. If he did not have any activist background and considered himself as a 'heretic' of the main trade union, this teacher explained his commitment by the fear which the presence of the Far Right's leader Jean-Marie le Pen at the second round of the French presidential elections inspired in him and the resulting risk of 'growing *communautarisme* (ethnic solidarities)'. As he was eager to harden the protest and was firmly against religion, he worked hard to convince the representatives of the general meeting and managed to reach a consensus on the defence of secularism.

Very often, the role of these 'alert launchers' is to raise the consciousness of others dulled by routine or blinded by the transparency of the ordinary world. Here, the teacher progressively incited his colleagues to drop their too conformist attitude towards school rules and the Council of the State's opinion because he was convinced that the issue was first and foremost a 'political' one and that a 'cause' had to be defended, while some teachers were considering only whether the bandana worn by Samira was discreet or conspicuous. During successive meetings, he developed convincing arguments to alert his colleagues about the 'trap' with which the local education authority was seeking to end the dispute as the latter was hiding behind the Council of the State's opinion to refuse the exclusion of the young girl, which was regarded by the teacher as excessive legalism. In keeping with his demonstration, he was supported by close colleagues, like the French teacher of the class who in the meantime had become the spokesman for his colleagues and was convinced about being the victim of an 'inch-by-inch war' and of being 'the prey to the enemy who chooses you'.

The process but also the pursuit of the movement called for an inventory of legal texts to make sure the complaint was highly publicized in a request based on legal terms. Once he became the spokesman of the collective, the economics teacher committed himself, with the help of a few colleagues who were familiar with legal proceedings, to a review and an analysis of the juris-prudence of the Council of the State's opinions and of the bills against the veil[3] before Parliament. The movement of protest, without the history and philosophy teachers who opted out of the group but with the support of school board representatives, also took the shape of posters and manifestos for the defence of secularism which were pinned up in the staffroom. Commitment was passionate but there was also an atmosphere of insecurity and fear so that, in the course of action, criticisms were addressed to spokesmen because they had a tendentious interpretation of legal texts, developed arguments with racist or anti-Muslim connotations, blew up some facts or events, or used sources which were thought to be unreliable.[4] In the wake of the issue, others deplored a form of 'terrorist intervention' which was contrary to the 'freedom of speech' and 'annihilated debate'. Some teachers were even compelled to 'self-censorship'.

The conditions of success for the complaint required that it be separated from the collective or the person who conveyed the message. That is why the protagonists generalized the cause in order to avoid the emotional register through rational arguments likely to drum up support and make sure that the request would be accepted in the public space. The philosophy teacher, the only one who really committed herself in her discipline, disputed the positions held by the spokesmen and wrote her own texts, which compelled them to change their arguments. She convinced them not to limit the issue to a quarrel with the principal, not to lampoon the local education authority, but rather to make the protest public through legal arguments and a reflection on the philosophical and legal stakes of the wearing of the veil. The female trade unionist, who was yet very attached to the principle of secularism, also found that some positions had been exaggerated and went against her anti-racism and anti-discrimination values. So she tried to contain the 'verbal excesses' of her colleagues and thus used her relationships within the trade union for the logistical aspects of the protest, the relationships with the press and for legal advice. The collective received the support of the principal who, in accordance with her personal convictions, said she could not accept the young girl and wished that the girl complied with the law.

However, in order to know whether the girl had broken school rules and then summon her to a disciplinary committee before her possible exclusion, the general meeting had to gather clues or tangible events in order to facilitate the management of evidence (Chateauraynaud 2004). To gather proof, teachers had to put the pupil in the wrong and to make her talk to express her religious convictions. Apart from proving that her act was intentional, thus breaking the school rules, the trial of confession enabled the moral character of the pupil to be defined and so support the criticism from the civic world emphasized by the group of teachers (Dulong 2001). Finally, given the different testimonies, it was necessary to go beyond the trust-based credibility test and support one's arguments on investigation-based checks to confirm that the girl had indeed broken school rules on tangible facts. Then, teachers in Samira's class were asked at the very beginning of each lesson to demand that Samira justify why she was wearing a headscarf. A report was written each time and her words were quoted in a notebook. It was agreed to ask her to take her headscarf off and, if she refused, she had to explain why and express her religious convictions, and ultimately she would be refused access to the classroom. Afterwards, her words were reported during general meetings.

Except for the history teacher who allowed her into his classroom and who was exposed to the scorn of his colleagues because he had broken professional solidarity, the pupil was kept outside the classroom. In compliance with the principal's and the lawyer's demands, teachers gave her schoolwork in order to respect the legal obligation of scholarship. On her side, Samira wrote down the words of teachers, taking notes in her pocketbook, sometimes in a provocative manner, and answered them according to the instructions given by her lawyer. The trial logic was gradually having effect in the classroom: it disrupted teaching, distracted, disturbed and discouraged pupils, and compelled disoriented and exhausted teachers to control their least gesture and word to avoid accusations or a complaint being lodged against them. The French teacher in particular was sensitive as, because of his own experience, he had warned pupils that he would lodge a complaint if he was personally slandered. On the initiative of this teacher, Samira was even put to the test in terms of the curriculum through the study of Voltaire's texts which condemned religion and through a commentary of Molière's *Tartuffe* against fundamentalism. Other colleagues also chose to use parts of official curricula to arouse a debate and to teach pupils the principle of secularism, but they eventually exhausted themselves in 'endless discussions', according to one teacher.

Moving the dispute into the public space and the horizon of the law

Through a classical strategy of delegation, the chief education officer, who was anxious to defuse what he estimated to be a conflict between teachers and the principal, dispatched his office director, the legal department manager, a chief inspector and a mediator from the Ministry of Education specializing in the settlement of conflicts over the Islamic veil. They met Samira's teachers, the representatives of the school board and the school management. They tried to explain the jurisprudence of the Council of the State in reminding teachers that their action was illegal and that they had to accept the pupil back into class. The teachers, who were standing firm on their positions, asked for a disciplinary committee to be convened by virtue of the legal dispositions and of the school rules which allowed them to decide whether they would keep or exclude the young girl. The mediator met the pupil and her family, had lunch with the principal and in the end devoted little time to the teachers because she had a train to catch. By reminding them of the jurisprudence of Council of the State, she tried to demonstrate that national statistics found a decrease in the number of veils worn and that the young girl was only seeking to trace her roots and was experiencing a teenage crisis. For the mediator, it was impossible to exclude the pupil since there was nothing like an Islamic veil in what she was wearing. Indeed, as her ears and neck were bare and her words were not a challenge to authority, there was no conspicuousness or proselytizing in her attitude. Therefore, the teachers had a choice to either reintegrate Samira or to hold a disciplinary committee. But if the latter was accepted by the local education authority, the pupil could nevertheless come with her lawyer and appeal to the administrative court. In any case, according to the mediator, teachers had to comply with the law regulating public services.

The mediator's opinion and the influence of active teachers united in the pursuit of a common good eventually convinced the principal that a disciplinary committee was needed to judge Samira's case. The principal had herself been affected by a chance meeting with the pupil, outside the school, who had adopted a challenging attitude. The day following the meeting with the mediator, the principal decided to convene a meeting with the pupil and her family. But the chief education officer, who was informed about the organization of a disciplinary committee, firmly ordered the principal to revisit her decision because he thought that the negotiation with the pupil and her family had been too short and that it was impossible to consider, with regard to the jurisprudence of the Council of the State, Samira's behaviour as an act of proselytism. He asked the principal to respect the law. The principal, who was feeling disavowed by her hierarchy, requested and received a written confirmation of the decision that she then posted in the staffroom. The majority of teachers then felt abandoned and betrayed because they had to accept the pupil back into the class, and because they thought that the chief education officer had exceeded his prerogatives, and pushed the process into scandal.

The collective then decided to publicize the news and alert the media while they also sent open letters to the Ministry of Education, politicians and associations for the defence of secularism. In an open letter addressed to pupils' parents, they reminded them that there 'should be sanctions against any breach of school rules' and expressed their will to 'maintain the neutrality of public space' in prohibiting 'clear signs of discrimination against women'.

As the staff regarded the school as a 'place of education, a place to learn rules and the law', a request was made to call upon the support of parents in the name of the 'obligation' of staff to 'remind about the rules' and to guarantee 'a place of rights and freedoms'. At the same time a one-day strike and a demonstration in front of the local education authority building were confirmed. The request of the general meeting was turned into a public cause. Besides, some teachers felt they were overtaken by this event over which they had absolutely no control.

Opposition hardened between teachers and the chief education officer. The latter refused to meet the spokesman of the collective and told the regional press that the protagonists were employing secularism as a 'pesticide' and that he would not turn the pupil into a 'candidate for martyrdom'. These declarations created a considerable stir and established a long-lasting crisis in the school while a debate emerged at national level. The issue of the Islamic veil in different media and political agendas, the awareness of new audiences and the propagation of favourable or unfavourable theses relating to the bill offered new opportunities for the spokesman of the collective to voice their arguments outside the classical spheres of institutional and political representation (Cefaï 2002; Thévenot 1999). The use of the electronic network of the district, the contacts with the regional and national media, the exchanges with associations defending state secularism, the information of right-wing or left-wing party members, were some of the resources and networks mobilized by teachers who were receiving many letters of support. The pressure exerted on politicians and the media led the chief education officer to call a meeting, the day after the demonstration, with the collective's spokesman, in the presence of a chief inspector and a general inspector representing the Ministry, but without the principal who had been dismissed shortly before the beginning of the talks. As the representative of the state, the chief education officer, who was convinced he had a trade union delegation in front of him, explained his conception of secularism in a half-hour monologue based on the legal texts in force and exhorted teachers to be more tolerant and adopt a more positive attitude. For their part, the teachers felt they were being lectured and that the chief education officer was denying the problem, and they were offended by this lack of concern which did not allow the seriousness of the situation to be appreciated to the degree that the statutory texts made them think appropriate. The general inspector, who was lending a friendlier ear, told them they held a lot at stake in their hands and that they should not despair of seeing a change in the law. He encouraged them to continue their educational work with pupils and added that the struggle was moving elsewhere, that is, on to the political stage and would no longer remain confined within the school now.

Under the direction of the collective and its spokesperson, the economics teacher who launched the alert originally, who then convened a new general meeting. They asked the principal to convene the school board for an extraordinary meeting. After stormy debates, the organization of a day on secularism within the school and a petition for the defence of neutrality were decided. On that occasion, a republican philosopher was invited. In the petition it was written that the school experienced a 'coloured Islamic headband' which testified to the 'trap' and the 'proselytizing work' led by 'fundamentalist groups' with 'their reading of the religious law above the republican common law'.

Therefore it was urgent for the 'teaching community' to provide a 'political and moral answer' to 'fluctuating secularism'.

Over the last few months of the school year, it proved obvious that the event had gone beyond the school framework and that the action of the protest group became more and more influenced by the public debate on the Islamic veil. The protagonists were confronted with a shift in the scales of publicity as the cause was now reported by the media and rallied by organizations accustomed to civic protest: the League of Human Rights, Associations for the Defence of Secularism, the Union of Families for Secularism, the Movement of Citizens, etc. The protest joined a larger movement in the defence of secularism against ethnic-based considerations and Islamic fundamentalism. Besides, the motives for action and the various arguments were increasingly based on ideology. However, prescriptive arguments were added as the 'bandana' issue influenced the debate and legislative work on the bill on secularism in French schools. Indeed, a new form of law procedure developed, before the parliamentary debate on the bill, which influenced the work of jurisprudence done hitherto by the Council of the State. Some spokespeople of the collective were called to testify before parliamentary committees and to explain the events, following contact or meetings at local level by members of parliament who were obviously involved in games of influence. These committees later played a major role in making politicians aware of the need for a bill. It is, however, difficult to prove that these meetings and the hearings of the different protagonists in the 'bandana' issue contributed to influencing the decision-making process which led to the vote of the law, but they definitely played a role in the presentation of a certain way of living together in a French secondary school.

Epilogue

At the end of the school year, the movement of protest in the school focused on the defence of pensions in the public sector. The principal broke her leg and nobody saw her again until the next September. Samira was accepted back into her class and streamed into a vocational training course as she had missed too many lessons over the year. The bill on secularism in schools was passed by Parliament. Some spokespeople from the collective group had become activists of the republican cause and posted information regularly in the staffroom. They recently became involved in the 'No' vote during the referendum campaign on the European Constitution and they organized a 'republican banquet' in the school.

Samira is still wearing her bandana in the school. It sometimes covers her chignon or her whole hair but nobody seems to be interested in it any more. She is also often dressed in loose tunics of vivid colours. Some pupils walk up and down the corridors with two-to-four-inch-long *fatma* hands around their necks. Other pupils put a four-inch wide ribbon in blue or black nylon around their heads. They are sometimes asked to reduce the surface of the cloth when they enter the classroom or when they enter the principal's office.

It seems that the presence of signs in the public space of the school no longer affects staff members despite recurrent face-to-face teaching situations, as if the closure of the event, the return to ordinary or routine activities and to a set of rules prevented any unveiling of the headscarf. As we have demonstrated, it must also be due to the fact that the perception of a sign in proximity only becomes a problem when the person oriented towards others is affected and when a set of events is examined and brought together to define and pass judgements on it. Then accountability and justice environments occur which raise debate around the common good. It is, as Hanna Arendt wrote, when a community of equals who are likely to get involved in words and action seek to strike a balance between forgiveness for past acts and the promise of future guarantees of living together (Arendt 1983).

References

Arendt, H. (1981) *La Vie de l'Esprit*. Paris: PUF.

Arendt, H. (1983) *Condition de l'Homme Moderne*. Paris: Calmann-Lévy.

Boltanski, L. and Thévenot, L. (1991) *De la Justification: Les économies de la grandeur*. Paris: Gallimard.

Cefaï, D. (2001) 'Qu'est-ce qu'une arène publique ? Quelques pistes dans une perspective pragmatiste', in Cefaï D. and Joseph I. (eds), *L'Héritage du Pragmatisme: Conflits d'urbanité et épreuves de civisme*. Paris: L'aube éditions.

Cefaï, D. (2002) 'Les cadres de l'action collective: Définitions et problèmes', in Cefaï D. and Tromm D. (eds), *Les Formes de l'Action Collective: Mobilisation dans des arènes publiques*. Paris: EHESS.

Chateauraynaud, F. (2004) 'L'épreuve du tangible: Expériences de l'enquête et surgissement de la preuve', in Karsenti B. and Quéré L. (Dir.), *La Croyance et l'Enquête: Aux sources du pragmatisme*. Paris: EHESS.

Chateauraynaud, F. and Torny, D. (1999) *Les Sombres Précurseurs: Une sociologie pragmatique de l'alerte et du risque*. Paris: EHESS.

Derouet, J.-L. (1992) *Ecole et Justice: De l'égalité des chances aux compromis locaux*. Paris: Métailié.

Derouet, J.-L. (Dir.) (2003) *Le Collège Unique en Question*. Paris: PUF.

Dulong, E. (Ed.) (2001) *L'Aveu: Histoire, sociologie, philosophie*. Paris: PUF.

Dutercq, Y. (Dir.) (2004) *Le Collège en Chantier*. Paris: INRP.

Gautherin, J. (2000) 'Au nom de la laïcité, Pénélope et Jules Ferry', in Derouet J.-L. (Dir.), *L'École dans Plusieurs Mondes*. Paris: De Boeck/INRP.

Hirschman, A.0. (1970) *Exit, Voice and Loyalty*. Cambridge, Ma: Harvard University Press.

Payet, J.-P. (1997) *Collèges de Banlieue: Ethnographie d'un monde scolaire*. Paris: Armand Colin.

Thévenot, L. (1992) 'Jugements ordinaires et jugements de droit', *Annales ESC*, 6, 1279–99.

Thévenot, L. (1999) 'Faire entendre une voix: Régimes d'engagement dans les mouvements sociaux', *Mouvements*, 3, 73–82.

Thévenot, L. (2000) 'Actions et acteurs de la procéduralisation', in Coppens P. and Lenoble J. (eds), *Démocratie et Procéduralisation du Droit*. Brussells: Bruylant.

Thévenot, L. (2004) 'Une science de la vie ensemble dans le monde', in Caillé A. and Dufoix S.

(eds), L'idée d'une théorie sociologique générale a-t-elle encore un sens aujourd'hui ?, *La Revue du M.A.U.S.S.* n° 34, 115–126.

Tromm, D. (2001) 'Grammaires de la mobilisation et vocabulaires des motifs', in Cefaï D. and Tromm D. (eds), *Les Formes de l'Action Collective: Mobilisation dans des arènes publiques*. Paris: EHESS.

Van Zanten, A. (2001) *L'École de la Périphérie: Scolarité et ségrégation en banlieue*. Paris: PUF.

Reflections on Normand's chapter

Normand tells the story of an incident that caught the attention of national and international media: a young woman who challenged school authority by gradually increasing the size of a head scarf from being a 'bandana' to that of the scarf associated with the Islamic religion. Effectively, it brought into relief a clash between secular and religious societies. There is considerable power in focusing on media cases in that they can dramatically put into relief structural, conceptual and philosophical issues. As discussed in Chapter 1, the media has long been seen as a tool for public relations manipulation of the 'public'. What is of 'public interest' and how it gets to be constructed as such is, of course, then of research interest. The key concepts employed in claims to 'fairness' by each side in the drama define the battleground. The ways in which the media represent claims, the emphases they give, the particular language they use in their descriptions of participants, arguments and actions provide insights into the manipulation or otherwise of what counts as 'news'.

Each universalizing concept – for example, freedom, equality, fairness, law and democracy – employed in demanding and representing 'rights' can be a focus for conceptual critique as well as media critique. In particular, the meaning of justice within a republic or, more generally, within Western liberal market democracies can be deconstructed by reflecting in detail on the ways in which the media represents the incident. It can of course be objected that generalization from a single instance is not possible. However, generalization in the statistical meaning of the term is not at stake here. Rather, it is the implicit or explicit universal 'concepts' and 'principles' that underpin judgements and claims that are the subject of critical analysis. What is drawn out are the implications of the key concepts of a debate concerning what is considered by the different viewpoints in the debate to be essential for producing the 'good society', or to be in the 'best interests' of individuals and social order. The range of arguments that can be drawn from the different viewpoints begins to establish a framework for developing the public sphere of debate. Such issues and the kinds of questions below are taken up in the Section *i* discussions (see p. 62).

Research questions

Media coverage of critical incidents provides a useful source of material for critical research. Of particular interest here are the kinds of questions that focus attention on the universalizing intent of key categories and principles. For example, a concept of 'fairness' is meant to apply to all, in all circumstances. However, what is considered fair by a rich person, is not necessarily so by a poor person. Illustrative questions that may be asked include:

- What examples of instances or 'stories' from the contemporary media can be used as a basis for exploring the strategic significance of educational, social, political, cultural, ethical and legal policies and practices for different theories of 'the good society' for all?
- What do media representations of instances say about the generalization, universalization, objectivity and validity of the incidents reported and the ways in which they are represented?
- How do the media responses to such incidents key into the universalizing or defining social, political, cultural, ethical and economic categories of social life?
- How are competing interpretations of incidents represented?
- Whose viewpoints are excluded from the media representations?

Chapter 5

Social research and 'race'[1]

Developing a critical paradigm

Gurnam Singh

Introduction

This chapter engages in a critical discussion of the different orientations of social research with black people (throughout the paper the term 'black' will be used in reference to black and minority ethnic (BME) groups). In doing so, it seeks to develop a model that is more responsive to oppressed groups whilst remaining committed to methodological rigour. The first section provides a historical context to the orientation of social research with BME individuals and communities, outlining, in particular, the ways social research has often acted to generate and reinforce racist oppression. The second section engages more directly with methodological issues and delineates the key components underpinning an emancipatory research paradigm.

Under conditions of relative powerlessness, black people are more likely to come under the gaze of state authorities and professionals. This has ramifications for both the practice of social research by members of these professions, and the collection and keeping of information relating to minority populations (Johnson 1996). Research activity in such circumstances takes on specific and conflicting functions. On the one hand, it can become complicit in reinforcing and reproducing oppression by seeking to explain the problems faced by black people in terms of their individual and collective (cultural) pathologies. One can see how through a process of racialization, research on minorities in Britain has tended to reinforce stereotypical and colonial constructions of black people (Ahmad and Sheldon 1993). Whilst the field of epidemiological research is particularly culpable in this respect (Bhopal 1992), there are many examples of the way researchers have legitimized racist oppression by making direct and indirect associations between physiology and real or imagined phenotypical characteristics and/or traditional cultural practice. Ahmad and Sheldon (1993) point out how such tendencies are evident in the ideological constructions of such things as "black people's reproductive capacity, sexuality, intelligence, ability to control the universe, 'rascality', mental breakdown, desire to run away from their slave-masters, lack of political achievements, and so on" (Ahmad and Sheldon 1993: 18).

In educational research there is a tendency to pathologize black people through the construction of deficit models which tend to focus on the individual weaknesses or differences as 'a problem' rather than on the institution as a whole. As pointed out in a recently published systematic review of widening participation:

> The terminology being used to refer to students from non-traditional backgrounds fuels the dominance of the 'deficit' model. Such students are frequently referred to as 'widening participation students', and moreover, contrasted with those from more traditional backgrounds. Institutions refer to the need to identify students from non-traditional backgrounds for tracking and monitoring purposes which, despite good intentions, fosters a 'them and us' divide.
>
> (HEFCE 2006)

On the other hand, through connecting individual problems to social, structural, economic and political domains, social research can and should function to counteract the processes of discrimination and oppression (Everitt *et al.* 1992).

Historical perspective: models of research

Although the level of interest in ethnic minority and refugee communities across Europe has never been greater, sadly, questions about their welfare have always been subservient to larger political concerns with the 'problem' of immigration and integration. It is not surprising then that, with few exceptions, much of the research on ethnic minorities has been problematic (Ahmad and Sheldon 1993; Humphries and Truman 1994). Three perspectives have characterized most public policy discussions and research about the provision of welfare services to members of minority ethnic communities in Britain: 'positivistic', 'phenomenological' and 'critical'.

Positivistic perspectives

The dominant and perhaps most enduring perspective is one that has set out to address 'race' from, essentially, an 'information-gathering exercise'. This policy-oriented research paradigm has been born out of both liberal sentiments to help black immigrants and refugees to integrate, and right-wing fears about maintaining social order and controlling immigration (Layton-Henry 1984). Primarily through the use of quantitative methodologies, certain facts about the scale and nature of minority populations, coupled with the range of problems they may be encountering, have been seen as critical to informing the decision-making process. In Britain, for example, throughout the 1960s and 1970s, large demographic surveys into 'race relations' set out to identify both the number of minorities in the country and the extent of discrimination and disadvantage they were encountering (Rose 1969; Daniel 1968; Smith 1977; Brown 1984). The positivist perspective has continued to hold the centre stage as can be seen in, for example, the work of Modood *et al.* (1997). Whilst there is no denying the value of empirical evidence that exposes discrimination and disadvantage, there are many problems with such an approach, mostly ones that echo the more general critiques of positivism made by feminist researchers (Roberts 1981; Harding 1987; Letherby 2003). Without delving into a detailed critique of the positivist empirical paradigm, I would like to offer a few words of caution.

First, whilst statistics may reveal interesting features about, for example, the age profile of a particular minority community, they are unable to tell us much about the particular needs of children and elders in that community, which may be influenced by a complex range of factors. Moreover, this type of policy research does little to help one understand the underlying social and political processes that may result in the production of social problems, such as, for example, higher rates of physical abuse and neglect amongst minority families (Creighton 1992). Further, the potential consequence of simplistic correlations based on statistical averages runs the danger of reinforcing stereotypical images of minority communities. Ahmad and Sheldon (1993), for instance, highlight examples where epidemiological studies that reveal disproportionate levels of disease or ill-health amongst minorities uncritically attribute these different levels to cultural and ethnic factors:

> Higher rates of consanguinity among Asians, particularly Pakistanis, in Britain has become the ultimate 'explanatory hypothesis' within medicine. This includes serious researchers who wish to disentangle the complex interplay between socio-economic, lifestyle, environmental and health service factors in influencing, for example, birth outcome – perinatal mortality and congenital malformations. A larger group, however, is happy to hang anything from poor birth 'outcome' to blood disorders, cancers, diseases of the eye, and much more onto this new found explanatory peg.
>
> (Ahmad and Sheldon 1993: 21)

Phenomenological perspectives

The second perspective is one that has sought to develop a more 'textured' dimension to 'race'-related questions in the lives of members of black communities. Here minorities with particular attributed labels (e.g. immigrants and asylum seekers) are not reduced to 'social facts'. To the contrary, through qualitative methodologies such as focus groups, participant observation and life-history work, researchers have attempted to map out the complex texture of their lives. Another important aspect of this paradigm is the rejection of the 'problem' finding/curing mentality and a corresponding concentration on describing the concrete interactions of minority communities, both between each other and with state agencies. Above all, this approach attempts to sub-jectivize otherwise highly objectified and abstract conceptualizations of black minority communities. At the most fundamental level there is a change from enumerating 'the exotic' to describing, with some level of understanding, the needs and aspirations of black ethnic minority communities in terms of their new cultural contexts and perspectives. These inevitably constitute a complex synthesis of past and present. By placing the concepts of culture and ethnicity as central to the analysis, texts written during the late 1970s and 1980s began to influence social work practice of the time (Cashmore 1979; Watson 1977; Khan 1979; Cheetham 1972).

However, a major criticism with what became known as the 'ethnic sensit-ivity approach' was the tendency to underplay the structural and political issues centred on the unresolved issues of racism, poverty and social exclusion (Ely and Denny 1987; Dominelli 1988). Indeed, by focusing too narrowly on black minority communities, explanations for the problems they were facing tended to reinforce and reproduce the kinds of frameworks emerging out of the black family pathology model, evident in much of the social work and health literature of the 1970s and 1980s (Lawrence 1982; Barn 1994; Prevatt-Goldstein 1999).

Emerging from these early attempts to address questions of ethnic and cultural difference (by mostly white researchers) was a series of misleading stereotypical representations of black communities. For example, studies often portrayed Afro-Caribbean families as being decadent, culturally deficient, disorganized and disintegrating – the high incidence of single parenthood, offending behaviour and low educational achievement being seen as evidence for this assertion (Cashmore and Troyna 1982). On the other hand, Asian family life was portrayed as an island of morality in a sea of (Western) decad-ence. It attempted to take a positive view of how the Asian community, in contrast to broader trends in society of chronic family breakdown (evidenced by high divorce rates and growth of single parenthood) and the contingent problems of juvenile delinquency and homelessness, had managed to retain a sense of piety, financial independence and social and familial cohesiveness. Ironically, the problems with such families were seen to lie in their inherent rigid traditional conservative outlook and repressive 'feudal' familial regimes (Singh 1992).

One of the major preoccupations of researchers was the issue of 'cultural conflict'. This referred to second-generation black young people who were seen to be trapped between the traditional expectations of their parents, on the one hand, and the conflicting social norms associated with Western culture into which they were being assimilated, on the other (Watson 1977). Particularly in relation to what became popularly known as the phenomenon of Asian girls running away from home to escape forced marriages, a number of influential social work texts during the 1960s and 1970s sought to construct 'cultural conflict' within Asian family life as a matter of fact (e.g. Fitzherbert 1967; Davies 1967; Cheetham 1972; Triseliotis 1972). These highly problematic and simplistic representations were given official credibility by organizations such as the Community Relations Council (CRC), which, ironically, was established to promote a better understanding of the 'ethnic minorities' and their respective cultures (Lawrence 1982: 112). It wasn't until the late 1980s that critiques of this approach began to register and somewhat ironically, it was young Asian women social workers and researchers that offered some of the most powerful challenges. Patel (1994), for example, in her research on homelessness amongst young black women, concludes that along with other factors they were running away because of "physical violence, emotional and sexual abuse" (Patel 1994: 35). Thus, whilst researchers were seeking to incorporate a 'race' perspective, there was a tendency to underestimate the importance of class, gender, sexuality and disability, particularly in the context of family violence (Mullender 1996; Mullender *et al.* 2002).

Leaving aside broader epistemological questions, at the level of research design and execution one can identify key elements that can characterize the failure of both perspectives described above. There has been the tendency to present ethnic identification as a given fact, and ethnic minority groups as being essentially homogeneous and self-contained. Such an approach, where policy makers and service delivery planners seek "to treat all Asian needs as one, or to wish to find a single point of access to the black and minority ethnic population", may be convenient, but it is inappropriate (Johnson 1996: 11). In doing so, a number of critical questions have been ignored.

First, as discussed earlier, quite apart from the variety of religious affiliations and languages involved, there are questions of gender, class and sexuality and their impact on both the ability of members of minority communities to resist oppression and on determining need for delivery of appropriate social services.

Second, research has tended to ignore the relationship between 'white ethnicity' as an undefined entity and 'black ethnicity' as something 'other'. Indeed, the whole question of identity formation and difference as social and psychological mechanisms has received little or no attention within social policy research until fairly recently.

Third, with the exception of feminist researchers, the importance of difference between researcher and researched, and how this may shape the research process – from question formulation through to dissemination of findings – has tended to be neglected. The failure to take into account the cultural, social and economic position of both the researchers and research subjects has resulted in a 'tendency of research to reinforce and contribute to the plethora of stereotypes and derogatory myths that prevail in the dominant society' (Mama 1989: 28) Indeed:

Alternative knowledge claims in and of themselves are rarely threatening to conventional knowledge. Such claims are routinely ignored, discarded, or simply absorbed and marginalised in existing paradigms. Much more threatening is the challenge that alternative epistemologies offer.

(Hill Collins 2000: 270–1)

Critical perspectives

As a direct consequence of the failure of academic and research institutions to develop critical understandings of the politics of research and their own Eurocentric bias (Ladner 1973; Mama 1989), debates within and outside social work emerged during the late 1980s and 1990s. In contrast to the previous perspectives which tended to take a functionalist approach, a critical perspective sets out to make politics, structural inequalities, power and oppression its prime concerns (Everitt *et al.* 1992; Barn 1994; Trinder 1996).

Drawing on many of the themes of community and radical social work of the 1970s and feminist, anti-racist and more recently anti-disablist, and service-user perspectives, this approach takes on very specific modes. By employing and developing skills and by linking individual concerns to wider social, political and economic factors, perhaps the singularly most important aim of a critical approach is to challenge oppression at all levels (Mullender and Ward 1991). Inevitably, in seeking to confront power relations, one immediately politicizes the process of research. Whilst the collection of good quality information remains important, it can no longer be the only concern for critical researchers. Trinder identifies two specific strands to research that is driven by political rather than 'scientific' or managerial imperatives. First, the researcher/practitioner needs to be located 'alongside members of oppressed groups in a non-hierarchical way, drawing links between an individual's situation and structural factors' (Trinder 1996: 239). The second strand seeks to disrupt the privileged location and knowledge of the expert in order to create space for 'the voices of the oppressed and their subjective experiences' (Trinder 1996: 239).

It is often assumed that in seeking to give 'voice' to the experiences of the oppressed, critical approaches are only interested in qualitative methodologies. Harvey (1990), however, emphasizes the danger of reducing critical social research to one domain alone. He argues that, with an overall aim of unmasking the nature of oppressive social structures, critical researchers should employ a range of methodologies and analytical techniques. Revealing a Marxist orientation, Harvey suggests that critical research can be characterized by a number of key elements of abstraction, namely, 'essence', 'totality', 'praxis', 'ideology', 'history' and 'structure'; but most importantly, they must be rooted in a materialist and dialectical conception of the world. More specifically, Mama (1989), in her study of professional responses to violence against black women in the home, identifies four specific steps that researchers can take to reduce racism in the research process: first, to minimize the possibility of miscommunication and to rectify some of the power imbalance, 'ethnic matching of researchers' should be considered; second, to give credence and priority to the accounts given by research subjects; and third, to analyse research findings in the light of the collective histories and cultures of minority groups, paying particular attention to colonial conquests, enslavement and economic exploitation. In short, critical researchers should not underestimate the ongoing legacy of the past and how this can affect relationships in the present.

Within the critical model, a three-way mutually beneficial partnership between academic researchers, frontline professionals and research subjects emerges. For academic researchers, one of the obvious benefits of such a partnership is the opportunity to overcome problems in obtaining access to research sites, subjects and, in some instances, funding. For professionals, the opportunity to participate in the construction, execution and dissemination of research offers the potential to enhance professional autonomy and to participate in a process that seeks to promote social change (Everitt *et al.* 1992; Broad 1994). Finally, for research subjects, the clearest benefits are the possibility of defining research agendas, gaining self-confidence, raising consciousness, and establishing support networks.

The language of classification

In nearly any case of social research, particularly when seeking to explore issues related to social diversity, it will be necessary to classify or label people. The point needs to be reiterated that such classifications need to be seen as a means to an end, and not the object of the study, as Humphries and Truman (1994) point out:

> Studies of different forms of inequality need to differentiate, for instance, the experiences of black people from the experiences of white people, disabled people from those of non-disabled people. However, it is neither the *blackness* or *whiteness* nor the *disability* or *non-disability* that forms the focus of the investigation but the differential *experiences* of being black or white that fundamentally reveal how inequalities are maintained.
>
> (Humphries and Truman, 1994: 3)

Many research texts warn against the dangers of essentialist assumptions, the use of a group label as if it was somehow real and by itself explained difference – and these are not confined to 'race and ethnicity' (Ahmad and Sheldon 1993). Similar dangers can arise in relation to gender (Humphries 1997), religion (Macourt 1995) or sexual relations and family structures – including the often uncontested nature of 'marriage' and household relationships (Graham 1993). Researchers should need no reminding that a person may be 'described' in all of these categories – for example, as a black, female, Buddhist and (lesbian) lone parent; and disadvantaged or advantaged by membership of each group. Equally, one should pay attention to the undefined 'control' 'white' majority category; very seldom is this group examined or explicitly defined (Frankenberg 1993; Dyer 1997). Therefore, in drawing attention to subdivisions amongst black groups, one should not forget the same consideration applies to the majority 'white' society.

The question may be rephrased – it all may be seen to depend upon how one addresses identity and difference (researcher and researched) within the research process. Spivak (1987) makes an important observation that for very specific, often political, purposes most people operate and deploy a form of 'strategic essentialism' whereby identity is presumed to be 'real' but cannot be said to be 'real' in any other sense that will determine their complete being. The danger is that the label becomes used in place of the person. Most importantly, one also needs to avoid categories that end up racializing individuals and groups. Arguably, if one argues against racism, then logically one must say that 'race' is an invalid empirical category (Miles 1989; Carter 2000). Yet, whatever category one uses, given the wider context, it is likely to assume some degree of racial intent. For example, the religious category Muslim, increasingly employed by social researchers (e.g. Modood *et al.* 1997), has, historically, within the context of Orientalism (Said 1978) and, more recently, Islamophobia, become extensively racialized.

For communication, it remains true that certain stereotypes and clichés, however dangerous, remain necessary; life is really a series of approximations and simplifications. Researchers must communicate, but at the same time be clear about the limitations of the terms and labels they use and how these are understood and mobilized by others. In sum, it is accepted that, as Humphries and Truman (1994) insist, there is no such thing as an unproblematic reality – even research is not based solely on objective knowledge, but on (as well as, in the process, making) constructed reality. Therefore, researchers are faced with the kinds of paradoxes, particularly so since it is often through deploying labels and categories that they exercise power. Perhaps the best that can be hoped for is that labels are used consciously and with the sort of footnote that Barn feels constrained to add to her discussion of anti-discriminatory research in social work: "Although the author accepts the concept of race to be a social construction and not a biological entity, the term is being employed here in the absence of other suitable terminology" (Barn 1994: 55).

It follows that when conducting social research of any kind, one needs to be explicit and aware in our use of such words in conducting and writing up research.

Towards an emancipatory paradigm

So far, I have concentrated on developing a broad discussion of a range of research approaches and how these have historically been deployed to research black people. I have argued that critical research perspectives are most suited to promote emancipatory goals. In the remainder of this paper, I will develop a more sustained discussion of the research paradigm that underpins emancipatory research. I begin this section with a discussion of the qualitative versus quantitative debate.

Theories of research are often divided into quantitative (emphasizing the collection of numerical data and statistical analysis) or qualitative (emphasizing the non-numerical and interpretative analysis of social phenomena). However, Silverman (2000) suggests that such polarities are problematic in that the resulting antagonisms do not help one group learn from another. Whilst this may be true, in some cases the use of mixed methodologies shows that researchers do value both approaches, but that each paradigm will answer a different question. For some, either approach may be emancipatory. Scott (1999), for example, identifies the strength of quantitative research in revealing the extent and systematic patterning of social inequalities in health and illness, whilst qualitative research brings into focus personal experience.

When it comes to research funding, quantitative is still seen as the gold standard (Forbes and Wainwright 2001). This may in part be due to methods employed within quantitative research tending to produce clear answers, which are easy to reject or accept according to whether or not they favour government policy. The most powerful defence of quantitative research is its claims to objective and value-free enquiry, although this is a claim that has been questioned, notably by feminist researchers (Harding 1987; Letherby 2003).

Bryman (1988) and Hammersley (1993) suggest that qualitative methodology is more likely to empower as it focuses on the self-generated meanings and understandings of participants, rather than on their actions and behaviours alone. It is also particularly useful for the study of sensitive topics and marginalized and/or difficult-to-access groups. This is mainly due to its flexible (and naturalistic) approach, typically using small samples for semi-structured, individual and group interviews intimately linked to agendas that are important to the research subjects. However, the intimacy involved in qualitative research raises additional questions about the identity of the researcher and the influence this may have on what respondents reveal. To conceptualize the knowledge and power differentials, which may facilitate or impede researchers from pursuing anti-racist goals, Boushel (2000) develops a notion of 'experiential affinity' and 'experiential interdependence'. She suggests researchers need to develop a 'costs and benefits' framework to decide what might be the most appropriate course of action. One needs to insert a word of caution about an uncritical acceptance of 'ethnic matching' in research. No one individual possesses by virtue of their ascribed identity, a 'natural' inclination to empower 'their kind'. Whilst, matching may open up the possibility of greater affinity, it doesn't guarantee it. As Ratcliffe points out, 'simply being black is not enough' (Ratcliffe 2004: 163).

Jayartine and Oakley (cited in Hammersley 1993) suggest that researchers using qualitative methodologies should work towards minimizing power differentials and exploitation. For example, in conducting face-to-face in-depth interviews, researchers should adapt, rephrase and clarify questions. Moreover, they should 'check out' answers as well as observe the body language and demeanour of participants, and query them if necessary. The potential benefits are clear: participant involvement is promoted; through the development of trust and empathy, respondents feel more able to tell their own stories and voice their own views; misunderstandings are likely to be reduced; rapport and validity may be enhanced; and more in-depth information is gained as a result.

Although the benefits outlined above are difficult to deny, qualitative research can be exploitative, particularly when interviews are conducted within a sensitive environment and/or when researching sensitive topics (Finch, quoted in Hammersley 1993). Therefore, the establishment of integrity must be a priority with study participants, and study findings must not be used to increase their oppression. Qualitative approaches are criticized by Forbes and Wainwright (2001) as overly focusing on the micro level at the expense of the macro level. Concentration on lived experience alone may 'blind' researchers to the wider social context.

Whilst qualitative research may also be criticized for its lack of structure, its relative flexibility allows researchers to be more responsive to the requirements of the participants. Conversely, there is a danger of a flexible approach that is not in some way accounted for. As Humphries (1997) warns:

> Commitment to self-reflexivity is fundamental, although this can deteriorate into a self-indulgence which places the researcher as the norm. An emancipatory intent is no guarantee of an emancipatory outcome. A self-critical account that situates the researcher at the centre of the text can perpetuate the dominance our emancipatory intentions hope to fight. Our own frameworks need to be interrogated as we look for the tensions and contradictions in our research practice, paradoxically aware of our own complicity in what we critique
>
> (Humphries 1997: para 4.10)

Research as politics

Whilst the purpose of all research is to generate new insights, a critical anti-racist perspective would seek to extend this remit by identifying political imperatives that transcend the desire to generate new knowledge, theory and insights alone. Thus, anti-racist researchers must seek, as a bare minimum, to diminish the effects of racist oppression for the research subjects. French and Swain (2004), speaking from a disability perspective, propose that emancipatory research needs to goes further in its liberation of the participants: participants should control the research agenda, process and outcome, and the researcher/s should place their knowledge and skill at the disposal of the researched. Whilst such perspectives offer an important ideal, a more realistic position may be to ensure a high degree of reflexivity and openness between researcher/s and researched in order to develop sensitivity to the potential for oppression at each stage of the research process. Cotterill and Letherby (1993) point out how, even if one has managed to be inclusive and participatory from the outset, participants have little control at the writing-up stage. Ribbons and Edwards (1998) point out that, more often than not, the researcher chooses what to leave in and what to discard. A way to deal with this power imbalance could be to make findings available to research subjects for them to offer their own critiques and conclusion, which in turn could be incorporated into final reporting.

Despite good intentions, social researchers need to be aware of the near impossibility of equalizing the power relationship. In analysing qualitative researchers, Fine (1994) draws attention to the potential for self-deception and the dangers therein. She argues that qualitative researchers often reproduce a 'colonizing discourse' of the 'other' whilst maintaining a self-delusion that they have given voice to the oppressed. The challenge, therefore, for the critical anti-racist researcher is to relay the story of the research subjects; interpretation yes, but total reconstruction, no. Even where the researcher is from the researched 'other' group, s/he cannot assume that membership alone will be sufficient to prevent this from occurring.

Conclusion

Whether or not one feels that research should be a neutral, dispassionate, fact-finding activity, one cannot escape the historical, political and social contexts in which it takes place. The distribution of power within society is undoubtedly influenced by 'race', gender, class and other axes of social differentiation. It follows that the process of research – from funding, the types of questions asked, the methodologies adopted, and the writing-up and dissemination – becomes implicated as political activity, even if this goes unacknowledged. Social research is rarely a benign activity; it serves to explain and explain away, and therefore it can serve different functions. Moreover, depending on such disparate factors as personal motivation, circumstance, funding sources and access arrangements, conflicts of interest will always be a factor. An approach that is complacent about the insidious modalities of power is likely to lead to oppressive outcomes, even where there is no obvious intent. Since people's lives are structured by the unequal distribution of power, social research can either be used to ignore, obscure or reinforce such inequalities, or it can be used to uncover, confront and reduce them (Trinder, 1996). In this paper, I have sought to outline key aspects of an approach that is capable of doing the latter. Yet one needs to be realistic about what can be achieved given the inherent power inequalities in the research process. For example, as no two human beings share exactly the same experience of living, degrees of ontological separation will always exist. A more realistic and honest approach will be where the researcher seeks to maximize and encourage participation, whilst recognizing the limits of one's own subjectivity.

References

Ahmad, W.I.U. and Sheldon, T.A. (1993) '"Race" and statistics', in M. Hammersley (ed.), *Social Research: Philosophy, politics and practice*. London: Sage.

Barn, R. (1994) 'Race and ethnicity in social work: Some issues for anti-discriminatory research', in B. Humphries and C. Truman (eds.), *Re-thinking Social Research: Anti-discriminatory approaches in research methodology*. Aldershot: Ashgate.

Bhopal, R. (1992) 'Future research on health of ethnic minorities' in W.I.U. Ahmad, *The Politics of 'Race' and Health*. Bradford: Bradford University Race Relations Research Unit, 51–4.

Boushel, M. (2000) 'What kind of people are we? "Race", anti-racism and social welfare research', *British Journal of Social Work*, 30(1), 71–89.

Broad, B. (1994) 'Anti-discriminatory practitioner social work research: Some basic problems and possible remedies', in B. Humphries and C. Truman (eds.), *Re-thinking Social Research: Anti-discriminatory approaches in research methodology*. Aldershot: Ashgate.

Brown, C. (1984) *Black and White Britain: The third PSI survey*. London: Heinemann.

Bryman, A. (1988) *Quantity and Quality in Social Research*. London: Unwin Hyman.

Carter, B. (2000) *Realism and Racism: Concepts of Race in Sociological Research*. London: Routledge.

Cashmore E. (1979) *Rastaman: The Rastafarian movement in England*. London, Boston: Allen & Unwin.

Cashmore, E. and Troyna, B. (eds.) (1982) *Black Youth in Crisis*. London: Allen and Unwin.

Cheetham, J. (1972) *Social Work with Immigrants*. London: Routledge and Kegan Paul.

Cotterill, P. and Letherby, G. (1993) 'Weaving stories: Personal autobiographies in feminist research'. *Women's Studies International Forum*, 15, 5/6, 593–606.

Creighton, S.J. (1992) *Child Abuse Trends in England and Wales 1988–1990 and an Overview From 1973–1990*. London: NSPCC.

Daniel, W. (1968) *Racial Discrimination in England*. London: Penguin.

Davies, J. (1967) 'Thursday's child has far to go'. *Case Conference*, 14(8), 298–303.

Dominelli, L. (1988) *Anti-Racist Social Work*, London: Macmillan. 2nd edition. 1997; 3rd edition. 2007.

Dyer, R. (1997) *White*. London: Routledge.

Ely, P. and Denny, D. (1987) *Social Work in a Multi-Racial Society*, Aldershot: Gower.

Everitt A., Hardiker P., Littlewood J. and Mullender, A. (1992) *Applied Research for Better Practice*. Basingstoke: Macmillan Press.

Fine, M. (1994) 'Dis-stance and other stances: Negotiations of power inside feminist research', in A. Gitlin (ed.), *Power and Method: Political activism and educational research*. London: Routledge.

Fitzherbert, K. (1967) *West Indian Children in London*. London: G. Bell & Sons.

Forbes, A. and Wainwright, S.P. (2001) 'On the methodological, theoretical and philosophical context of health inequalities research: A critique', *Social Science and Medicine*, 53, 6, 801–16.

Frankenberg, R. (1993) *White Women, Race Matters: The social construction of whiteness*. Minneapolis: University of Minnesota Press.

French, S. and Swain, J. (2004) 'Researching together: A participatory approach', in S. French and J. Sim (eds), *Physiotherapy: A psychosocial approach* (3rd edition). Butterworth Heinemann: Oxford.

Graham, H. (1993) *Hardship and Health in Women's Lives*. London: Harvester.

Hammersley, M. (ed.) (1993) *Social Research: Philosophy, politics and practice*. London: SAGE/ Open University.

Harding, S. (ed.) (1987) *Feminism and Methodology*. Milton Keynes: Open University Press.

Harvey, L. (1990) *Critical Social Research*. London: Unwin Hyman.

HEFCE (2006) *Review of Widening Participation Research: Addressing the barriers to participation in higher education*. A report to HEFCE by the University of York, Higher Education Academy and Institute for Access Studies. Available at: http://www.hefce.ac.uk/pubs/rdreports/2006/ rd13_06/barriers.doc.

Hill Collins, P. (2000) *Black Feminist Thought: Knowledge, consciousness and the politics of empowerment* (2nd edition). London: Routledge.

Humphries, B. (1997) 'From critical thought to emancipatory action: Contradictory research goals?' *Sociological Research Online*, 2, 1. Available at: http://www.socresonline.org.uk/2/1/3. html (accessed August 15, 2009).

Humphries, B. and Truman, C. (1994) *Rethinking Social Research*. Aldershot: Avebury.

Johnson M.R.D. (1996) *Good Practice and Quality Indicators in Primary Health Care*. Leeds: NHS Ethnic Health Unit.

Khan, V. (1979) *Minority Families in Britain: Support and stress*. London: Macmillan.

Ladner, J. (ed.) (1973) *The Death of White Sociology*. New York: Random House.

Lawrence, E. (1982) 'Just plain common sense: The 'roots' of racism, in CCCS', in *The Empire Strikes Back: Race and racism in 70s Britain*. London: Routledge.

Layton-Henry, Z. (1984) *The Politics of Race in Britain*. London: Allen and Unwin.

Letherby, G. (2003) *Feminist Research in Theory and Practice*. Buckingham: Open University Press.

Macourt, M. (1995) 'Using census data: Religion as a key variable in studies of Northern Ireland', *Environment and Planning*, 27, 4, Apr, 593–614.

Mama, A. (1989) *The Hidden Struggle: Statutory and voluntary sector responses to violence against black women in the home*. London: London Race and Housing Research Unit.

Miles, R. (1989) *Racism*. London: Routledge.

Modood, T., Berthoud, R., Lakey, J., Nazroo, J., Smith, P., Virdee, S. and Beishon, S. (1997) *Ethnic Minorities in Britain: Diversity and disadvantage – fourth national survey of ethnic minorities*. London: Policy Studies Institute.

Mullender, A. (1996) *Rethinking Domestic Violence: The social work and probation response*. London: Routledge.

Mullender, A. and Ward, D. (1991) *Self-Directed Groupwork: Users take action for empowerment*. London: Whiting and Birch.

Mullender, A., Hague, G., Imam, U., Kelly, L., Malos, E. and Regan, L. (2002) *Children's Perspectives on Domestic Violence*. London: Sage.

Patel, G. (1994) *The Porth Project: A study of homelessness and running away amongst young black people in Newport, Gwent*. London: The Children's Society.

Prevatt-Goldstein, B. (1999) 'Black, with a white parent, a positive and achievable identity', *British Journal of Social Work*, 29, 285–301.

Ratcliffe, P. (2004) *Race, Ethnicity and Difference*. Buckingham: Open University Press.

Ribbons, J. and Edwards, R. (1998) *Feminist Dilemmas in Qualitative Research: Public knowledge and private lives*. London: Sage.

Roberts, H. (1981) *Doing Feminist Research*, London, Boston: Routledge & Kegan Paul.

Rose, E. (1969) *Colour and Citizenship: A report on British race relations*. Oxford: Institute of Race Relations/Oxford University Press.

Said, E. (1978) *Orientalism*. London: Routledge and Kegan Paul; Harmondsworth: Penguin, 1995 (with new afterword).

Scott, P. (1999) 'Black people's health: Ethnic status and research issues', in S. Hood, B. Mayall and S. Oliver (eds), *Critical Issues in Social Research*. Buckingham: Open University Press.

Silverman, D. (2000) *Doing Qualitative Research: A practical handbook*. London: Sage.

Singh, G. (1992) *Race and Social Work: From black pathology to black perspectives*. Bradford: Race Relations Unit, University of Bradford.

Smith, D.J. (1977) *Racial Disadvantage in Britain*. London: Penguin.

Spivak, G.C. (1987) *In Other Worlds: Essays in cultural politics*. London: Methuen.

Trinder, L. (1996) 'Social work research: The state of the art (or science)', *Child and Family Social Work*, 1, 4, 233–42.

Triseliotis, J. (Ed.) (1972) *Social Work with Coloured Immigrants and Their Families*. Oxford: Institute of Race Relations/Oxford University Press.

Watson, J.L (Ed.) (1977) *Between Two Cultures: Migrants and minorities in Britain*. Oxford: Blackwell.

Reflections on Singh's chapter

Singh's chapter critically discusses the different orientations of social research with black and minority ethnic groups (BME). He argues that a new model for research is needed, as mainstream models are inappropriate. In particular, being relatively powerless, BME groups more frequently attract "the gaze of state authorities and professionals" who commission research. In this context, research can become "complicit in reinforcing and reproducing oppression". Thus, Singh "seeks to develop a model that is more responsive to oppressed groups whilst remaining committed to methodological rigour". To do so he describes the three perspectives that, for the most part, public policy and research on provision of welfare services have adopted: 'positivistic', 'phenomenological' and 'critical'. In his view, "Social research is rarely a benign activity; it serves to explain and explain away, and therefore it can serve different functions". Conflicts of interest will always be a factor. Indeed, in analyzing and writing up, self-deception lurks in the dark shadows ready to overwhelm the writer into the possessive act of "a 'colonising discourse' of the 'other'", whilst being self-deluded into thinking that a voice has been given to the oppressed. In response to such a view, Singh considers what would be needed for a genuinely emancipatory research practice.

Research questions

In the work of research:

- Where does interpretation end and reconstruction begin?
- How can the political stakes be changed? Would it amount to reversing

prevailing practices, where participants might control the research agenda? Or is such an intention too ambitious?

- Is it possible to bring about "a high degree of reflexivity and openness between researcher/s and researched in order to develop sensitivity to the potential for oppression at each level of the research process"?
- Should research findings be offered to the researched in order that they are able to add their own critiques and conclusion?
- In reality how exactly can one equalize the power relationship between researcher and researched?

Chapter 6

Violence, social exclusion and construction of identities in early childhood education

Concepción Sánchez Blanco

In this chapter, Blanco writes of the violence born of poverty and prejudice in a culture of excess. She writes, too, of teachers needing to be aware that they may "involuntarily be fostering the sort of structural violence against less privileged children (Ross Epp and Watkinson 1999) which is so ubiquitous in a neoliberal society extolling ownership and consumption as the basic principles of existence".

Very young children can be fully aware of the circumstances of their lives:

> *Little children's drawings and discourses with regard to the poor show us their awareness of extreme poverty due to illnesses, the lack of housing or half-destroyed buildings and houses, tattered clothes, the lack of food. This is a world which they have access to by means of the discourses from their own families, their schools, the mass media, although the influence exerted by the kind of stereotyped leisure promoted by the multinational companies of child entertainment must not be forgotten.*
>
> *(Steinberg and Kincheloe 2000)*

How then should schools respond?

To begin with

The reflections in this chapter draw upon qualitative and ethnographic research conducted in school playgrounds and second-stage early childhood education classrooms in government schools situated in the city of A Coruña (in the autonomous region of Galicia, in north-western Spain), as well as from interviews that were made with teachers working in this particular age group within the Spanish educational system. The aim of the research was to explore the physical violence taking place and to try to find ways to analyze and understand the phenomenon of violence in the context of schools. Efforts were focused on the behaviour of children whose ages ranged from three to five years old. Fundamentally, the most interesting thing was to investigate those processes that emerge in school environments which may promote a culture in which children learn to use violence, from the very earliest of ages, to solve their social conflicts, under the perception that this is a socially legitimate strategy.

Observing, discussing and analyzing issues related to economic inequality and social exclusion, as well as promoting the construction of a culture of peace as the central point of teaching work, played a fundamental role in this research. This was precisely because of the weight such issues and values have on children's identities from the very earliest days of their schooling.

Values and teaching: Remembering the basics

In our context, that there is a presumed loss of values taking place in our society is an argument with conservative overtones typically used to account for physical violence in schools from children's first years at school. It is an argument that needs to be reviewed and questioned. Where teaching is concerned, arguments such as this are often accompanied by teachers complaining about the loss of their authority in the eyes of pupils. Now, what sort of authority are we talking about? Although it may be true that there has been an erosion or disappearance of the political messianisms of previous generations, as Lipovetsky has pointed out, it may also be the case that this weakening of previous positions also facilitates a reconciliation between competing democracies themselves and their basic moral principles in the development of 'human rights' (Lipovetsky 2006; Lipovetsky and Charles 2006).

It is therefore time to reconsider the value and importance of teaching, particularly if it is true that teachers have lost authority vis-à-vis families, pupils, the school community and society in general. Such a loss of authority is particularly apparent in the context of a world where information is hyper-multiplied and can be seen as a manifestation of consumer society's culture of excess, and, as such, may be devalued for that very reason. That is to say, if we defend teachers' authority by claiming their superiority in terms of the transmission of 'information', we are lost, because Google, the search engine, clearly outdoes teachers in this respect. That is why it is so urgent to focus on the ethical dimensions of the teaching role in relation to the representation of human rights in schools. To do so involves thinking ethically about all the activities schools organize and to present them as such to their pupils from the very earliest of ages.

I suggest a Copernican turn in teaching that involves working in favour of dismantling the metaphor according to which teachers and pupils are enemies from the very earliest of ages and which does nothing whatsoever to make coexistence in classrooms and schools any easier. From such a confrontational stance, teachers may come to believe that it is easier for pupils to spend their time going around causing trouble and acting like vandals, disrupting and boycotting lessons rather than getting involved in school activities. This sort of scenario culminates in devaluing teachers' initiatives because pupils may end up believing that the teaching staff only do the things which are interesting to them, and even that, as some older pupils state, they are nothing but a 'heap of lazybones' who think of nothing except their holidays and who live the grand life. Both parties need to come to know each other better. The children must become aware of the fact that being a teacher, like being a pupil, entails a number of unavoidable duties and indisputable rights. These need to be known by both parties from the very beginning of schooling. There is no better manner of achieving this than by organizing classroom projects to work at these issues in a serious and committed way (Le Gal 2005).

Even though there are teachers who are disappointed with their pupils, the fact that there are also young boys and girls who are equally disappointed with their teachers should also be taken into account. This feeling of disappointment is built gradually from the very beginning of their schooling. However, the type of schooling I propose takes on the commitment of fostering a context where families have a sufficient degree of trust in the school culture, from the beginning of their children's education, in order to encourage them to send their children to school to learn, rather than this being a question of compulsory schooling. Children, for their part, need to feel that they truly want to go to school, rather than feeling the need to pretend to be ill or to stay away from school by playing truant so as to run away from a reality that does not recognize them.

The fiction of a happy world

Isolating little children in a space of their own, with protective candy-flossed walls which prevents them from seeing the calamities of the world, during their first years at early childhood education is most risky (Starratt 1994: 23), leading perhaps to a process of gradual disillusionment as they confront the harsh realities of everyday life when they later start in primary school. This process of illusion versus disillusion often results in little boys and girls becoming aggressive or shy and reserved. What they are really doing, though, is nothing but expressing the frustration that follows this manifest deception that stems from a real reluctance during the time of early schooling to analyze the frustrations and misfortunes that take place in the lives of many children.

Early childhood education institutions ought to take on the commitment of helping little boys and girls learn to reflect upon the meaning of their own lives in their community, which includes both their pleasant situations and their suffering, and to try to find ways to explain and understand them. Even other issues, such as the fact that pleasant occurrences also include an unpleasant part, need to be treated and worked through in classrooms, for example, even though breaking-up for the school holidays means spending more time with one's family, it also means a farewell to friends and other kind people (Sánchez Blanco 2000).

An early childhood education ought to offer little children contexts where they might learn to analyze the things that happen in their everyday lives and to look for ways of bearing the disillusion that they may cause. There should be no question that either they themselves or other people actually deserve such a fate. Therefore, as well as play, there is also a need to generate more projects which directly raise issues that do anything but amuse and which are, nonetheless, a part of our everyday lives, such as war, illnesses, hunger, physical abuse or traffic accidents. It goes without saying that matters related to violence fall on the other side of the fence to, for example, films that reinforce the view that everything has to be funny and entertaining (Sarabia 1998: 51–2). Such films try to exploit the funny side of violence, even though there is evidently and emphatically no such side to it in reality.

This world of 'sugar' is in tune with that perverse socialization process focused on showing children 'the best', which is often promoted by the mass media as being synonymous with a responsible paternity/maternity. In short, it is about ideas closely linked to a culture of excess, in an era when shortage and hardship prevail in an ever-growing sector of the population and which succeeds in trapping many families in an uninterrupted production process in order to pay their debts even, in some cases, to the point of searching for other less legitimate ways of fulfilling their obligations. Thus, constructing that happy world in early childhood education often corresponds more to a construction of the adult world, which is often commercialized, than it does to the real needs of little boys and girls.

Violence, class ethnocentrism and exclusion

A segregationist ideology believes that it is impossible to have a climate of coexistence when certain types of pupils are present in schools. The truancy of those considered troublesome or problematic turns out to be enormously useful for the continued reproduction of segregationist ideas, particularly those very pernicious ones which consider that such childhood behaviour as truancy leads to future criminal behaviour (Carlen, Gleeson and Wardhaug 1992: 62–3). The cause of the problem in this view is perceived to be the children. This is a position which buries any debate about the relationship between violence and exclusion. Sadly, such views hamper the development of measures aimed at making it easier to include pupils from socially marginalized groups.

Such a conservative and segregationist ideology does nothing but lend support to clashes between the middle class represented by teaching staff and 'well-off families', and the working class represented by poor pupils, foreign immigrants feeling rootless, ethnic minorities and traditionally marginalized groups, such as the gypsy ethnic group in our research. Debarbieux (1997: 38) makes reference to the fact that it is not a question of painting a picture of these children as if they were 'savages' or 'barbarians', nor painting a picture of teachers as if they were some privileged people getting rid of marginalized ones; rather there is the lack of a sense of civic responsibility revealing a painful economic and social rift tainted by aspects of ethnic discrimination (cf. Kozol 1991). This ideology leads to very young children constructing their school experience in terms of 'they and we' and 'foes and friends', as Debarbieux (1997:

89) would put it. According to this author, democratic societies are faced with one of their greatest challenges through the perspective of violence: whether being different from an ethnic point of view is to be considered as something positive or whether, on the contrary, xenophobic deviations or self-exclusion is to be viewed in a positive light. The social hope for integration by means of schools and employment grows smaller as the gap between 'them', the excluded ones, and 'us', the more privileged, included ones, becomes wider. A possible solution to this problem (and not in schools alone) could consist in transforming the desire for equality into a demand for a differentiated and ethnified identity on the part of the teaching staff and the pupils alike. Such a solution clashes with the effort that has lately gone into a number of political initiatives aimed at turning the neoliberal socio-economic model, together with its social manifestations, into a supposedly progressive and scientific one. The aim is to put an end to the power of collective action by specific groups (ethnic ones, for instance), even to the point of making them effectively disappear since they interfere with the dynamics of the market. The end result thus causes the excluded collectives to be restigmatized. Teaching ought to be used with the objective of allowing the voice of minorities to be heard, as well as bringing those minorities whose protests attack everyone's rights, back to the path of dialogue and democratic participation.

However, rather than dialogue and democratic participation, a whole discourse is appearing around the so called 'school security policy' (Mooij 1997: 42), which goes beyond rethinking issues related to the presence of secure school spaces and school equipment. These matters often place certain characters who come from groups that are exposed to marginalization at the 'centre of the controversy'; little girls and boys who personally suffer campaigns guided by the 'secure schools' motto which suggests that there is a type of population that makes the rest of the pupils feel insecure. The 'security in schools' motto has become yet another element used for marketing certain products such as metal detectors, teaching materials designed to prevent or defend oneself against school violence and judo lessons, and this is all in line with the demand that is generated by the lucrative security business in the market society.

As Tonucci points out (1997: 32), money itself has generated a number of defences which we consider to be legitimate: reinforced glass, armed security guards, policemen and alarms. All of these things have come to be viewed as natural by us, and even legitimate. This idea has extended itself to the field of education and it is plain to see that its influence reaches all the way into our schools. This whole discourse and the measures which are all about creating, supposedly, more secure spaces do nothing but contribute to the population making their fear of certain groups visible beforehand. However, even if the school community's wish for security is legitimate, the questionable issue here, as we are beginning to see, is the way that such security policies look and the ideology of exclusion that supports them, not only in schools but in other social environments as well. Drastic coercive and punitive measures are conceived as useful with a view to putting an end to violence in schools, because they are based on identifying the supposed risk groups; and establishing special class-rooms and/or schools for these groups contributes once more to stigmatizing these children from the very earliest of ages. Far from privileging democracy in the social relations which develop in school environments, such strategies instead contribute to creating hierarchies that are supported by the fact that only certain subjects are considered to enjoy particular rights.

Conceptions such as those find themselves strengthened by perceptions that are characteristic for this time and age and which end up turning schools, just like homes, into a sort of hyper-reinforced refuge, in all respects, sheltering us from a world which is considered to be particularly hostile and violent. In this context, it is easy for children to learn that talking to or receiving gifts from strangers is dangerous, and all the more so if the groups concerned are socially stigmatized as threatening and criminal, and not as a set of individuals who have got something important to offer.

Thus, there are certain situations and practices which do nothing at all to help to construct spaces where social heterogeneity is perceived to be associated with and not contrary to coexistence. At a very early stage, early schooling has got to offer children experiences of environments far removed from the zonification which so frequently takes place in towns and cities (children at school, poor people in the suburbs, the upper classes in the leafy suburbs) and the idyllic and isolated rural areas which are offered as a guarantee of freedom from social clashes and fractures.

This spirit of zonifying may very well be introducing itself into schools, not only by turning classrooms into watertight social compartments functioning as separated individualities or closed social worlds (Sánchez Blanco 2006: 231–5), but also by certain teaching strategies developing in early childhood education classrooms, some of which are deeply rooted in the pedagogical tradition of this particular stage. For instance, this is the case when it comes to dividing the classroom into fixed work corners and work zones where the space they take up, as well as the equipment that is used, the way it is used, the amount of time it is used for, and the little boys and girls who take up this space are perfectly well-organized and regulated, so that any inflexible alteration of this established order is suppressed and even punished by the teacher. One might therefore ask what the point of such strategies is when we live in a world in which, as Guéhenno points out (1995: 32), human activity is freeing itself from spatial limitations when the mobility of women and men is blowing geographic demarcations into bits and pieces?

Therefore, we must rid ourselves of practices such as the ones we have been criticizing, in order to deconstruct the belief that living a zonified and confron-tational existence is something perfectly normal. Rather, it is the separation of human beings into 'they' and 'we' and 'friends' and 'foes' which needs to be transformed (Schostak and Schostak 2008). We would have to think about the fact that children's rights to security necessitate an environment which has not been degraded either socially or physically. This requirement clashes openly with the living conditions of some children within and outside our context and we cannot remain impassive before this situation. We need to continue our work of denouncing and transforming it by involving the children themselves in this task at a very early age.

By way of final considerations

We cannot allow those pupils who, for whatever reason, break the norms of coexistence to end up being labelled in such a way that they become prisoners of these categories, such as: 's/he's a bully', 's/he's a pervert', 's/he's given to violence', 's/he's a troublemaker', because these individual labels cause the subjects who receive them (whether they are classmates, schoolmates, teachers or other adults) to remember their 'reprehensible' acts rather than their 'good' sides; that is, that which places them outside the sort of everyday practices that fall within the rules of normal behaviour, thus labelling them as 'deviant', as outside the accepted social rules (Schostak 1983: 65). When the culture of prejudice is passed on from one generation to another, just like the culture of control, we end up viewing it as something absolutely 'natural' when it is actually something culturally or socially constructed. We have to try to understand the dialectic relationship between deviation and control; one acts on the other; they both work to form and support each other.

The social dramas of everyday life include deviance. There is a great variety of theories that endeavour to answer questions about deviance. Some forms of deviance are aggressive and violent, whereas others are passive and mild. In popular language, typical explanations of violent or aggressive behaviour include: no one is perfect, it's due to bad company, we have innate violent and aggressive impulses, or it is the fault of parents or of society (cf. Schostak 1983: 16–17). The very tension found between generations, which has always existed, has sometimes been interpreted as a deviation, meaning that a fear of the young is generated in adults to a point where it becomes irrational. Carrión (1999: 64) points out that the most reactionary politicians, cheered on by the mass media which are always thirsty for stories of blood and violence featuring juvenile delinquents, stoke up that fire by announcing terrible disasters and by distorting and manipulating facts and statistics in order to cast a shadow over the outlook. The fact that the number of crimes committed by minors in comparison to general crime in this country (Spain) as a whole is very low does not seem to matter.

All of this leads us to believe that teachers have to reflect upon and learn from children's ways of resisting teachers' authoritarianism and despotism in school environments. Is it truly a question of deviant behaviour which is worrying us because it may affect coexistence in schools? Or is it a case of children rebelling against or denouncing the exclusion to that which they find themselves subject? It must be borne in mind that these manifestations may often aim at re-establishing equal relations, even though the roads chosen to do so may not be lawful. However, they end up establishing themselves as rituals of active resistance aimed at sabotaging a school institution that excludes them (Giroux 2003; McLaren 1995). Therefore, it is vitally important for schools and classrooms to generate a vast number of channels which reflect the pupils' discontent and are capable of generating strategies of change through which they can solve issues in a peaceful manner.

References

Carlen, P., Gleeson, D. and Wardhaug, A.J. (1992) *Truancy: The politics of compulsory schooling*. London: Open University Press.

Carrión, I. (1999) 'Niños en cárceles de adultos', *El País*, Sunday Supplement 1178, 25 April, 56–72.

Debarbieux, E. (1997) 'La violencia en la escuela francesa', *Revista de Educación*, 313, 79–93.

Guéhenno, J.M. (1995) *El Fin de la Democracia: La crisis política y las nuevas reglas de juego*. Barcelona: Paidós.

Giroux, H.A. (2003) *La Inocencia Robada: Juventud, multinacionales y política cultural*. Madrid: Morata.

Kozol, J. (1991) *Savage Inequalities*. New York: Crown Publishers.

Le Gal, J. (2005) *Los Derechos del Niño en la Escuela: Una educación para la ciudadanía*. Barcelona: Graó.

Lipovetsky, G. (2006) *La Felicidad Paradójica: Ensayos sobre la sociedad del hiperconsumo*. Barcelona: Anagrama.

Lipovetsky, G. and Charles, S. (2006) *Los Tiempos Hipermodernos*. Barcelona: Anagrama.

McLaren, P. (1995) *Critical Pedagogy and Predatory Culture: Oppositional politics in a postmodern era*. London: Routledge.

Mooij, Ton (1997) 'Por la seguridad en las escuelas', *Revista de Educación*, 313, 29–52.

Ross Epp, Juanita and Watkinson, Ailsa M. (1999) *La Violencia en el Sistema Educativo: Del daño que las escuelas causan a los niños*. Madrid: La Muralla.

Sánchez Blanco, C. (2000) *Dilemas de la Educación Infantil*. Vol. I. Sevilla: M.C.E.P.

Sánchez Blanco, C. (2006) *La Cooperación en Educación Infantil*. A Coruña: Universidade da Coruña.

Sarabia, B. (1998) 'Violencia adolescente', *Rev. Cuenta y Razón del Pensamiento Actual*, 106 (April–May), 49–52.

Schostak, J. (1983) *Maladjusted Schooling: Deviance, social control and individuality in secondary schooling*. London: Falmer Press.

Schostak, J.F. and Schostak, J. (2008) *Radical Research: Designing, developing and writing research to make a difference*. London: Routledge.

Starratt, R.J. (1994) *Building an Ethical School: A practical response to the moral crisis in schools*. London, Washington DC: Falmer Press.

Steinberg, SH.R. and Kincheloe, J.L. (Comps.) (2000) *Cultura Infantil y Multinacionales*. Madrid: Morata.

Tonucci, F. (1997) *La Ciudad de los Niños*. Fundación Sánchez Ruipérez, Madrid.

Reflections on Blanco's chapter

Blanco's chapter argues from the standpoint of a researcher and teacher committed to building a culture of peace in the context of early childhood education in Spain. Her focus is on those pervasive processes that promote the use of violence as a natural means to solve conflicts. She argues for a reconception of and revaluation of the importance of teaching. This involves thinking ethically about all aspects of schooling in the lives of young children. Blanco argues forcefully for a "Copernican turn in teaching", that is, a revolution in thinking and practice in working with very young children. It involves a commitment to "dismantling the metaphor according to which teachers and pupils are enemies" (see p. 103).

She describes the "fiction of a happy world" that is, fostered for very young children, arguing that this leads to a process of disappointment that can in turn lead to the frustration that generates confrontation and violence. Rather than the fiction, teaching ought to focus on the realities and provide the means by which to deal with these. For many children, such realities include various forms of discrimination, such as racism as well as poverty. In addressing such issues, teachers need to look at their own profession, their own practices, their own discourses and make changes where necessary.

Research questions

Practitioners may carry out research in schools and on their own practice in order to generate the possibilities for change and so ask:

• To what extent are teachers implicated in forms of structural violence that are present in the prevailing neoliberal market philosophies?
• What forms of disappointment, frustration and inequalities are experienced by children?
• What are the ways in which children resist the processes of schooling?
• How may schools contribute to the development of social justice?
• How can schools and teaching be organized to promote dialogue that includes all voices through democratic participation and the construction of a culture of peace?

Methodological discussion section *ii*

Resisting identities and boundaries

Jill Schostak and John F. Schostak

The discussion of Section *i* focused principally upon the contextual conditions within which methodologies to research violence, democracy and people's rights are constructed in order to contribute to the creation of the conditions for the emergence of a public in which none are excluded. The discussion in Section *ii* now focuses more upon the intricacies of contestation where boundaries are challenged, Power(s) resist and categories become 'shifty', that is, where Power is unhinged and individuals exercise their powers to redefine, transform and create the conditions for alternative social forms. In the gaps that open up, what are the methodological possibilities for the emergence of alternative 'spheres of justice' and thus of a new model of education and democratic practice? How may research methodology be employed to open up the spaces of questioning and critique?

In Chapter 4, Normand relays the story of a young ethnic minority girl wearing a 'bandana' in school. The school, a public place, a common space, operates a dress-code. However, when is a bandana (judged as acceptable) not a bandana (thus becoming unacceptable)? The events that happen in the account throw into question the 'validity', 'objectivity' and 'reliability' of the naming of the object that appears in public. The questionability of the name makes the application of the school rules problematic and contestable. In routine circumstances where the names of things are relatively stable, and the school rules are taken for granted by all, the underlying tacit rules and regulatory powers of social order remain invisible; once, however, what constitutes routine is broken, once the 'taken for granted' becomes problematic and the forbidden is inscribed in the public space (that is, the scarf can now be named in terms of its function as a religious symbol), the invisible becomes visible. By describing the transformation of the bandana into a scarf that can be named as a religious symbol, Normand begins to address the play of tensions between private (faith) and public (political values and principles through which the concept of, say, a republic is constituted), between the invisible and the visible, and between the mode of living in a faith community and the polis composed of citizens of the republic. These tensions continue to play out throughout the entire narrative like a game of hide and seek, and Normand ensures that the reader realizes this by attending to the smallest detail within the dense complexities of social interaction. As the bandana gradually enlarges to cover more of the young girl's hair, when does it take on the appearance of a headscarf and not a bandana, and to whom? Who has the authority, the state backing, to assume the gaze of Power in order to decide and impose decisions? Whose voice judges the limit case, the point at which the bandana has crossed the line and become the headscarf? When does that transition occur, when is the instance of fixing or of baptizing, which names the precise moment of transgression from bandana to forbidden headscarf? Through her action of gradually changing the width of the cloth, she creates a symbolic space where in the personal domain of apparent fashion, choices are made that gradually transmute into a symbol of faith. This symbol is bit by bit inscribed and thus made visible in what Power has constituted as a 'public domain'. In this space, faith is positioned as 'private' and is thus debarred. However, faith here demands to be public and poses a challenge. Hence in a small way the young ethnic minority girl disturbs and destabilizes the routine structures and processes in which the school, as a representative of the 'majority' or of Power, defines what is 'proper' to appear in public. A major battle, in this seemingly trivial incident, is invoked: that between reason as the antithesis of faith where 'reason' through the French Revolution gave birth to the contemporary republic and its constitutional definitions of public space. There is a lot at stake for each side.

Crudely, there is a contest of universals in the tiny particulars of everyday life. The one universal principle of order – reason – does not leave space within the public for the other universal principle of order – faith – which must always remain an expression of private opinion. And faith demands that its law replaces the law of reason. An identity formed under reason does not leave space for an identity formed under faith. For both to coexist there must be a space that supports plurality rather than reducing all to a single system: that is, either faith or reason but not both. If identities are framed by universals then under conditions of plurality, a sense of identity is produced in the interplay, or clash, between reason and faith as they are articulated in the interactions that compose the dramas of everyday life through which public space is constituted.

The meaning of public spaces is contested, boundaries are disputed and territories are staked out, as claims are made towards a particular personal and collective identity. The move from fashion statement to religious statement in a system that excludes religious expression is a provocation on the one hand and an assertion of identity on the other. Thus, the young girl is seeking a voice to give substance to what she may consider her 'real' identity, which is rendered invisible by the official identities of the school and classroom; while some of the teachers seek to restore and reinforce the status quo, putting an end to permitting a pupil to have a faith-based voice. There is much at stake here. It is not the mere application of one set of rules rather than another. There is the emotional binding of an identity with one way of life rather than another. The bandana changes the emotional tone as its width increases to become ever closer to being the forbidden scarf. This emotional charge that binds identity to a particular object and its appearance is the little bit of *jouissance*, the *petit a* of Lacanian psychoanalysis which is employed as a theoretical mechanism to explain expressions of desire and demand that underlie everyday behaviours and the explosions of frustration and anger that accompany seemingly trivial events.

Others, more 'at home' with themselves in Arendt's sense, may strive to recognize the apparently sudden otherness of this particular pupil and to accommodate it. Normand's narrative style is constructed to illustrate how such teachers think through the problem of the young girl's appearance and how they engage with each other to assert a definition of public space. At one level, they try to reconcile her unexpected challenging behaviour to their memories of the pupil they have taught in their classes and therefore come to know in terms of her contribution to class discussion, her work, her relationships to themselves and to classmates. In other words, they reflect upon what they have seen in the past, and what they know about the young girl and they question what has happened in the light of what they know and, in what Kristeva would call the intimate space, they try and think it through and come to some decision about the justice of what should happen next. By engaging in this life of the psyche, in this intimate space, they become aware that the pupil they thought they knew does not fit into the stereotype of the troublemaker she has now become through the process of wilfully flouting the school dress code. They seek to find explanations. Although the narrative focuses attention on details, on particularities, these can only be understood by engaging with the universals of what counts as 'good', 'justice', 'right', 'wrong' and what it means to be a member of a republic, a faith or a democracy and to have an 'education' and to explore the question of 'how to live together' when there are so many fundamental disagreements.

Normand's account, although framed in terms of the particular, has both generalizable and universal implications. It is generalizable in terms of the structures, the mechanisms and the everyday encounters engaged in by pupils and teachers in classrooms in the context of mainstream schools. These structures, mechanisms and everyday encounters provide a necessary vehicle for generalizable theorization to the extent that they are essential to the definition of schooling or particular models of schooling locally, nationally or globally. Furthermore, the universal is drawn into play through the concepts of justice, law, freedom and equality that arose in the process of claim and counterclaim during particular encounters. Hence, alongside the empirical there is the conceptual through which the empirical realities of everyday life are configured, explained, justified and contested, whether in debate through critique or by conflict using the law or violence. The universal, as Laclau (1996, 2005) puts it, is an empty signifier where the actual contents (signifieds) that give the signifier meaning are open to contestation by different sides to a debate or conflict.

This essential conflict at the heart of demands based on universals is also at work in Singh's argument. Inasmuch as there is no unproblematic reality confronting power relations, this inevitably politicizes the research process. Under the gaze of state authorities and professionals, black minority ethnic groups are vulnerable to pathologization, even demonization (see Chapter 3), and thus are vulnerable research subjects. His concern is to address the injustices that research can [un]wittingly visit upon research subjects. Methodology, research design, data collection and the analytic process itself, he argues, require a critical theoretical approach to avoid visiting further oppressive and violent action upon the research subjects. Since social realities are constructed and "research is not based solely on objective knowledge" (Humphreys and Truman 1994), Singh thus opens up a space in which to question what might be called 'the issue of the fact'. But what is the status of a 'fact'? It plays a key role in what might be characterized as 'hard science' in that facts have their being in 'reality' and are thus presumed to stand apart from theory. However, as Kuhn (1970) argued in his historical discussions of scientific revolutions, facts have to be seen, and different ways of seeing alters what counts as a fact – hence, methodology and theory are implicated in the production of 'facts'.

Taking this seriously actually challenges the nature of the methodological strategy undertaken during the research process. Quantitative and qualitative strategies thus come under scrutiny as Singh explores what is at stake in, first, selecting one or the other, and, second, in signing up to one or the other methodology. Their respective values, objectivities, validities, truths, and notions of what constitutes evidence and representations differ. They answer different research questions. They create different realities – where 'reality' is a function of the ways in which sense or 'pictures in the mind' (see Chapter 1 on Lippmann 1922, 1927) can be made of sensory experiences. Having explored the evidence for his argument, Singh proposes that what is needed is a new methodological strategy. An emancipatory approach is essential, he suggests, in order to build symbolic spaces where love of difference can contribute to ensuring participation and action. Singh argues for an emancipatory research paradigm that would incorporate critical theory and critical methodological strategy.

How does criticism take place? One form of criticism takes place when inconsistencies or contradictions are discovered in the workings of a system. So, for example, in a particular industry or place of employment, it may be that women or members of a minority group of either sex are found to receive earnings significantly below that of men or the dominant ethnic group. This would contradict any principle of equal earnings for equal work. However, as pointed out by Fraser (2009), the act of seeking parity of earnings for equal work plays into the hands of neoliberal politics where it is claimed that work should be differentially rewarded according to talent and hard work. Since the principle is internal to the system, by making the system more consistent, the system itself is never challenged. Thus, the alternative form of criticism, or perhaps better named *critique* to distinguish it from the first, takes place from a point external to the system into order to call into question the whole system. Socialism has claimed to provide such a point of critique. Or, to refer again to the principle of *égaliberté* (see Chapter 1), this provides a point of critique at the level of what in Figure 2 (see p. 68) is called the multitude, the totality of individuals, where no one individual – or group – is able to dominate the rest. It provides a criterion by which to critique the operations of a system by questioning that system in terms of whether it reduces the freedom and the equality of individuals or particular groups.

Critique involves asking questions, questioning everything and taking nothing for granted. Questioning involves a shift in attitude where what was certain is, during the moment of questioning, uncertain or doubtful. For Descartes (2001) the method of doubting was essential to distinguishing the false from the true by founding knowledge upon the thinking subject. After doubting everything, what escapes doubt is the subject itself performing the act of doubting. By building structures of reasoning upon this first principle of certainty, Descartes argued, true knowledge could be constructed as in geometry where thought is able to engage logically with the real. This doubt reveals the existence of the 'I' who states – I think, therefore I am. However, for Freud, the 'I' was not a foundational place, a place of certainty rather than doubt; there is a process of suspicion that consciousness is not the point of origin of actions. In explorations of dreams, slips of the tongue and physiological 'symptoms' the effects of the unconscious could be analysed and the structure and processes of the psyche theorized. Through 'free association' the connections between images, ideas and feelings could be explored. The focus then is upon the ways in which associations can be organized. In this, the structure of language – particularly for Lacan (1977) – provided a way of thinking about the operation of the unconscious, where the unconscious is structured like a language. If this is so, then to understand people's lives it is not simply enough to ask for the conscious meanings they give to their actions since there may be unconscious processes at work. As Derrida would put it, the conscious reasons, meanings and 'facts' need to be questioned to see if they are built upon largely forgotten levels of association between distinct, arbitrary, even contradictory elements and processes – that is to say, they need to be deconstructed in order to reveal their temporal or historical composition.

Something of what is at stake here is seen in Normand's discussion of the bandana/scarf that becomes the focus of a question, a question that challenges the meaning of 'right' and 'liberty' in a republic. And in doing so it challenges what it means to be 'me' as framed within a world that is 'mine'. I am aware that the eyes that address me with their question are positioned in and see a different world. And yet in seeing each other, or addressing ourselves to each other, each from our different 'worlds', neither can be simply dismissed. A doubt drifts into the scene as a question takes hold of 'me' – as if it comes to me, becomes of me: that is to say, the question arrives here in this intimate space that is me, unannounced, uninvited, touching me before letting itself be seen, in the spirit of a visitation. And so, this "question could not happen to *me* except by being *said* as much as *touched upon* – by the other – belonging first to the other, come to me from the other who was already addressing it to the other" (Derrida 2005: 1–2).

I am suddenly 'other' to another who addresses me with a question, a question that places a doubt at the centre of my being. There is always an 'otherness' of the question, a strangeness. That is to say, a question can only be posed from a point exterior to the world view, or belief systems that are 'mine', a position that is other than the one I occupy and that sustains me. However, the question cannot be avoided because it is addressed to me by the other. This other addresses it to me because I am the other's other. There is, too, something intimate about a question in that it takes hold in the place where a sense of 'me' resides, also rendering this me strange, disturbing it in its sense of being 'at home'. The possibility of reasoning in public concerning what is right, objective and valid begins with this kind of questioning that arises from the other. The question in this sense, then, challenges at the most fundamental levels. We occupy or seek to occupy the same space. But this space has a history of occupations and of struggles to occupy. How were those occupations accomplished? At whose expense, if any? And why is one occupation thought to be more 'natural' than another?

The justifications, if any are possible, have to do with what is 'universally' valid/true/real as well as what is most intimately 'me', as that which existentially distinguishes 'me' and 'my history' from everything else. For Hegel, occupation involves the primordial struggle for domination of a space; it is a struggle till death or surrender. Where the victor becomes master, the loser submits and becomes slave or servant. Both inhabit the space but only the master occupies it, wilfully controlling all aspects. The contest of wills was clearly seen in Normand's story. Its resolution was the appeal to the law which occupies the place of the master in a democratic republic, a place that was constructed through the violence of the French Revolution and its aftermath during The Terror. Underlying the peaceful occupation of this space of cohabitation is thus a history of violence. In order to have and be possessed by the peace, there is first a necessary submission to the law that guarantees the peace. In the time of terror, all hint of questioning of the law has to be rooted out. However, the law only has its being by the act of those in submitting their powers to it, provide it – as an aggregation of powers – with its Power. Teachers thus take their legitimacy from Power; their structural position has its everyday logic only in the occupancy of a given space by Power. However, since Power depends on the powers of individuals, its occupancy of a given space can never be total or fixed. It is always, in everyday life, potentially open to contestation by the powers of individuals and thus always, potentially, deconstructable until occupancy is contested and control reimposed through struggle and violence.

This everydayness of struggle, violence and the assertion of mastery can be seen in Blanco's chapter in its discussion of violence in the context of the school.

Blanco first considers violence in early-years education. What is revealed is a space for foment that encourages violence, that inside school and outside school the routinized violence of the everyday practices of inequality and social exclusion are reinforced (see also Pearce's discussion of 'violency' in Chapter 9, in relation to Blanco's discussion of 'secure spaces'). In the spaces that very young children are encouraged to occupy or are prevented from occupying inside and outside school, whether in classrooms, corridors, playgrounds or at the gates of school, what is learnt? In particular, if school is initially regarded as a place of education, then what is learnt concerning how people can live together so that young children can feel included, safe and peaceful as a basis for developing their talents and sense of self in community with others? For Blanco 'children are foreigners in the world of modernity'. How is this to be understood? If modernity represents a victory of reason over tradition and faith, where divine right and class are replaced by the rights of individuals as equals, then it would seem there should be no obstacle to the use of powers in common to achieve the social good that is also a personal good. However, the freedoms of modernity are articulated through the market driven by profit, wealth accumulation and the protection of private property. Here the worth of an individual, just as much as things and services, is measured by market value. There may be, as Thévenot and Boltanski (2006) argue, multiple realms within which value – a sense of self worth – may be recognized, but the predominant means through which the material supports for life is allocated is through the private market, which privileges the accumulation of wealth for the few. Talent may be recognized for itself, but its worth is also measured by money.

Does this mean, Blanco asks, that what is wrong at school and in everyday life, is due to a loss of values or a lack of respect for human rights, whether it is rights for the child or rights for the teacher? No, the situation as it unfolds is much more complex than that. In a society of excess and of consumerism, Blanco contends, there is nothing that children cannot have or cannot do; unless of course they are underprivileged. It is a question of surplus to the point of excess side by side with scarcity. If there is democracy underpinned by Kant's principle of freedom being exercised through the use of reason publicly in all matters, then the question of how to deal with scarcity for the many and surplus for the few becomes a critical issue because the voices of those who experience scarcity will predominate. However, in 'leadership democracies' (see Chapter 1 and the discussion in Section *i*) where elites 'manufacture consent' and control the legitimate means of force through the police and the military (see Chapter 12 and the discussion in Section *iv*) then workable solutions through wider participation in democratic decision making are buried. Thus, Blanco argues, the necessity for solidarity in the face of poverty, powerlessness and disadvantage is easily dispensed with. The notion of fairness and codependency has all but disappeared, having been replaced by the contrived, the false and the emptiness of the mere spectacle. A notion of custodial democracy (Murray 2005) is not too far away. By this it is meant that the 'underclass', as he called them, is to be cordoned off from the property owners, the employed and the middle and elite classes. Democracy is reserved for the rich with policing guarding the poor.

As a response to poverty and the need for the reconstruction of human rights, Blanco argues that in this era of the Internet with its wealth of search engines, teachers are no longer restricted by being guardians of information but can transform their professional lives by becoming civic agents working towards a culture of peace through supporting heterogeneity, promoting values of hope and difference via action which takes the form of a kind of talking through, espousing radical reaction and the development of new hegemonies through giving the children given time to sit down and reflect on the social conflicts they have experienced whilst playing their games. In this time-out, in this quiet, reflective space, they can learn to question and critique and thereby become voices to be counted and heard. Moreover, it is argued, the learning of how to handle the difficulties they face in their world in this particular manner at so young an age, will stand them in good stead for their future and for future democracy. Children, it is often said, are the hope for the future. To Arendt (1998), with each birth, there is a new voice, a new demand, a new viewpoint to be taken into account. As such, children bear society's hope for change as well – as Blanco points out – as the fear of being 'other'.

References

Arendt, A. (1998) *The Human Condition*, Introduction by Margaret Canovan. Chicago: University of Chicago Press; first published 1958.

Derrida, J. (2005) *On Touching – Jean-Luc Nancy* (trans. Christine Irizarry). Stanford: Stanford University Press.

Descartes, R. (2001) *Discourse on Method* (trans. R.E. Sutcliffe). Harmondsworth: Penguin Books.

Fraser, N. (2009) 'Feminism, capitalism and the cunning of history', *New Left Review*, 56, 97–117.

Humphries, B. and Truman, C. (1994) *Rethinking Social Research*. Aldershot: Avebury.

Kuhn, T. (1970) 'The Structure of Scientific Revolutions' (2nd edition). Vols. I and II, in O. Neurath, R. Carnap and C.F.W. Morris (eds), *Foundations of the Unity of Science*. Chicago: University of Chicago Press.

Lacan, J. (1977) *Écrits: A selection*. London: Tavistock/Routledge.

Laclau, E. (1996) *Emancipation(s)*. London and New York: Verso.

Laclau, E. (2005) *Populist Reason*. London: Verso.

Lippmann, W. (1922) *Public Opinion*. New York: Harcourt Brace and Company.

Lippmann, W. (1927) *The Phantom Public*. New York: Macmillan; 13 Transaction Publishers, New Brunswick, New Jersey.

Murray, C. (2005) 'The advantages of social apartheid. US experience shows Britain what to do with its underclass – get it off the streets', *Sunday Times*, 3 April; American Enterprise for Public Policy Research, posted 4 April at: http://www.aei.org/publications/filter.all, pubID.22252/pub_detail.asp (accessed August 15, 2009).

Thévenot, L. and Boltanski, L. (2006) *On Justification: Economies of worth* (trans. Catherine Porter). Princeton, NJ: Princeton University Press.

Chapter 7

'(Don't) change the subject. You did it'

Media and schooling *as* violence

João Paraskeva

Paraskeva's purpose in this chapter is "to disclose the interplay between media and schooling". He sees this as "part of an intricate process of meaning making" that is "deeply rooted within a politics of common sense". For him, this politics of common sense naturalizes and domesticates "social constructions such as violence in such a way that the border 'violence/nonviolence' becomes profoundly blurred". In this case, he proposes that there is a "need to see both media and schools as violence" and draws upon discussions in relation to the US, South Africa and Portugal to show how violence has to be situated within particular social formations that are pervaded by class, race, gender, economic and cultural segregation. The aim, he says, is not to change the subject but to try to understand one of the foundational motives of school violence. He is concerned with the "lack of relevance and dehumanized pedagogies found in schools". In the media, he argues:

> *We are facing a particular form of ideological control that is profoundly related to what Bourdieu (1996) calls a 'show and hide' strategy. That is to say, "{paradoxically} television can hide by showing" (Bourdieu ibid: 19), since journalists (and neither Bourdieu (ibid) nor I are claiming an essentializing position here) "select very specific aspects {of a given event} as a function of their particular perceptual categories, the particular way they see things {categories} that are the product of education, history; {in other words} they used {specific} {eye} glasses" (Bourdieu ibid: 19). Thus, as Fiske and Hartley (1998: 17–21) highlight, since "television is a human construct and the job that it does is the result of human choice, cultural decisions and social pressures", reading television is being radically aware of its "manifest {and} latent content". In essence, one should be aware that in the tension between "giving news vs. giving views" (Bourdieu ibid: 42), the mainstream media aligns with the latter.*

Drawing on Bourdieu's argument, Paraskeva argues that to analyse the media requires being aware of its convoluted dynamics involving "economic and political censorship, the 'game' of showing and hiding, the 'circular circulation' of information, and the relation between market and competition". It is in this context that he turns his attention to schools, as follows.

There is an inexorable connection between school violence and the media. Such a connection is quite explicit, not only in the way particular media apparatuses characterize and code violence both in society and in schools, but also through the cultural politics of advertisements, as well as what constitutes news. Children and adolescents are systematically exposed to particular social formations deeply structured by violence, sex and commercialism. Commercialism is a key issue that establishes a clear distinction between public and private interests (Williams 1974). Contrary to the common public interest, commercial television, for instance, has an ideological and cultural agenda that relies on rounding up the largest possible audience it can and delivering that audience to an advertiser (Levine 1996). We are facing a cultural struggle that is engaged in a non-stop process of gaining audiences, and of creating false perceptions of the world, in which there is no border between reality and fiction, to those audiences.

Volokh and Snell's (1998: 17) research is quite clear about this as well. They identify 11 possible sources of school violence, within which they clearly identify how violent cultural imagery, from TV shows to sympathetic news coverage of militaristic foreign policy, numbs children to the effects of violence, as well as how materialism and advertising creates a culture where children are manipulated and feel exploited. The media is not innocent in the escalation of violence in society and in schools. *Channel One* in the United States is a good example.

Through their analysis of the impact of *Channel One* within schools, Molnar (1996a, b), Apple (2000) and McLaren and Farahmandpur (2002) demonstrate the segregated economic, ideological and cultural dynamics underpinning the advent of *Channel One* which creates a captive audience. One should not ignore the fact that television inside and outside of schools is involved in the struggle for meaning (Fiske 1987). *Channel One* provides clear evidence of the way the mainstream media 'plays' in the complex process of reconfiguring 'common sense'. It is in this context that we need to understand how violence in schools and societies becomes domesticated. We are witnessing, as Molnar (1996a), Apple (2000) and McLaren and Farahmandpur (2002) documented, the emergence and consolidation of a commercially produced television news program that is now invading and colonizing thousands of classrooms and schools in the United States. This is a powerful device that also has a strong effect on the intricate process of knowledge regulation, and the way children construct and interplay with violent/nonviolent social formations.

Since "not only are students sold as commodities to advertisers, but the satellite antennae themselves are 'fixed' to the *Channel One* station and cannot be used to receive other programs" (Apple 2000: 95), it is a political, economic and cultural scheme to construct a 'captive audience' and a daily praxis that is 'selling our kids to business' (Molnar 1996a). Hence we need to understand the "ways that meanings are made and circulated" (Apple 2000: 97). In fact, it is quite crucial to situate *Channel One* at the very core of an ideological reconstruction that is going on in schools. This particular ideological construction is overtly palpable in the way violence is constructed in the news. Media apparatuses have been able to put violence together in particular ways, thus naturalizing it.

As Steinberg (2006: 60) reminds us, "as Arabic [and African] peoples and Muslims continue to emigrate in large numbers to the West, it becomes an obligation of critical teachers to facilitate a critical media literacy in which our students are able to acknowledge the construction of stereotypes and racism by Hollywood and the BBC". This diet "is not innocent, it is constructed on obsession, stereotype, fear, and most importantly, what sells" (Steinberg 2006: 60). In fact, we need, as Chomsky (1989: viii) stresses, "to undertake a course of intellectual self-defense to protect [us] from manipulation and control and to lay the basis for more meaningful democracy".

By distorting reality intentionally, the media changes the (real) issue. For instance, in South Africa white eugenic dominance, based on an inhumane segregated state, considered and treated black and non-white people as not human. Mainstream media had a record of defending eugenic policies and practices to defend and perpetuate a "white supremacist power bloc" (Steinberg and Kincheloe 2001: 17; cf. also Mphahlele 2006; Biko 2004). The way the media glamorizes particular forms of violence (George W. Bush's pompous proclamation that the war in Iraq was over; the over-proud announcement by Paul Bremer about Saddam Hussein's capture – "Ladies and Gentlemen, we've got him") and the way it silences forms of mass death/genocide (Rwanda, Congo, Gaza), is a vivid example that the media is engaged in producing and reproducing 'artifactualities', a set of intricate processes working at the very core of common sense. Such 'artifactualities' are interlinked with what one might call the cultural politics of the megaspectacle. OJ Simpson's megaspectacle trial, Kellner (2003) argues, clearly shows how the media play a key role in what constitutes (non)violence. To further complicate the argument, particular media apparatuses really play an active role in what counts as official violence, and is thus condemned by a biased judiciary system.

Particular media apparatuses have been able to cultivate particular cultural perspectives, in which violence is the only way out to address particular social conflicts (Levine 1996). Žižek's approach on violence helps a great deal here. In his notable work *Violence*, Žižek provides quite an acute account:

A German officer visited Picasso in his Paris studio during the Second World War. There he saw *Guernica*, and shocked at the modernist 'chaos' of the painting, asked Picasso: "Did you do this?" Picasso calmly replied: "No, you did this".

(2008: 11)

Although the media does not kill people, it provides ideas, the social sanction and instructions that encourage aggressive behaviour (Levine 1996). It provides a juicy ideological and cultural germ that fuels a particular, dangerous common sense. The very leitmotif 'if it bleeds, it leads' shows how powerful the media message is, especially in its puzzling audible silences. Reality's dictatorship does not lie though.

> Firearms play a central role in the morbidity and mortality of American children. [However] the United States leads the Western world in handgun availability and handgun deaths. Firearm use is portrayed in the media as an acceptable means to resolving conflict. [Also] easy access to weapons is highly associated with suicide. Tobacco kills 434,000 Americans per year, and the tobacco industry spends $3,27 billion per year to find new clients to keep the market share. Over 3 million adolescents smoke cigarettes, and more than 1 million use smokeless tobacco. Over $900 million per year is spent on beer and wine in the media. Television exposes children to more than fourteen thousand sexual situations and innuendoes per year, while less than 175 of the episodes depicted make any reference to one of the following: birth control, self-control, or abstinence.
>
> (Derksen and Strasburger 1996: 67–9)

Thus, violent realities are something doable by the media in particular, lethal ways. It is interesting that in trying to perceive the interplay between the media and violence (and schools) we stumble upon a crude reality. Media needs to be seen *as* violence. An accurate examination over the interplay 'media and school violence' implies a serious analysis, not only over the way the particular media apparatuses 'construct', 'describe' and 'code' violence in society and in schools, but also over the way the media edifies (constitutes) news and advertisements that needs to be understood as a form of cultural politics. We need to question what 'we' mean by violence. Who benefits? Whose violence is of most worth? What kinds of violence become official and legitimate? Who's been affected? More than ever before, one needs to pay attention to such questions in order to unveil the compounded nexus between media apparatuses and school violence. These are not minor issues or rhetorical questions since the media play a key role in the way individuals perceive reality and truth. As Freire (1974: 34) argues, when excluded from the sphere of decisions being made by fewer and fewer people, man is manoeuvred by the mass media to the point where "he believes nothing he has not heard on the radio, seen on television, or read in the newspapers".

One good way to address such issues is to challenge school's lack of relevance. In so doing we will be able to claim that, in fact, we need to see schooling *as* violence. In the US and elsewhere (Paraskeva 2004), I was able to examine at great length the struggle for curriculum relevance at the very emergence of the curriculum as a field of study. Such a struggle achieved a superior level of complexity in the middle of the last century. School's lack of relevance was socially unsustainable. The belief in the necessity for an 'open education' was beginning to crystallize, a belief which broke free of the obsolete schemes of a traditional education and which implied, among other things, a strong inter-action between the students, the curricular activities centred on the students, the flexibility of spaces, the scope and the relevance of the topics dealt with and, most importantly, a radical break from the existing status quo, in which every-thing was to be conducted in perfect order to reach a previously determined objective. At the forefront of this movement in favour of an open education were the voices of many educators, writers and journalists including Dennison, Friedenberg, Goodman, Henry, Holt, Illich, Kohl, Kozol, Leonard, McLuhan, Roszack and Silberman who associated themselves with the struggle against the alienation of the youth perpetuated by an irrelevant pedagogy. This group, labelled the *Romantic Critics*, the *Radical Critics* or even the *Radical Reform Movement* was opposed to what was understood as the depersonalization of the youth. A new direction in the schools was mandatory as was the need to prevent the schools from compartmentalizing knowledge, from continuing to be an important force of alienation, and from being insensitive to differences bet-ween young people (Friedenberg 1962). They advocated that teachers should place the emphasis of their work on the individual interests of the children and be able to mould the previously determined curriculum according to these interests (Holt 1969), resorting to various strategies to captivate the interest of the students (Holt 1970).

Despite these multifarious struggles for pedagogy and curriculum relev-ance, one clearly sees that the divorce between schools and society is vividly visible. The task is to fight for a relevant curriculum content as a way to address violence in schools. Although it is just a movie, *Freedom Writers* is a crystal example of how an upper middle-class white female new teacher of freshman English (Erin Gruwell) at a racially divided California high school was able to staunch school crime and ballistic violence by, among other things, dramatically changing curriculum content, to make it profoundly relevant for the school's context, with serious and profound implications in the students' daily lives. Without any attempt to romanticize the approach – there are actually some puzzling audible silences in the 'story' – it is undeniable that one cannot minimize the nexus between a school's lack of relevance and viol-ence and crime in schools. *Freedom Writers* needs to be seen, as well, as a call for the urgent end of dehumanized forms of pedagogy (Freire 2003); it needs to be seen as a wake-up call for the fact that, as teacher Gruwell claims, the real battle for social justice should be fought in schools, and precisely in each classroom, as well. Gruwell's approach shows us that it is possible to change an intricate and hostile environment. Facing a 'racist attitude' towards African Americans, Gruwell was able to make a connection between the toxic classist, racist and gendered gang environment that undermined the classroom, and the Holocaust. With such a strategy [one that reminds us of Hawkins' (1973) *How Do You Plan for Spontaneity?*] the students were beginning to consciously assume a different posture. They are now quite interested in writing a different curriculum. *Freedom Writers* is also about curriculum writers. The daily episodes of violence experienced in such a California high school are quite similar to other schools in other nations of the world.

Freedom Writers is an example of a massive generation of children that have been growing up embedded in dangerous sentiments like hate, revulsion, odium, and twisted constructions about particular social formations. It is also an example of how particular, lethal perspectives about education in general and curriculum in particular (e.g. integration is a lie; multiculturalism is hopeless) are assumed in consciousness (yet not so explicit) in teachers' thoughts and practices in such a way that they constitute real obstacles to producing any change, however timid. *Freedom Writers* is a crude and painful illustration that generations of children are engaged daily in a struggle to survive. It is the survival of the fittest in its worst sense. The challenge over school's knowledge is also quite visible in other movies (it is one of the leitmotifs of *Dead Poets Society* and *Elite Squad*). Here, such a lack of school's relevance is deeply connected with an authoritarian culture quite dominant in formal schooling that actually instigates several forms of violence in schools. As Harber (2004: 38) argues in relation to real schools:

> The hegemonic model of schooling internationally is authoritarian. Pupils have little say how schools are run, what is taught or how it is taught and this situation is perhaps at its most pronounced in large schools. It is this authoritarianism that provides the context for school's role in the reproduction and perpetration of violence.

In this regard I do concur with Harber that schooling needs to be seen as violence. All too often, Harber (2004: 1) argues, the "hallmarks of conventional schooling are authoritarianism, boredom, irrelevance, frustration and alienation". School's lack of relevance needs to be understood within what Freire (2003: 46–7) sharply denounced as prescription, "one of the basic elements of the relationship between oppressor and oppressed".

In the context of the neoliberal strategy of 'selling kids to business' what we really have is schooling as a lethal path that (re)produces what Freire (1974: 17) calls "semi-intransitive consciousness". That is, beings of "semi-intransitive consciousness cannot apprehend problems situated outside their sphere of biological necessity [in other words] their interests center almost totally around survival and they lack a sense of life on a more historic plane" (Freire 1974: 17).

According to Freire (1974: 17) we need to fight for an educational platform where men and women "amplify their power to perceive and respond to suggestions and questions arising in their context and increase their capacity to enter into a dialogue not only with other men but with their world". In so doing, Freire (1974: 17) argues, man and woman "become transitive [and] transitivity of consciousness makes man 'permeable'".

In essence, one of the major arguments with regards to the toxic interplay between the media, school and violence is the insidious covert construction of semi-intransitive consciousness. By silencing particular kinds of knowledge, both the media and schooling are in fact explicitly engaged in a cognitive genocide, a cultural fascism that only fosters violence. By perpetrating direct violence (deliberate injury to the integrity of human life), indirect violence (omission or lack of protection against poverty, hunger, disease and accidents), repressive violence (deprivation of fundamental human rights such as freedom of thought, freedom of religion, freedom of speech, right to a fair trial, equality before the law, freedom of movement and freedom to vote) and alienating violence [alienating working conditions, racism (and presumably sexism), social ostracism, cultural repression and living in fear] (Salmi 1999; cf. Harber 2004: 44–5), schooling needs to be studied as a form of societal fascism, quite engaged in a kind of cultural cleansing.

Summing up, the task is to understand both the media and schooling *as* violence. Avoiding such understanding is clearly 'changing the subject'. Žižek's approach teaches us a great deal here.

> There is an old joke about a husband who returns home earlier than usual from work and finds his wife in bed with another man. The surprised wife exclaims: "Why have you come back early?" The husband furiously snaps back: "What are you doing in bed with another man?" The wife calmly replies: "I asked you a question first – don't try to squeeze out of it by changing the topic". The same goes for violence: the task is precisely to change the topic.
>
> (Žižek 2008: 11)

The point is precisely *to change* the topic. The point is paying serious attention to school's lack of relevance and its nexus with school violence. In so doing we will engage in a struggle for epistemological diversity.

Challenging epistemologies: another knowledge is possible

A very good way to challenge media and schooling as violence and the way they have been used and abused – by what I call the 'neoradical centrist dominant stream' to win the battle over common sense – is to engage in a struggle that respects what Sousa Santos, Nunes and Meneses (2007) call epistemological diversity. As they argue, there is no such thing as "global social justice without cognitive justice" (2007: ix). In fact, by claiming as 'official' particular kinds and forms of knowledge, truth and reality schooling does participate in what Sousa Santos (1997) called espistemicides – a lethal tool that fosters the commitment to imperialism and white supremacy (Hooks 1994). In fact, Sousa Santos, Nunes and Meneses claim quite astutely that the "suppression of knowledge is the other side of genocide" (2007: ix).

Further, we need to engage in a battle against the monoculture of scientific knowledge and fight for an ecology of knowledges, which is "an invitation to the promotion of non-relativistic dialogues among knowledges, granting equality of opportunities to the different kinds of knowledge" (Sousa Santos, Nunes and Meneses, 2007: xx). The target of our fighting should be the coloniality of power and knowledge. In so doing, we will end up challenging the notions, concepts and practices of multiculturalism which are profoundly:

> ... Eurocentric, created and describ[ing] cultural diversity within the framework of the nation-states of the Northern Hemisphere (...) the prime expression of the cultural logic of multinational or global capitalism, a capitalism without homeland at last, and a new form of racism, tend[ing] to be quite descriptive and apolitical thus suppressing the problem of power relations, exploitation, inequality, and exclusion.
> (Sousa Santos, Nunes and Meneses 2007: xx–xxi)

In so doing we will be allowing for fruitful conditions, or what Sousa Santos (2004) calls the sociology of absences that will challenge invisible subjectivities (Ellison 1952). Undeniably the struggle for school's relevance implies a non-negotiable commitment: challenging epistemologies.

What we have here is a call for the democratization of knowledge, a commitment towards an emancipatory non-relativistic and cosmopolitan knowledge. We need to learn from the South (since) the aim to reinvent social emancipation goes beyond the critical theory produced in the North and the social and political praxis to which it has subscribed (Sousa Santos, Nunes and Meneses 2007: xiv).

It is the role of teachers as public intellectuals, Giroux (1994) argues, to decentre the curriculum, in a way to separate it from its westernizing forms and content, to fight savage inequalities (Kozol 1999). Both media and schooling have to play a leading and key role in addressing one of the most challenging issues that we have before us – democratizing democracy. It is undeniable, Vavi (2004) claims, that democracy is bypassing the poor.

Sousa Santos (2005) is quite accurate when he claims that we are living in an era with modern problems without modern solutions. In order to re-democratize democracy, Sousa Santos (2005) suggests that we need to reinvent social emancipation since traditional social emancipation has been pushed into a kind of dead end by neoliberal globalization.

However, a different form of globalization, a counter-hegemonic globalization that will propel a myriad social movements and transformations, has challenged such globalization. It is exactly within the very marrow of such counter-hegemonic forms of globalization and in its clashes with the neoliberal hegemonic globalization that new itineraries of social emancipation are developing.

Thus, the struggle for democracy, Shivji (2003: 1) argues, "is primarily a political struggle on the form of governance, thus involving the reconstitution of the state and creating conditions for the emancipatory project". Somehow, we are clearly facing what Sousa Santos (1998) coined as a state that should be seen as a spotless new social movement. That is, a more vast political organization in which the democratic forces will struggle for a distributive democracy, thus transforming the state into a new – yet powerful – social and political entity. The task is to daily reinvent how to democratize democracy. A new struggle must, in fact, begin. This is the best way, as the Mozambican writer Couto claims, that we have "to challenge a past that was portrayed in a deformed way, a present dressed with borrowed clothes and a future ordered already by foreign interests" (Couto 2005: 10). Public education does have a key role in claiming that (an)other knowledge is possible and needs to address how such knowledge is crucial for the transformative processes of democratizing democracy.

References

Apple, M. (2000) *Official Knowledge: Democratic education in a conservative age*. New York: Routledge.

Biko, S. (2004) *I Write What I Like*. Johannesburg: Picador Africa.

Bourdieu, P. (1996) *On Television*. New York: The New York Press.

Chomsky, N. (1982) *Towards a New Cold War: Essay on the current crisis and how we got there*. London: Pluto.

Chomsky, N. (1989) *Necessary Illusions: Thought control in democratic societies*. Cambridge: South End Press.

Couto, Mia (2005) *Pensatempos*. Lisboa: Caminho.

Derksen, D.J. and Strasburger, V. (1996) 'Media and television violence. Effects on violence, aggression and anti-social behaviors in children', in A. Hoffman (ed.), *Schools, Violence and Society*. London: Praeger, pp. 61–77.

Ellison, R. (1952) *Invisible Man* (reprinted 1995). New York: Vintage Books.

Fairclough, N. (1992) *Discourse and Social Change*. Cambridge: Polity Press.

Fiske, J. (1987) *Television Culture*. New York: Methuen.

Fiske, J. and Hartley, J. (1998) *Reading Television*. London: Methuen.

Freire, P. (1974) *Education: The practice of freedom*. London: Writers Readers Publishing Cooperative.

Freire, P. (2003) *Pedagogy of the Oppressed* (3rd edition). New York: Continuum.

Friedenberg, E. (1962) *The Vanishing Adolescent*. New York: Dell Publishing.

Giroux, H. (1994) *Doing Cultural Studies: Youth and the challenge of pedagogy*. http://www.gseis.ucla.edu/courses/ed253a/giroux/giroux1.html (accessed August 2008).

Harber, C. (2004) *Schooling as Violence*. New York: Routledge.

Hawkins, D. (1973) 'How do you plan for spontaneity' in C. Silberman (ed.), *The Open Classroom Reader*. New York: Random House, pp. 486–503.

Holt, J. (1969) 'How children fail', in R. Gross and B. Gross (eds.), *Radical School Reform*. New York: Simon and Schuster, pp. 59–77.

Holt, J. (1970) *What Do I Do on Monday?* New York: Dutton.

Hooks, B (1994) *Teaching to Transgress: Education as the practice of freedom*. London: Routledge.

Kellner, D. (2003) *Media Spectacle*. New York: Routledge.

Kozol, J. (1999) *Amazing Grace: The lives of children and the conscience of a nation*. NY: Bt Bound.

Levine, M. (1996) *Viewing Violence: How the media affects your children and adolescent's development*. New York: Doubleday.

McLaren, P. E. and Farahmandpur, R. (2002) 'Freire, Marx and the New Imperialism: Towards a revolutionary praxis', in J. Slater, S. Fain and C. Rossatto (eds), *The Freirean Legacy – Education for social justice*. New York: Peter Lang, pp. 37–56.

Molnar, A. (1996a) *Giving Kids the Business: The commercialization of America schools*. Boulder CO: Westview.

Molnar, A. (1996b) An interview with Alex Molnar, by Jay Huber. *Stay Free*. Available at http://www.stayfreemagazine.org/index.html (accessed October 2006).

Mphahlele, E. (2006) *In Corner B*. London: Penguin Books.

Paraskeva, J. (2004) *Here I Stand: A long revolution*. Braga: University of Minho.

Salmi, J. (1999) 'Violence, democracy and education: an analytic framework'. Paper delivered at the Oxford International Conference on Education Development, September.

Shivji, I. (2003) *The Struggle for Democracy*. Available at: http://www.marxists.org/subject/africa/shivji/struggle-democracy.htm (accessed August 15, 2009).

Sousa Santos, B. (1997) *Um Discurso sobre as Ciencias*. Oporto: Afrontamento.

Sousa Santos, B. (1998) *Reinventar a democracia*. Lisboa: Gradiva.

Sousa Santos, B. (2004) 'A critique of lazy reason: Against the waste of experience', in I. Wallerstein (ed.), *The Modern World System in the Longue Duree*. Boulder CO: Paradigm Publishers.

Sousa Santos, B. (2005) *Another Knowledge is Possible*. London: Verso.

Sousa Santos, B., Nunes, J. and Meneses, M. (2007) 'Open up the canon of knowledge and recognition of difference', in B. Sousa Santos (ed.), *Another Knowledge is Possible*. London: Verso, pp. ix – lxii.

Steinberg, S. (2006) 'Usar a capacidade de leitura crítica dos meios de comunicação para ensinar aspectos sobre o racismo contra Muçulmanos e Árabes', in J. Paraskeva (ed.), *Currículo e Multiculturalismo*. Lisboa: Edições Pedago, pp. 51–62.

Steinberg, S. and Kincheloe, J (2001) 'Setting the context for critical multi/interculturalism: The power blocs of class elitism, white supremacy, and patriarchy', in S. Steinberg (ed.), *Multicultural Conversations: A reader*. New York: Peter Lang, pp. 3–30.

Vavi, Z. (2004) 'Democracy has by-passed the poor', *Sowetan* (newspaper) 13 January. Available at: http://www.marxists.org/subject/africa/vavi/poor-bypassed.htm (accessed August 12, 2009).

Volokh, A. and Snell, L. (1998) 'Strategies to keep schools safe', *Policy Study*, 234, January, 1–75.

Williams, R. (1974) *Television: Technology and cultural form* (2nd edition). E. Williams (ed.), 1990. London: Routledge.

Žižek, S. (2008) *Violence*. New York: Picador.

Reflections on Paraskeva's chapter

Paraskeva's chapter explores the relationship between media and schooling and how this complex interplay, lying at the heart of an intricate process of meaning making, has far-reaching implications for social justice and democracy. In this constant struggle for meaning making, where and how does violence as portrayed in the media and the violence that occurs in schools interact and with what effect? Neither can be detached from the other.

Paraskeva argues that, for a variety of reasons, the media puts reality together in particular kinds of ways that thus call into question whether the media actually gives news or gives views. In this milieu of 'a reality effect' hand in hand with 'an effect on reality', boundaries – for example, those between violence and non-violence – become profoundly blurred. Violent realities in war-torn countries therefore become naturalized, domesticated and 'commonsensically unavoidable'. Particular kinds of 'communities of interpretation' build up but these are confined within the set semantic borders as defined by the 'show and hide strategy' that the media engages in, locked into 'false perceptions of the world where there is no border between reality and fiction'.

Violence in schools, it is argued, is due to 'a violent silence' produced by those processes, practices and curricular materials of schooling that bring about a 'cognitive passivity'. Paraskeva says that in order to counter such a silent violence as well as the media representations, we need what Chomsky described as "a course of intellectual self-defense" as a protection against "media manipulation and to lay the basis for a more meaningful democracy" (1982: vii; 1989: 6). Indeed, as Paraskeva raises as a key issue: what is the new role for schools in democratizing democracy?

Research questions

This chapter prompts us to identify ways in which research can contribute to the creation of an everyday course of 'intellectual self-defense' and 'democratizing democracy' through the development of school processes, practices, organizations and curricula.

- What kinds of teaching methods are needed to contribute to the critique of media representations?
- What contemporary school processes contribute to the production of violence?
- Who determines the curriculum and for what reasons?
- How, when and for what purposes are curriculum changes made? Who determines those changes?
- Who are the protagonists involved in the struggle for 'curriculum relevance'?
- Whose voices are included and whose excluded at school? Why?

Chapter 8

'Charlie why ya hideing'

The role of myth and emotion in the lives of young people living in a high crime area

Kaye Haw

This chapter is based on research of ethnic minority communities living in a small geographical location in the United Kingdom, with a reputation for gun crime, gang-related violence and drugs. It is written by a researcher who works in urban communities from a social action participatory research perspective using video as a research tool. The focus of this approach is on the 'voice' of young people and how this can be articulated through making their own films about their everyday lives and concerns. The work with video has been developed over many years on a diverse range of research projects. In each project, video has been used slightly differently depending on the objectives of the research and the type of users it aimed to engage. Each piece of research though has a common aim, to legitimate a range of 'voices' through creating a series of spaces for critical dialogue and action. To do this, video is used as a community consultation tool drawing on Melucci's (1989) approach to exploring group self – representation, and collective and individual identity.

Urbanfields was chosen as a place to carry out the research because it was one of the first areas in Britain to be patrolled by armed police after dark and has a reputation, across the city, built up over several generations, for its gang and drug cultures. The region in which Urbanfields is located is considered one of the top four most dangerous British places to live in terms of gun crime (Povey and Kaiza 2005: 49). It also has very specific boundaries but is connected by a bridge to a wealthy suburb, populated by 'middle class' professionals due to the reputation of its schools. A number of the young people from Urbanfields now go to these schools because of the closure of the only secondary school in Urbanfields.

The focus for the research was to understand more about the social processes around risk and resilience. The aim was to support young people to articulate their perspective by focusing on their agency and through this develop a theoretical critique of a debate, dominated in criminology by notions of the predictive power of 'risk factors' and intervention strategies so-called 'risk factorology' (Kemshall 2003). This alternative approach is important because in criminology the coupling of the notion of a criminal career with the causality

Figure 3.

behind risk and protection has given rise to the notion of a pathway into and out of crime. The internal logic of the pathway has encouraged researchers and practitioners to search for risk and protective factors that could be affected by interventions prior to offending and to guide 'treatments' afterwards. Its 'natural' analytical trajectory, spurred on by policy makers and politicians, has been a concern to predict offending behaviour and to devise strategies to prevent delinquent development.

Current risk literature in the area of youth crime is therefore heavily dominated by biological (see Rutter *et al.* 1998) and psychological models (see Wikstrom 1998: 2004; Wikstrom and Loeber 2000) that claim to predict offending through the identification of key risk factors, incorporating these into models that are both additive and causal. To put it simply, the more risk factors possessed by an individual, such as being from a single parent family, or a minority ethnic group, or excluded from school, the more likely that an individual will become involved in antisocial behaviour and/or criminal activity.

Given its focus on the social construction of risk, the research was concerned to critique this kind of risk-factor research with regard to its claims of validity and generalizability and reveal the failure of most risk-factor research to generate sufficiently sophisticated models to show how key factors interact (Armstrong 2004). At the heart of this failure is the tendency of the vast majority of such models to undertheorize the relationship between individuals and their contexts. For example, although more recent models are likely to discuss 'resilience' factors, such as being a member of a formal group like a church or a warm supportive family, they still contain a very limited notion of the forms of agency, either individual or collective, that might account for how 'resilience factors' might influence the risk taking of an individual. In a similar vein, more 'structural' factors such as social class, ethnicity or gender are conceptualized in a way that means they cannot account for the wide variations in behaviour and outcomes of individuals sharing similar or identical risk profiles (Bessant *et al.* 2003; Pitts 2003). At this point, these models tend to retreat into their statistical roots and a weak discussion of probabilities and correlations, often dressed up in the language of causality in order to reconcile the anomalies of how similar structural arrangements amongst individuals give rise to very different patterns of risk behaviour between individuals (see Goldson 1999). Risk-factor models also tend to operate with such macro definitions of the structural arrangements that surround individuals that they distance the individual from the immediate social contexts and localities in which they operate and live (see Douglas 1992). When combined with the previous criticism of their limited sense of agency, it means they fail to understand or account for how individuals and groups actively create the immediate context through which risk factors are mediated, moderated and experienced.

Underpinning this research was a belief that there was a need for a new level of analysis, situated somewhere between the discursive and the cultural, because in a late modern British context, a need has developed to understand the connections between the external lived worlds of individuals and their internal 'felt' worlds. This is important because of the nature of the micro-cultural world we now live in, and the way individuals are increasingly recognized as active consumers and producers of culture. This chapter therefore outlines the development of the methodological and analytical frameworks. These frameworks use the notion of a 'mythic feedback loop' as a heuristic device to understand how individuals combine and link their internal worlds to their external environment. The loop designates a narrative movement by individuals from their internal worlds to their external worlds, looping from one to the other. This movement is a dynamic flowing from internal 'felt' contradiction, then synthesized as fact in the social world, which then takes on a symbolic function to shape the internal sense-making of individuals. The loop therefore breaches the boundary between the internally 'felt' world of the individual and the external world of social action by linking thinking, feeling and action.

The first two sections of this chapter introduce the notions of 'myth', the 'mythic' feedback loop and 'mythcourse' through a discussion of the 'Charlie' graffiti. The purpose is threefold: first, to highlight that 'myths' are more than just sense-making practices because they function as a connective structure used reflexively by individuals; second, to show how video as a research tool is uniquely placed to capture this generative looped dynamic between thinking, feeling and action; and third, to show how the methodological and analytical frameworks were developed. These sections conclude by applying the analytical framework to the 'Charlie why ya hideing' graffiti. The final section brings the discussion full circle by returning briefly to examine the implications the research has for current risk-factor research.

The research design

The research combined young people making videos and, therefore, mapping the social context through what the participants chose to film, with a second approach that encouraged reflection and reflexivity by 'triggering' a series of technical and creative discussions about the content of each video and what the participant film makers wished to convey to their audience.

The theoretical development required by the work partially positioned it within existing research in the UK on social exclusion, youth transitions and criminal careers (MacDonald and Marsh 2005; MacDonald 2006). Such work is illuminating in its emphasis on a structural analysis of discourses linked to agency, using locality as a means of providing a nuanced view of how wider social discourses operate. However, it tends to treat locality/context as only a moderating factor in the lives of young people and fails to encapsulate how it becomes a mediating space that is actively created by them. The research therefore required a methodological approach and an analytical framework that could account for young people simultaneously constructing, inhabiting and moving between different groups and localities while accounting for apparently 'different' and 'contradictory' behaviour as they did so. This was required if the research was to position itself within interpretations of resilience that better account for cultural and contextual differences in its expression by individuals, families and communities (see Ungar 2004a, b). Ungar's work in this area is apposite because he explores at least two limitations of the current risk/resilience approach. The first is a tendency to locate the source of antisocial behaviours amongst 'at-risk' young people in the young people themselves rather than in the relationships and contexts to which they belong. The second is with the failure to adequately incorporate the agency of the young people into attempts at understanding what is going on in their lives, and intervening within them.

The project worked with six groups of young people aged between 11 and 21. One of these groups was made up entirely of young men of Asian origin and another of young women of a similar age of African-Caribbean descent. The four remaining groups were younger and more mixed in terms of gender and ethnic background. In total this was between 50–70 participants, although the number is significantly reduced if only those who worked to the completion of their video are counted. All the participants had a combination of risk factors that identified them as potential offenders. Some of them were, or became, part of the British Criminal Justice System over the life of the research. Others did not. At least two of them became involved in serious criminal activity including grievous bodily harm and murder while several others were the recipients of Anti-Social Behaviour Orders. The priority was to work with young people on sensitive subjects and for this reason alone it was not considered to be in the interests of the quality of the research to 'frighten off' participants through intrusive personal questioning. The project also worked with and serially interviewed 16 adults representing a range of services. These were the police, social workers, youth offending team workers, probation officers, community drugs workers, youth workers and teachers. The outcomes of the research were two trigger films, six films by young people and one final DVD.

Data generation occurred over three phases. The first phase began with interviews with professionals about their personal theories of risk and resilience. These views were incorporated into a short 'trigger' video that combined footage of the area, with local and national media coverage of violent events in Urbanfields. This trigger video was then used in the recruitment of groups of young people, a technique that has been used in other projects (see Haw 2008). During this phase, six community researchers were recruited from within Urbanfields. Their role as part of the research team was to provide: an insider's view of the happenings within Urbanfields, encouragement and support, and advice on ethical aspects to do with preserving anonymity and confidentiality.

The second phase of data generation was based on participatory methods as the participants, with their families and friends and help from the research team, created videos that captured aspects of their lives. The discussions that occurred while each film was edited and produced were tape recorded and filmed by the researchers to give a further layer of data and formed the first stages of the analytical process. The footage collected by the researchers over this phase together with elements of the tape-recorded discussions were then incorporated into the original trigger video to make a second trigger video for use in the third phase of the research. The selection of material in this second trigger was now based upon the themes that had arisen from the young people juxtaposed with 'voice overs' from young people and professionals.

The third phase involved multiple group and individual interviews with professionals and participants after the second trigger video had been viewed. Each of the different phases throughout the research provided yet another level of data. The process allowed us not only to juxtapose the themes that had arisen from different groups but also to capture their reactions to them, and reflections on them, and for these to be incorporated at the end of this third phase into a final DVD. Central to it were the tensions felt by the participants and many of the professionals about young people being 'done to' versus approaches that attempted to 'work with' them.

Developing an adequate methodological approach: Critical voice and theoretical critique

Methodologically, the approach had to be one that was capable of helping the young people of Urbanfields articulate their own in-depth descriptions of their direct experiences of 'risk' and then analytically connect these accounts with the project's overall aim of critiquing current risk-factor research. The design criteria for the methodology was threefold. First, it needed to support the participants to reflect on aspects of their lives they perceived to be everyday or commonsensical as well as the more dramatic, difficult and potentially painful. Second, it needed to encourage a reflexive awareness of their agency at certain moments, and how this might change in similar situations. Third, it needed to expose and analyze the linkages between their internal personal 'felt' narratives, and the external social discourses that surrounded them. To connect these three aims, the presence of some quite strongly held local cultural beliefs or 'myths' around risk taking and criminality became a nexus for the development of the reflective dialogues and processes required to support these participants to critically articulate their own experiences of risk.

How 'myths' were used to support the participants: Critical reflections and articulations

As the participants discussed their videos, several key mythologies emerged from their conversations. These included drug dealing and the lifestyle surrounding it, gang violence, notions of 'territory' and rivalry, sexual relation-ships and the status of being the 'number one' girl. It became clear that some participants were talking from direct experiences, whereas others were talking from either indirect experiences or from a 'wannabe' perspective. Either way, what began to be interesting was that these mythologies were being shaped by 'myths' that functioned to rationalize, normalize and bring people together by providing causal explanations and resolving the contradictions presented to them by living in Urbanfields. However, these 'myths' were clearly being used differently. One set of 'myths' related to some graffiti, 'Charlie why ya hideing', that appeared all over Urbanfields at the beginning of the research. Initially, to explore why the participants were drawing on locally held myths in a certain way, the 'trigger' videos were used. A mixture of explicit messages and more oblique messages were incorporated into these videos. These 'trigger' tapes deliberately included within them myths 'in action', such as the 'Charlie' graffiti, and myths that were being 'acted out' by the participants such as that of the 'gangsta'.

As these filmed materials were viewed over the different phases of the research, different audiences commented on the myths, making them a good source of reflection because each myth was differently interpreted. In terms of the first aim, to develop criticality and support reflection, the 'Charlie' graffiti became important for several reasons. First, it was a myth specific to Urbanfields, a community myth. Second, it was important because of the way it was being used by different groups of participants to both 'big up' and normal-ize an extraordinary happening in Urbanfields. Last, it allowed the research to focus on difficult and sensitive issues that 'lived' in a community where there were a lot of tensions around drug dealing and gang violence. As a community myth it reflected the application of wider social discourses to specific events within Urbanfields that then took on their own mythic status. In this sense, the graffiti was a reflection of events that had already been processed, creating a safe place for collective reflection because it was part of common parlance. In a piece of research dealing with difficult and sensitive issues where there was a great deal of tension around what could be talked about and what could not, the graffiti provided the space to discuss and 'play' with these wider issues.

In terms of the second aim, to encourage a reflexive awareness of the agency of the participants, the myths circulating around the graffiti were also important because they 'lived' sufficiently within the locality for a range of participants and professionals to be aware of them, and hold different understandings of them. The production and consumption phases of the video process were helpful in focusing on, and accounting for, the agency of the participants by allowing for discussions on the extent to which they rejected or took on board these myths, and therefore used them in the construction of their own contexts.

This way of researching with 'voice' and video combines a mixture of approaches drawing on that of visual ethnographers and anthropologists interested in researching the construction of individual lives and representation within the media (Banks 1995; Banks and Morphy 1997; MacCanell 1994; Margolis 1998). The 'Charlie' graffiti was a reflection of this mix of approaches. By 'grabbing the moment' of its appearance it was able to explore the way in which the Urbanfields community was applying wider discourses to what was happening in it.

As the participants made numerous decisions about the content of their videos, their 'internal narratives' – spaces for critical subjectivity – were opened up, reflecting the agency of the film makers. Crucially though, as these videos were produced and shown to different audiences, the potential to enhance this reflexivity and criticality was developed. This is because images bring with them an analysis of their internal narrative through critical engagement with how successfully they convey its story and an 'external narrative' as audiences reacted to this content. The external narrative then, is "the social context that produced the image embedded at any moment of viewing" (Banks 2001: 11–12). An analysis of images therefore means 'a reading of the external narrative that goes beyond the visual text itself' (Banks 2001: 12), one that combines an internal 'felt' reaction to the images and commentary fed through a reflexive feedback loop to the external world. Social relations of visual images are therefore key to understanding their meaning because they are the product of individual action set within a nexus of social contexts and their interconnections.

The third aim of the methodological framework was to expose and analyze the linkages between the internal personal 'felt' narratives of the participants and the external social discourses that surrounded them. Getting the participants to engage with the collectively held myths such as those of the 'gangsta', the dealer, the gang member and the 'number one girl' in their own videos involved incorporating elements within the video process of what they considered ordinary and everyday within their locality with what was perceived as extraordinary by those outside it, and to explore why this was so. An exploration of these mythologies relied on the collective experience of the participants and professionals. In this way the internal and external narratives of the different videos revealed through the production and consumption process also highlighted the connections between the 'felt' worlds of the participants and how they then fed these back into the wider social discourses operating around them.

'Charlie why ya hideing': The process of coming to an analytical framework

If 'myths' supported the aim of getting participants to articulate their views, could they also provide a basis for critiquing current risk theories? As a piece of participatory action research, the analytical framework arising from this methodological underpinning had, at least in part, to be capable of 'living' within the world of the participants, if it was to form part of the discussions with them and support their 'voicing' of their perspectives. It was recognized early on in the research that as emotionally charged accounts, certain 'myths' conveyed an explicit or implicit invitation to assent to a particular ideological or discursive standpoint and potentially to act in accordance with it.

This made these myths useful as a starting point to explore agency with regards to the extent the participants could reject or take on these myths. Discussions with the participants moved the analysis on from ideas of acceptance and rejection to a broader exploration of agency because they revealed the participants to be both 'myth consumers' and 'myth producers and promoters' as they connected with various local 'myths'. As consumers, myths appeared to function as a way of making the world of Urbanfields 'natural' and as they were used over time to make 'reasonable' the notions and intentions of others (Barthes 2000). These same myths were also used by 'outsiders' to make sense of young peoples' agency. For example, a youth worker working in the area talked about the way in which myth and fantasy created a false reality, in the sense of a strong disjuncture between one set of experiences and other 'lived' experiences that at the same time 'intensified' and 'distanced' the reality of living in Urbanfields:

> They buy into image and sometimes it's a false image. I am not saying it's all false because some of the things is the real truth of their life. But it's glossed up now in a way that, you know, if you see a guy driving a real fast car, with lots of women hanging off his arm, fur coats and lots of diamonds and long gold chains it can have two impacts. One it can say if you do this you can achieve these things. Others see the other side of it which is all the badness that goes on with it.

The analysis of the roles played by these community myths began feeding back into the developing theoretical framework around what shaped the agency of the participants. It appeared that as these local myths moved between individuals and different contexts, they moved beyond them, and as they did this, they gradually took on broader symbolic meanings through this intensification process. This process resulted in these myths shaping the actions of others and therefore shaping their environment. In a small community such as Urbanfields the intensification process was made most transparent in different interpretations of specific violent events such as the 'Charlie' graffiti or the behaviour of certain notorious individuals. The framework therefore began to move between the dispassionate tool of discourse to reveal the influences operating in Urbanfields to do with wider social phenomena such as gang culture and 'neotribes' (Bennett 2005; Hall and Jefferson 1979; Maffesoli 1996; Muggleton 2000) and began to develop into one that was capable of identifying and exploring the connection points between these external narratives and the internal narratives of individuals.

Once they were conceptualized as more than 'sense-making' practices, myths played a role in making these connections. Increasingly, it began to seem that they functioned as a connective structure used reflexively by the participants to mediate and connect their lived worlds to wider social discourses and, most importantly, their own internal narratives, both consciously and unconsciously. In doing so this also enabled them to move between the different social contexts that made up their lived world. As these community myths were consumed, promoted and produced, different linkages were revealed. To provide a shorthand description of this trail and the multiple connections it encompassed, the term 'mythcourse' was used as a means of mapping the trajectory of these myths as they spanned the links between wider social discourses, different communities and groups, and the internal and external worlds of individuals, and back again.

The analytical power of 'mythcourse' was its apparent potential to reveal how individuals were positioned as actors in the social world through connection to, and disconnection from, different myths and how they also constructed this social world through these connections. The question then, was whether others had considered the role that myths might play beyond being an internal sense-making apparatus. Had myths previously been viewed as a point of connection between the external worlds of individuals and their internal worlds? These theoretical questions led to the work of Losev (2003) and his notion of the 'mythic feedback loop'. This loop is a dynamic that breaches the boundary between the internally 'felt' world of the individual and the external world of social action. 'Myths' in Losev's work do this because they serve to deal with internal contradictions and tensions but when these resolutions are enacted in the social world they take on symbolic meaning through integration into wider social, community, family and individual narratives and memories. In this research these mythic feedback loops were captured through the internal and external narratives revealed in the process of making and viewing the videos of the participants.

Losev's theory was also important to the ongoing analysis of the agency of young people with regard to perceptions and constructions of risk because of its emphasis on contradiction, unsurprising because of his interest in dialectics, and the emphasis it placed on the ontological resolution of such contradictions as a means of understanding the social world of individuals. In this sense, myths possess a dynamic that, once internalized, form a deep structure, acting as intermediaries between the unconscious and consciousness (Bennett 1980), the individual and the social, functioning through this looped process to resolve contradictions and tensions.

The data generated via the video production process and the discussions around it was reinterrogated using an analytical framework based upon the overarching notion of 'mythcourse'. This analysis centred around the identification of possible feedback loops operating on the one hand between the individual and a range of wider social discourses and on the other hand between the internal lives of individuals and their external lives through a range of local social contexts. In this way, the analysis began to move through the different levels of the social world of these participants, as they were driven in part by their need to resolve or avoid the contradictions they felt, or those that had become 'facts' or real, and shaped their engagement in risk taking. The point here is to demonstrate that Barthes' somewhat passive analysis of individuals as myth consumers and producers fails to fully account for the emotional responses of individuals to the myths surrounding them.

This analytical framework is now applied to the 'Charlie why ya hideing' graffiti. The role played by graffiti in the lives of individuals is complex. Graffiti as an urban practice in Western countries has two main roots. The first is associated with the spread of propaganda, revolutionary ideals and the bringing down of the establishment. The second emerged in the mid 1970s on the American East Coast in association with the hip-hop culture [for a

Figure 4.

detailed description of the origins and mechanics of graffiti as a subculture see Castleman (1982), Ferrel (1996) and Kim (1995)]. In both cases graffiti fulfils the function of being an immediate medium that physically supports a desire for social and cultural change. More recently, it has been used as an advertising medium and has become "one of the most expressive signals of cultural stimulation in the late capitalist status quo" (Alvelos 2004: 185). In the case of the 'Charlie' graffiti, its role was to make public personal drama feeding into mythic loops around the 'hard man', the 'number one girl', messing with other people's women, machismo and retribution. It also inspired others to tell their versions of the exploits of the anonymous writer. The graffiti writer utilized walls all over Urbanfields as media to both track down and threaten Charlie. This was not just 'myth' as a speech act but more importantly revealed firstly, how a community myth can take on a symbolic function in the lives of others and secondly, the role of emotions in this process as others dramatize the events around it.

In the discussions focused around their video productions, many different accounts were given of the 'Charlie' graffiti, and the narratives were subtly transformed depending on the group that was talking. Groups of younger males imagined the graffiti writer, Ian, as a baseball-wielding urban ninja determined to take revenge on Charlie. The nature of the dispute between Charlie and Ian changes from 'having tension' between them, to it being an argument over a girl, as do the graphic descriptions of the violent consequences when 'Charlie' is found, from little more than harassment, to having his arms chopped off. These are 'comic strip' representations of a ninja that take on the creation of the man Ian as the ninja. In its use by different individuals and groups, the urban myths that sprang up around the 'Charlie' graffiti touched upon the nature of sexuality and masculinity as the unfaithfulness of relationships between adults was being questioned. These accounts were mostly about virtual violence. In one account the ninja, Ian, chops Charlie's arms off while he was sleeping. In another, Charlie's arms are cut off at 'night-time' presumably while he was out in the area, and the fear of being around Urbanfields as an isolated individual is highlighted.

But the graffiti writer is not only a ninja; he is also Ian, as presented by another participant with a more direct association with him. In this account, Ian becomes a pushbike-riding Ian, making plans for his mum to look after his dog and furniture if anything should happen to him as a consequence of his behaviour. As the graffiti was discussed amongst the group in the process of making their own video, rivalry, violence and the status of the 'number one girl' also referred to but in a more distanced way. But even though the account appeared far less dramatic, in this discussion the violence was actual because Charlie, not Ian, stabbed somebody as he became emotionally 'caught up' in the chase:

I remember that morning my step-dad was standing on the front talking.

Ian was just the re and I could hear him and he was like saying "if I see him I'm going to kill him when I find him". And he had this big box on his back like a long thin box across his back on some straps. He goes "I've got my knife. I'm hunting him down. I've got my sword and I'm going to kill him when I find him. I can't believe he's done this". Apparently he was going to kill the girl as well. I heard down the line that he had this little dog and he'd given it to his mum and sold all the furniture in his flat because he was ready to kill Charlie and willing to take the consequences and go to prison for it. I don't know. Maybe it's his pride or something like that. Charlie obviously must have seen all the graffiti and stabbed a guy outside a shop in the Meadows. Charlie got arrested but then he got let off somehow. He'd stabbed the guy quite bad. I don't know how he got off, he probably paid them off [the police] or something like that. Now I always see Charlie and Louisa together all the time. Ian was like hunting around on his little bike. Just a little pushbike. Louisa, I think she left Ian for Charlie thinking I'm going to be his number one girl but I don't think she is, to be honest. Apparently Charlie's one of the drug dealers as well so they all have their many girls on the go.

This discussion in the telling and re-telling and picking over of the events around the graffiti also makes emotional connections or disconnections to Ian, Charlie or Louisa. Part of the intensification process is connected to these emotional linkages and it is here that we get an insight into the series of feedback loops operating in the lives of individuals as they emotionalize their context. Emotions are created and exist, intensified and downplayed in the spaces created by the mythic feedback loops generated around violence, machismo, drugs and being a 'number one girl' feeding into wider social discourses around the family, relationships and police corruption. In this process, individuals 'switch' between emotions to justify contradictory behaviour like that of Ian's as he 'hunts' Charlie down.

The function of the various myths within these narratives is not only to provide simplified causal accounts of Ian and Charlie's complex and contradictory behaviour but to elicit emotional responses that can switch between the ordinary and extraordinary. In the process between thinking, feeling and action, fundamental contradictions between what is risky and what is not, accepted and acceptable behaviour within a family and extraordinary behaviour outside of it, are resolved. The stories circulating around the graffiti become powerful as they are used differently by individuals to feed into and feed off the 'mythic feedback loops' they generate. Their mythological status accretes over time, through different generations within Urbanfields, making it possible to shape what people do by providing explanations of what does and what does not happen in the area. In Urbanfields 'risky' behaviour is practised, sometimes through 'play acting' and play fighting that is then sometimes acted out for real because it is considered necessary to maintain a certain 'protective' reputation.

Often the 'myths' drawn upon in maintaining this volatile and complex balance had historical antecedents passed down between the generations through a series of mythical feedback loops concerning the notorious but heroic status of the big drug dealer, maintenance of a number of different sexual relationships, and notions of gangs and gang rivalry.

While a discursive analysis is illuminating in that it gives a wider understanding of the gang and drug dealing culture that individuals like Charlie and Ian are part of, it cannot account for the complexity of the relationship between risk and resilience because it fails to unpick the contradictory feedback loops operating in the lives of these individuals. A 'mythcourse' analysis highlights the part played by locality and its role in mediating and moderating the connections between broader social discourses and individual actions. Tracing different 'mythcourses' reveals how individual intentionality is set within a series of feedback loops created between very specific community myths and different aspects of their own personal narratives. An analysis of the responses to the local and localized 'myths' generated by the 'Charlie' graffiti shows individuals as myth manipulators and promoters even as they produce and consume them.

Conclusion

In justifying small – or more serious – acts of violence concerned with respect or territory, dealing in and taking drugs or the break-up of relationships, these participants revealed in their discussions as they made their videos the ability to actively use myths by switching between different emotional responses to them. In the process they demonstrated a sophisticated understanding of the 'dangerousness' and attractiveness of an otherwise uneventful every day:

> It's just boring mate. We're all bored even on a Friday, it's just boring. I'm bored. I just smoke weed. Nothing to do. I do every day what I do every day. Just hang around the streets.

These times were also punctuated by extreme events and the kinds of acts of violence as revealed through their discussions of the 'Charlie' graffiti. The recognition of the participants of the cache attached to drawing in the 'wannabes' and wider 'wannabe' culture of other young people, who liked to play with danger simply because they could leave it behind them, was also linked to their own risk taking and their perceptions of the relationship between the risks they took and the protection this offered as they moved through different contexts. Being from Urbanfields was influential in their risk-taking behaviour because their perceptions of risk were linked to their ability to play with the 'dangerousness' and attractiveness of their everyday and a sophisticated notion of the protection it could offer them.

Methodologically, video is a useful way of exploring this risk-resilience loop for four reasons. First, it has the potential to support participants to reflect on aspects of lives perceived to be everyday and mundane as well as the more dramatic, difficult and potentially painful. Second, it has the potential to encourage a reflexive awareness of agency at certain moments, and how this might change as they discuss similar situations such as reactions to the 'Charlie' graffiti. Third, it can expose the linkages between internal personal 'felt' narratives, and the external social discourses through its intrinsic internal and external narrative arcs as it is created and viewed. Last, it allowed the research to focus on difficult and sensitive issues that 'lived' in a community where there were a lot of tensions around drug dealing and gang violence. As a community myth the 'Charlie' graffiti reflected the application of wider social discourses to specific events within Urbanfields that then took on their own mythic status. In this sense the graffiti was a reflection of events that had already been processed, creating a safe place for collective reflection because it was part of common parlance. A combination of these reasons means video has the potential to access the emotional aspects of individual lives because of its unique potential to develop critical subjectivity through reflection, reflexivity and criticality.

Theoretically a 'mythcourse' analysis that allows for an exploration of the mythic feedback loops operating in Urbanfields is useful because as an heuristic device it has the potential to give insights into how individuals combine and link their internal worlds to their external environment. This is important because of the need to more adequately understand what is happening within specific communities such as Urbanfields and in individual lives as they manoeuvre the space to make different choices about how they act within it. The role of myth and the 'mythcourses' through which they operate gives a fuller understanding of this agency for three reasons. First, it reveals how myths normalize by making the extraordinary ordinary and the ordinary extraordinary; second, it reveals how myths function to dramatize through intensification as they become symbolic; and third, it reveals their role as a means to fantasize about escaping often 'humdrum' everyday lives. In each case myth is used differently to help resolve contradictions presented to individuals through the external and internal 'felt' narratives operating in their lives.

Finally, the necessarily brief analysis of the 'Charlie' graffiti presented in the chapter reveals individuals who prioritize emotions above almost all else in the short term, at least in respect to the risks they take and the moral consequences of any act as they justify small, or more serious, acts of violence concerned with respect or territory, dealing in and taking of drugs or the break-up of relationships. This differentiates what constitutes resistance behaviour and sources of resilience as they learn how to manipulate spaces within which to make choices about what they take part in and what they do not and make temporary or partial resolutions to the tensions and contradictions facing them. The argument presented in the chapter is that the 'fine grained' choices of young people, living as they do in a world of ontological insecurity where emotional distance from its problems is being replaced by emotional engagement with them cannot be fully explained by decision-making models or behaviour repertoires because their choices are value laden and evolve out of a series of generative dynamic loops connecting thinking, feeling and practice.

References

Alvelos, H. (2004) 'The desert of imagination in the city of signs: Cultural implications of sponsored transgression and branded graffiti', in J. Ferrel, K. Hayward, W. Morrison and M. Presdee (eds), *Cultural Criminology Unleashed*. Sydney: Glasshouse Press. Portland: Routledge.

Armstrong, D. (2004) 'A risky business? Research, policy, governmentality and youth offending', *Youth Justice*, 4, 2, 100–16.

Banks, M. (1995) 'Visual research methods', *Social Research Update*, 11, Winter, University of Surrey.

Banks, M. (2001) *Visual Methods in Social Research*. London, Thousand Oaks, CA, New Delhi: Sage.

Banks, M and Morphy, H. (1997) *Rethinking Visual Anthropology*. New Haven: Yale University Press.

Barthes, R. (2000) *Mythologies*. London: Vintage.

Beck, U. (1992) *Risk Society: Towards a new modernity*. London: Sage.

Bennett, A. (2005) *Cultures and Everyday Life*. London, Thousand Oaks, CA: Sage.

Bennett, W.L. (1980) 'Myth, ritual and political control', *Journal of Communication*, 30, 1, 66–79.

Bessant, J., Hill R. and Watts, R. (2003) *'Discovering' Risk: Social research and policy making*. New York: Peter Lang.

Castleman, C. (1982) *Getting Up: Subway graffiti in New York*. Cambridge, MA: MIT Press.

Douglas, M. (1992) *Risk and Blame: Essays in cultural theory*. London: Routledge.

Ferrel, J. (1996) *Crimes of Style: Urban graffiti and the politics of criminality*. Boston: Northeastern University Press.

Goldson, B. (1999) 'Youth (in)justice: Contemporary developments in policy and practice', in B. Goldson (ed.), *Youth Justice: Contemporary policy and practice*. Aldershot: Ashgate, 1–27.

Hall, S and Jefferson T. (eds) (1979) *Resistance Through Rituals: Youth subcultures in post-war Britain*. London: Macmillan.

Haw K. (2008) 'Voice and video: Seen heard and listened to?', in Pat Thomson (ed.), *Get the Picture: Visual research with children and young people*. London: Routledge.

Kemshall, H. (2003) *Understanding Risk in Criminal Justice*. Maidenhead, PA: Open University Press

Kim, S. (1995) *Chicano Graffiti and Murals: The neighbourhood art of Peter Quezada*. Jackson, MI: University Press of Mississippi.

Losev, Aleksei Fyodorovich (2003) *The Dialectics of Myth* (trans. Vladimir Marchenkov). London and New York: Routledge, Taylor and Francis Group.

MacCannell, D. (1994) 'Cannibal tours', in Lucien Taylor (ed.), *Visualizing Theory: Selected essays from V.A.R. 1990–1994*. New York and London: Routledge.

MacDonald, R. (2006) 'Social exclusion, youth transitions and criminal careers', *Australian and New Zealand Journal of Criminology*, 39, 3, 371–84.

MacDonald, R. and Marsh, J. (2005) *Disconnected Youth? Growing up in Britain's poor neighbourhoods*. Basinstoke, UK: Palgrave.

Maffesoli, M. (1996) *The Time of the Tribes: The decline of individualism in mass society*. London: Sage.

Margolis, E. (1998) 'Picturing labour: A visual ethnography of the coal mine labour process', *Visual Sociology*, 13, 2, 5–37.

Melucci, A. (1989) *Nomads of the Present*. Philadelphia: Temple University Press.

Muggleton, D. (2000) *Inside Subculture: The postmodern meaning of style*. Oxford: Berg.

Pitts, J. (2003) *The New Politics of Youth Crime: Discipline or solidarity* (2nd edition). Lyme Regis, Dorset: Russell House Publishing.

Povey, D. and Kaiza, P. (2005) 'Recorded crimes involving firearms'. Chapter 2 in D. Povey (ed.), *Crime in England and Wales 2003/2004*: Supplementary Volume 1: 'Homicide and Gun Crime' (pp. 27–50). *Home Office Statistical Bulletin* 02/05. London: Home Office. See: www.homeoffice.gov.uk/rds/pdfs05/hosb0205.pdf.

Rutter, M., Giller, H. and Hagell, A. (1998) *Antisocial Behaviour by Young People*. Cambridge: Cambridge University Press.

Wikstrom, P-O. (1998) 'Communities and Crime', in M. Tonry (ed.), *The Handbook of Crime and Punishment*. New York: Oxford University Press. pp. 269–301.

Wikstrom, P-O. H. and Loeber, R. (2000) *Do Disadvantaged Neighbourhoods Cause Well-adjusted Children to Become Adolescent Delinquents?* Thousand Oaks, CA: Sage.

Ungar, M. (2004a) *Nurturing Hidden Resilience in Troubled Youth*. Toronto: University of Toronto Press.

Ungar, M (2004b) 'A constructionist discourse on resilience', *Youth & Society*, 30, 3, 341–65.

Reflections on Haw's chapter

Haw's chapter tells the story of how research can give a 'voice' to young people of ethnic minority communities. The setting is a small geographical location in the United Kingdom called Urbanfields in which live ethnic minority communities with a reputation for gun crime, gang-related violence and drugs. With well-defined geographical boundaries, it is contained, apart from a bridge that connects it to a wealthy suburb and it is one of the top four most dangerous British places to live in terms of gun crime. Recently, however, its social boundaries are less defined due to the closure of the only secondary school in Urbanfields. The use of video as a "community consultation tool" was adopted in order to "legitimate a range of 'voices' through creating a series of spaces for critical dialogue and action" (see p. 129).

Focusing on risk and resilience, the "aim was to support young people to articulate their perspective by focusing on their agency and through this develop alternative approaches" (see p. 129). Currently, literature and debate in criminology is "dominated by biological and psychological models" (see p. 134), with statistical foundations that effectively distance the individual from the "immediate social contexts and localities in which they operate and live" (see p. 131). Using a new approach to analysis, "situated somewhere between the discursive and the cultural", the need to "understand the connections between the external lived worlds of individuals and their internal 'felt' worlds" was addressed (see p. 131). The young people were allowed the freedom to make videos of their own choosing to offset the pervading sense of 'being done to' and replace it with an intention to 'work with' and to promote reflection and reflexivity.

Key mythologies emerged, including drug dealing and its associated life-style, "gang violence, notions of 'territory' and rivalry, sexual relationships and the status of being the 'number one' girl" (see p. 134). Such community myths combined in complex ways to produce 'mythcourses' which linked thinking, feeling and practice in ways that represented the choices of young people living in their own worlds better than the dominant models in criminology.

Research questions

Ethnographies are produced in order to get close to and engage with people in their everyday lives. Such a close focus on the details of lives provides a way of critiquing and thus deconstructing dominant theoretical models and prevailing taken-for-granted perceptions. Research questions focus on the lived experiences of people:

- What methods enable people to articulate their experiences?
- What kinds of images, narratives and 'myths' are employed by people and for what purposes?
- What feelings are connected to the narratives that are told about everyday life?
- How do stories construct identities? And do identities change as a result of telling and reflecting?
- What possibilities for the development of different responses, actions and ways of seeing and interpreting arise when critical reflection takes place?

Chapter 9

Passionate places and fragmented spaces

Cathie Pearce

A sense of place matters to us all. We can hardly imagine our existence without thinking 'place' in one way or another; as real, imagined, remembered, lived, experienced. We talk of *having* a place, *being in* a place, *being out* of place, *going to* a place, *coming from* a place. Places have significance in our cultural world; they demarcate what, where and how we do things or not! Yet what we mean by the term 'place' is not at all well understood.

Philosophers are no clearer either. There are both contradictory and paradoxical conceptions of how we might think of both 'place' and 'space'. We talk of violence *taking* place as an event, an act that unfolds or happens. But what exactly is being taken? How is violence being 'placed' or, perhaps more importantly, what is being 'displaced'? Why do so many conflicts and disagreements take the form of violence? And why is violence so often experienced as irruption or of being incomprehensible? According to some of the early empirical philosophers such as Edmund Burke, "the sublime is the strongest emotion that the mind is capable of feeling" (Battersby 2007: 24). Is it any wonder then, that one of philosophy's most noble words – the 'sublime' – can be linked with terror, violence, power and fear?

This chapter aims to draw upon sociological and philosophical approaches to reconfigure some understandings of violence. Sociology has traditionally focused on the causes and effects of violence. Such emphases necessarily focus on exterior dimensions but not on how violence *might be made to happen*, the spaces in which violence is assembled and the ways in which violence *'touches on the sublime'*.

Philosophy has traditionally thought of the sublime as a place of terror and a place that 'temporarily took man out of the human' (Battersby 2007: 2). However in doing this we appeal to transcendental notions that devolve us of any response-ability or indeed agency. Christine Battersby in *The Sublime, Terror and Human Difference* (2007) makes a detailed exploration of how traditional philosophical notions of the sublime have worked against lived experience and, in particular, women's lived experience. She goes on to explore how the sublime can be reclaimed and rethought in terms that might enable us to assess human differences anew. Our interest in this chapter is in exploring how such a philosophical approach, along with other philosophies of difference, can help in creating new resources both theoretically and methodologically, especially in relation to violence.

In this chapter the task will be to work both with and against a notion of the sublime – the term **violency**[1] might be a more productive mode of appropriation which enables us to assemble violence in its various senses rather than reducing it to its exterior dimensions. A focus that objectifies violence tends to negate any role of our human awareness, whilst subjectifying violence – as Žižek so clearly points out (2008) – leads us to miss more insidious forms that generate its production. Instead we will try to map different kinds of spaces where it might be possible to work the spaces between subject and object.

And so, in a dual sense that isn't a binary, the emphasis will be on using empirical data from a research project to explore how spaces and places can be configured and reconfigured; deterritorialized and reterritorialized in Deleuzian terms, to see what new understandings can emerge from such a complex interplay of differences. Any easy or clear-cut distinctions between empirical particularities and abstract universals will be resisted. Such workings of the data are a necessary experimentation that attempts to make space for new thoughts. It is to work with the unknown and the unthought in ways that offer a promise of alternative ways of knowing and doing, rather than by considering what systems, processes and structures lead us to see, or indeed, expect us to see. It is to place an importance on exploration and experimentation whereby one cannot possibly know in advance and where it is necessary (temporarily at least) for desire to be separated from any notion of rights.

It is perhaps "to theorise a tenuous new form of freedom. In space one has the liberty to experiment, to try new things but the price is that one cannot keep what one gains" (Buchanen and Lambert 2005: 3).

Encountering spaces and places

> [T]hought thinks its own history (the past), but in order to free itself from what it thinks (the present) and be able finally to 'think otherwise' (the future).
>
> (Deleuze, in Gatens and Lloyd 1999: 7)

Between 2003 and 2007, a leading financial company in the UK spent £30 million pounds developing a community investment programme. The programme was called Spaces for Sports and aimed to work with communities and areas that were deemed to be in need of 'regenerating'. Many of the 'local sites' (of which there were more than 200) were therefore on disused land and were subsequently developed into a 'space for sport'. Consultation processes took place, as did negotiations and dialogues between various local projects and the programme's dedicated personnel. As researchers, our task was to follow the programme as it unfolded, to see the extent to which the developments were having an impact within communities and to see what could be learned from such large-scale community investments. The independence of our research was paramount and our engagements gave us critical and significant access to interviews and personnel at all levels within the research project and across a wide range of personnel in the field.

One such interview was with a police architectural liaison unit (ALU) within a large metropolitan city in north-west England. The interview had come about after a visit to a local community group who were planning to install a multi-use games area on what was previously a piece of common land. In an early interview with a community project worker for the site, a comment had been made that "the early plans had changed" and that "the pitch was to be turned sideways to the road" following the advice of the police architectural liaison unit. As this was being said, she demonstrated the move by drawing a diagram. She went on to say that the advice had been taken up by the steering group, who were in agreement with the police architectural liaison unit, and that the developers were working to take this new shift in direction into account.

Such a change both in and of the plans invoked interesting questions, not least as to why this was signalling a preferred position? On what basis? What was at stake? How was it imagined that such a change would make a difference? And how might any thinking move between a 'reasoning' and a 'sense' of things?

An in-depth interview with one of the leading personnel in the ALU found both researcher and interviewee exploring areas that were both simultaneously disconcerting and revealing of the ways in which our thoughts were being assembled and disassembled in trying to make sense of what had happened, as well as account for any changes that were made. At a pragmatic level, as a researcher I was asking about the history of the officer's involvement, a sense of his role within the project, the ways in which he was viewing social and cultural contexts, and at another level I was also exploring the logic and boundaries of thought, action, theory and practices without really knowing it. On reading the transcripts through I was struck by the ways in which when something is deemed as being necessary then any account, texts and narratives that follow tend to provide the norms by which the account justifies itself – both mine and his. Working on the basis that a moral view from nowhere or one that is not acknowledged tends to work in favour of a capitalist position or at least in the interests of those who hold power, I reread the transcripts with a view to considering what else might be opened up if I were to take both social and affective dimensions into account: a working out of the inner logic and effect of our social constructions with a view to expanding the possibilities rather than destroying or denying the discomfort that they created.

There were curious points of disjunction where discourses were operating within the account. The officer commented:

The architectural liaison unit ... basically our function is twofold; one is promoting the principles of crime reduction and design and prevention which is structured in all kinds of documents from academics from all over the world and the other is to advise on measures to limit crime and disorder so it involves almost exclusively anything in the built environment whether it is buildings, whether it is structures whether it is landscaping, parkland, any structure at all we believe that we are in a position to try and limit the possibility of crime being generated by the virtue of a building that is effectively created.

But out of what force fields is this response being composed? And how are they operating in this account? Moving between belief and desire with a mandate that is offering protection, the spaces that the officer is referring to could be conceived in terms of 'environments of enclosure' where space is demarcated in terms of boundaries, fixedness, location and structure, indeed "any structure at all". It is an account of space that does yet reflect any awareness of mobility at all. It proceeds by the 'limiting of possibilities' (negation) 'of what is generated by the virtue of a building' (what exists) and what is 'effectively created' (by man, humanism).

Deleuze, in *Negotiations* (1995), considers how we conceive of our social worlds. He refers to 'environments of enclosure', examples of which would be institutions, buildings and cities as spaces where our social and individual worlds connect and enter into production with one another. Deleuze invokes an analogy with the mole who burrows its way through various territories and works through disciplinary fields. He writes that the crisis of any environment of enclosure is that they can "at first express a new sense of freedom" but he argues, it is also possible that "they could participate in the mechanisms of control in ways that would be comparable to some of the harshest of confinement" (Deleuze 1995: 177). Do conceptions and compositions of place and space where the former is considered as being determined and the latter indetermined repeat and reinforce even more insidious and violent forms of control?

The task in Deleuzian terms is to consider how thought '*thinks* its own history' rather than '*has* its own history' [my emphases]. Deleuze makes reference to a society of control in much the same way as Foucault but he goes further than Foucault in that he argues in *A Thousand Plateaus* (Deleuze 1988) that the model of the panopticon does not go far enough to convey the continuous modes of monitoring and surveillance that we are subjected to. We are not just under 'a gaze', we are under 'a *continuous* gaze' and are 'banked' in data systems, information sets, numerical tags and codings of all kinds that transform us into what Deleuze terms 'dividuals'.[2] We are mapped into the system by codings and these codings come from a range of forces, whether they be economic, social, genetic, environmental, etc. It is a serpent, not a mole, that is a better analogy for Deleuze's social 'animal' in this space, one that coils and recoils even within its own movements.

Change is reality and we need to apprehend both its movements as well as the force fields from which change is emerging or arising out of. We cannot refer to any of our usual practices and processes of forming mental representations for these tend to inscribe what we already know in one form or another. This involves letting go of our usual tripartite divisions: the fields of 'reality', 'representation' and 'subjectivity'. Yet neither can we entirely shirk such spaces from apprehending any logic at all or it would be impossible for us to navigate our way, let alone, to find any alternatives. How do we proceed then?

Although Rancière does not explicitly refer to Deleuze as a philosopher who influenced his thought, his thinking is nonetheless rather closely connected. Ranciere's notion of policing is associated with 'the supervision of places and functions' rather than with any uniformed presence. In this sense it enables the data to be read both with and against a sense of ordering, of assemblages and of a sense of what holds 'the proper' in place. In other words, to explore what holds our conceptions 'in place' and explore our passions and allegiances to them rather than imposing any layers of meaning that might seek to justify or explain.

In methodological terms, however, it is sometimes difficult with such engagements not to 'other' the other especially when we are confronted with perspectives and positions that are alienating and perhaps even an affront to our own beliefs and values. It is also difficult not to fall back on history in the sense of doing so in a liberal, tolerant way that would see such thinking go unchallenged or offer no resistance to its effects. However, we fail perhaps because we do not understand the dynamics involved and no less our own dynamics in relation to the dynamics that we are caught up in. Later in the same ALU interview:

> What it [the development of the site] is doing bit by bit is closing spaces. Whereas before it was one big vast open area and you could see well over to the river, bit by bit now it is being enclosed with sports centres and fencing and football pitches and so on ... the argument that the police have is this – any sort of youth facility like that is that it needs to be close enough to properties for people to be able to see what is going on and to police it but far enough away so that it doesn't create any nuisance or noise or antisocial behaviour and I think that was a lot of the debate in this forum that I went to.

The ways in which 'space' is conceived within our social understandings has been studied by many theorists: Walter Benjamin theorized the arcades as a way in which we were encouraged to 'pass through' places; Kracauer with his example of hotel lobbies that explore both the visibility of the urban and the 'waiting waiting' of modernity; Simmel explored a notion of strangers in places that induced fear and seduction (Harrington 2004); and, we might add, for Auge, the anonymous 'non places' that speed up our transcience through places and spaces (Auge 1995). How might we theorize conceptions of space in the above account? Again a language of enclosure is invoked whereby observation and surveillance, this time by the 'people', is called upon. It implicitly appeals to a rational consensus that people might 'be able to see what is going on' whilst being 'far enough away' to tolerate the incommensurable positions that might also be created.

Projects within the Spaces for Sports programme frequently drew upon processes of consultation whereby a language of consensus was either policed or enforced by the processes themselves. Funding required that people were consulted and agencies on the ground paid varying degrees of attention to the importance of community consultation; some with lip service and tick boxes, others with detailed and time-consuming participatory approaches. Whatever the variation, however, the press for a consensus was huge – there could be disagreement as long as there was agreement in time for various funding deadlines. Agree or lose the funding was often the choice that was presented implicitly or explicitly.

For Foucault the term 'policing' is equated with notions of governmentality. This is significant in that such an emphasis in association has a marked effect upon how we conceive of any agency in both space and place. Foucault draws our attention to the politics of the state within a society of control whereas Rancière urges us to separate our apprehension of politics from the politics of the state. Rancière along with theorists such as Laclau and Mouffe ask that we rethink our engagements in term of a *politics of emergence* and of "constituting a common stage or of acting our common scenes rather than governing common interests" (Rancière 2004). Common places nearly always involve couplings and binaries of more/less, near/far, here/there and invoke a language of approximation, similarity, recognition in ways that raise questions about how commonality may function if it is *not* to shore up a status quo of hierarchy and dominance or be reduced to a politics of special interests. What Foucault, Deleuze and Rancière have in common is a desire to open places up and to find the spaces in which we can deterritorialize the structures and practices that keep domination, oppression and exploitation in place and reterritorialize those aspects that would see us create fairer, productive and more equitable lives. All three philosophers emphasize active modes for our engagement and reject any notion that we can arrive at a consensual point through rational argument and debate.

Just as our social worlds are changing, so too is the political. Moving from a psycho-sexual conception of agency or subjectivity to a politio-ethical sense is both significant and important to the ways in which we might read an 'other' and engage with research that seeks to expand opportunities for people to become visible upon the public stage of discussion, debate, decision making and action.

There are important implications here too for how we might read, write and reconfigure the interview material. "There is no need to fear or to hope but only to look for new weapons." What new methodological and theoretical tools might enable us to open this space further? What would an ethics of discord look like? How can we understand a politics of the sublime or, rather, the sublime within politics, as Christine Battersby suggests, and how can we apprehend violency in all its variations?

Encounters which go back to the future

Many of the underlying assumptions about our social practices and institutional structures are heavily influenced by a history of Western philosophy. Traditional philosophical notions of the sublime have ranged across different theories, perspectives, philosophies and politics but have in the main focused upon how a notion of the sublime affects us as individuals and humans rather than perhaps asking how we could possibly affect or change our conceptions of the sublime.

Our interest here is to think again about the ways in which life touches against our conceptual and interpretative frameworks. It is both an experience and an experiment that attempts to unblock our thoughts in respect to the sublime. As Christine Battersby argues, traditional notions of the sublime take their norm from a Westernized and gendered psyche that "fears the other and the ultimate power of nature" (Battersby 2007: 12). It is therefore with an aspiration of discordant engagement with the sublime that seeks to make visible what is differently human whilst simultaneously exploring how any "representations of terror or fear touch on the notion of the sublime"?

In the same ALU interview, the officer theorizes about how crime potential is identified:

> ... in a very simple form, consider a cash machine, any cash machine or ATM which is located anywhere in the city of Northcity. If we take the basic premise that a cash machine in an urban environment, like Northcity, with a relatively high level of crime which in the crime surveys, we are the third-highest crime-ridden area in the UK ... so the ATM in the city of Northcity ... because it is a cash machine and it holds cash and it dispenses cash and it gives people cash that they can then walk away from, that facility is almost 99.9 per cent likely to generate crime so if we start from that basic premise that if we have an ATM in there it will generate crime, if there is no ATM there, there is no crime likely to occur due to robbery, violence, mugging etc. The fact is that we can't say we don't want an ATM, we have to live with that, so what we do is to try and advise on the measures most appropriate to limit the possibilities of crimes being committed because that is a new ATM ... certain situations we can identify as I have done recently that the level of street robbery and the level of violence is that the ATM would tip the balance to such a degree that it would be very difficult if not impossible to (a) police and (b) to expect crime levels to go down in any reasonable level because that ATM would

generate even more crime and exacerbate even greater problems that the local people are experiencing and the police ...

What is the logic of the event?

• an ATM or cash machine where money = robbery = violence = mugging

And conversely in a logic where:

• no ATM or cash machine = no money = no possibilities = no violence

There is also a troubling metaphysical logic underlying this premise, that is, if it exists, potentialities also exist and perhaps rather dangerously its converse is implied. It proceeds by exclusion, by eliminating, reducing, removing or limiting potential or even existence itself. Such accounts are inherently violent in both their representation and their violency that seek to present crime as a causal linkage between places with spaces; existence and potentiality; thought and action. Just how these events get evented is a productive space that works at the intersections of anticipation and remembrance but which can also be transformative when the emotional and psychic tricks of distancing are placed under strain. Indeed the 'balance can be significantly tipped' in terms of any imagined consensual agreement of 'rational men and communities' that is being implied along with any imagined human rights of protection that would seek to justify any universality.

The questions become: Are there multiple narratives in the account? Yes. Are there incommensurable frameworks of meaning? Yes. Are there irreducible tensions and contradictions? Yes. But a question remains that might ask: What happens when our understandings, frameworks and methods fail?

Žižek argues that violence is everywhere. He writes "we live with it and yet we can't easily explain it or accept it" (Žižek 2008). In his book *Violence* (2008), Žižek's premise is that there is a much more insidious violence that is taking place in our social and political worlds and which underpins our social structures, institutions and practices. He writes that acts of violence often appear to us as random irruptions in what would otherwise be our peaceful and 'normal' everyday worlds; in this sense then, an engagement with the sublime whereby we have learned to tame and domesticate – horror, terror, fear, the unknown and what is taken to be our otherwise safe, secure and known territories. Repetitive patterns of incomprehensibility are repeated whereby we no longer expect to make sense and where we have learned to maintain a safe distance from that which we think threatens to disturb our boundaries. Such thinking works to shore up a fear of the unknown, of what is 'out there', of infinity, of the sublime. The by now familiar language of 'shock and awe' tactics employed by the US and the UK in Iraq invoked a language of the sublime that worked precisely in these ways. Thus, "there is no representation of modern political terror which does not in one manner or another, touch on the idea of the sublime" (Battersby 2007: 3).

The task in reconfiguring more politico-ethical approaches to the sublime therefore becomes one of thinking both with and against our own continued attachments as well as our implicit allegiances to both philosophies of presence and consciousness as well as our philosophical conceptions of places and spaces. It is perhaps a mistake to think that in order to encounter an 'other' we need to be taken 'beyond' a conception of a space-time world.

The officer continued:

> The kids want these things [referring to youth shelters and multi-use games areas]. We are told that they want them away from prying eyes of adults, they want them away from authority. They don't want to be seen. They don't want to be overlooked but why? What goes on in these locations that they want to hide? And we are concerned about antisocial behaviour with inappropriate behaviour, drug taking etc., sexual deviation, whatever you want to call it ... all these factors are there for us to consider so although we want to work with these kids and we want to design something that they can accept, we have got to accept that, they should have, there should be a level of observation, we should, surveillance is an issue and we should know that they are there and what they are likely to be doing. The element of surveillance is probably our single most important crime deterrent.

The visibility/invisibility themes are striking in this part of the account. Kids become the 'targets' for surveillance and suspicion runs amok in what can be read as a general moralized discourse. Here a discourse of consensus reaches a recognizable limit in consulting with 'kids' in 'wanting to design something that they can accept' whilst simultaneously emphasizing that 'surveillance is an issue' and that not only that 'we should know that they are there' but 'what they are likely to be doing' as well. It is a discourse which tries to read into the future in ways that justify the actions of the present – a pre-emptive discourse which posits the future as a set of undesirable potentialities, possibilities and unknowns. But if we reconsider the task not as one which takes us into this 'non-human' place, this transcendental space of infinity, and consider instead how we might take a different relation to the present, what might happen then?

Thinking otherwise: reconfiguring places and spaces

What happens when two very different views collide with each other? How can differences be negotiated? Can they be negotiated? And what kinds of differences are they? In the interview, we have already seen how a white, male, Westernized view has been taken as the norm within both traditional philosophical notions of the sublime and in the sublimation of differences that any universal claims inevitably make. Differences (both mine and his) are smoothed over to enable us to say what we know, imagine and believe.

INTERVIEWER: What do you base your knowledge on?
OFFICER: I don't think we are any different from how we perceive crime than anybody else ...

[A little later on in the conversation and without any prompting or questioning he begins reflecting on his job and his role]

OFFICER: I think we work a lot with the negatives, I think we identify what problems we think will occur when we identify particular situations. If somebody offered us a piece of brownfield land on a site and said what would you advise that we build in here, I think that would cause us a few problems because I don't think we would know and to be frank with you we have never actually come across a scenario where we are presented with a flat patch which says OK tell us what to build here.

Moira Gatens, in her book *Collective Imaginings*, writes, "We become something different through the expansion of possibilities involved in a sociability which necessarily involves the past. Affect and imagination are both crucial in understanding these responsibilities and the kind of individuality in which they are caught up" (Gatens and Lloyd 1999: 82).

Thinking about a space, thinking in space, and thinking constructively and actively about space brings with it its own passion. Reason becomes an achievement, something made – something joyful in Spinoza's terms – that would see "a construction in time of something new, not a discovery of something that already existed" (Gatens and Lloyd 1999: 127). It is a collective endeavour that seeks to take responsibility for a past, not to condemn or carry a burden of guilt but so that we can rethink both our place and our futures.

In the ALU officer's view:

What we want to do is to create an environment where we don't need a fence and we don't need patrols and we don't need cameras and in certain cases we can try and create that ... really one of the main things we are concerned about is antisocial behaviour. Noise and nuisance are not crimes, antisocial behaviour is not a crime, per se it is not a crime Nuisance is not a crime – it is when it degenerates into personal attack and verbal assaults etc. then these become crime ... antisocial behaviour is the fastest-growing problem for the police and there is not sufficient facilities for the younger people who are generating antisocial behaviour to divert their mind towards ... and that is a culture thing ... there are huge problems here ... how do you? what do you provide for this group of people to try and disperse often violent, destructive attitudes they have? and I speak with people who come up with all different kinds of solutions and you wonder why they don't work?

It is up to us all to participate in what is necessarily ongoing in the formation of our social structures and institutions, as it is through these very structures and institutions that our conceptions of places and spaces (passions and fragmentations) can be negotiated, formed and re-formed. "We will never be without passion", write Gatens and Lloyd as they explore the ways in which we are both passive and active, acted upon and capable of acting. Fragmentation is inevitable in our multiplicitous lives, registers and pasts but where we all strive to make sense of our worlds, at least provisionally. Is it possible to speak of *passionation* then? Would that work?

How the past perishes is how the future becomes
(Whitehead 1993: 304–5)

If only we reposit the questions, turn them sideways and ask: how are we being made to comply with either fear or hope? And how could it be otherwise?

References

Auge, M. (1995) *Non Places: Introduction to an anthropology of supermodernity*. London: Verso.
Battersby, C. (2007) *The Sublime, Terror and Human Difference*. Abingdon: Routledge.
Buchanen, I. and Lambert, G. (2005) *Deleuze and Space*. Edinburgh: University Press.
Deleuze, G. (1995) *Negotiations 1972–90, European Perspectives: A series in social thought and cultural criticism* (trans. Martin Joughin). New York: Columbia University Press.
Deleuze G. and Guattari, F. (2002) *A Thousand Plateaus: capitalism and schizophrenia*, translation and foreword by Brian Massumi. Athlone Contemporary European Thinkers. London: Continuum.
Gatens, M. and Lloyd, G. (1999) *Collective Imaginings: Spinoza, past and present*. London: Routledge.
Harrington, A. (2004) *Art and Social Theory*. Cambridge: Polity.
Magid, Jill (2004) *Evidence Locker Story*. Available at: www.evidencelocker.net/story.php (accessed August 2008).
Ranciere, J. (2004) *The Politics of Aesthetics*. London: Continuum.
Whitehead, A. N. (1993) *Adventures of Ideas*. New York: The Free Press, in Shaviro, S. 'Pulses of Emotion: Whitehead's Critique of Pure Feeling' at www.shaviro.com/Othertexts/Pulse.pdf (accessed July 2008).
Žižek, S. (2008) *Violence*. London: Profile Books Ltd.

Reflections on Pearce's chapter

Pearce's chapter takes the reader on an exploration of the notion of space and its possible meanings, following a number of pathways from a "sense of place matters to us all" through detours of violence to the emotion of the sublime, all the while focusing on how the space is assembled. It is this process of configuring and reconfiguring that comes under particular scrutiny in the exploration. A meaning of space crystallizes out, becoming fixed, providing the norms for the desire for a framework and justifying rationale of explanation, description, account and so on. The researcher is assailed on all sides by the "limiting of possibilities" and has to learn to 'let go' whilst yet holding on to some sort of framework that allows sense-making to occur. It is this violence of arriving at a framing logic that is at the heart of the ethical dilemma for the researcher.

Pearce draws upon philosophical as well as sociological approaches, employing the concept of the 'sublime' in relation to terror and violence and uses the term 'violency' as a way of not reducing violence to its external forms but to bring together its multiple senses. She applies her philosophical approach to the analysis of data.

Research questions

In research, care has to be taken in the development and definition of the categories that will be used to 'explain' and 'interpret' data as a basis for building theories or models.

• What are the key terms and categories employed by people in their accounts of and explanations of 'events' and courses of action?
• What is the relationship between the universal categories employed by people in their explanations and descriptions and the particulars, the incidents, the experiences, the individuals and groups they are meant to contain, describe or explain?
• What new understandings might be derived from a philosophical scrutiny of the concepts employed in everyday life?
• How are spaces conceived by different people?
• What effect do different ways of conceiving of space have upon people?

Chapter 10

The return of the repressed

Loïc Wacquant

This chapter is adapted from The Return of the Repressed: Violence, 'race',
and dualization in three advanced societies, *Working Paper # 24 (Russell Sage
Foundation, New York, 1993). The following adaptation made for this chapter is from
an article revised for inclusion in Loïc Wacquant's book* Urban Outcasts: A comparative sociology of marginality *(Cambridge, Polity Press, 2007).*

*In the lead-up to the extract Wacquant describes the expansionary decades of the
Western democracies following the Second World War. However, the image of peaceful
development was "shattered by spectacular outbursts of public unrest, rising ethnic tensions, and mounting destitution and distress at the heart of large cities". Wacquant goes
on to describe the 'violence from below' that results. He describes three incidents:*

*The first: "October 1990 in Vaulx-en-Velin, a drab and quiet working-class town on
the periphery of Lyon, France: several hundred youths, many of them second-generation
immigrants from the Maghrib, take to the streets to confront police after a neighbourhood teenager dies in a motorcycle accident caused by a patrol car. For three days and
nights, they clash with law enforcement officials and the Compagnies Républicaines de
Sécurité (CRS, riot brigades) hastily dispatched by the government, pelting police vans
with rocks, ransacking shops, and setting two hundred cars on fire. When calm finally
returns, tens of injured are counted, damage is estimated at some 120 million dollars,
and the country is in a state of shock".*

*The second: "July 1992 in Bristol, England: a nearly identical chain of events trig-
gers several nights of rioting on the Hartcliffe estate, a dilapidated industrial district
on the southern edge of town. Violence breaks out after two local teenagers joyriding on a
stolen police motorcycle are killed in a collision with an unmarked police car. Later that
night, some hundred youths go on a rampage through the local shopping centre. When
police counter-attack, they are showered with bricks and stones, steel balls, scaffolding,
and gasoline bombs. The confrontation quickly spills throughout the neighbourhood. Over
five hundred elite troops have to be called in to restore order to a one-square-kilometer
area temporarily turned urban guerrilla zone. Similar large-scale incidents break out
that same summer in Coventry, Manchester, Salford, Blackburn, and Birmingham".*

*The third: "April 1992 in Los Angeles: the acquittal of four white police officers
implicated in the brutal videotaped beating of Rodney King, a defenseless black motorist
arrested after a car chase, sets off an explosion of civil violence unmatched in American*

history in the twentieth century. In the ghetto of South Central, white motorists are snatched out their cars and beaten, stores are vandalized, police cars are overturned and set aflame. The Korean-owned liquor outlets, swapmeets and markets that dot the area are targeted for systematic destruction. So overwhelming is the eruption that neither firefighters nor the police can prevent the torching of thousands of buildings. Rioting promptly mushrooms outwards as scenes of mass looting multiply. A state of emergency is proclaimed and 7,000 federal troops, including 1,200 Marines, are drafted in and deployed. Sniper fire and shootings between rioters, police, and storeowners who take up arms to defend their shops bring the death toll to 45. By the end of the third day of upheaval, nearly 2,400 have suffered injury and over 10,000 are under arrest; a thousand families have lost their homes and 20,000 their jobs. Total destruction is estimated at a staggering one billion dollars".

"A closer look at their anatomy suggests that these urban disorders led by lower-class youths have, to a varying extent depending on the country, combined two logics: a logic of protest against ethno-racial injustice rooted in discriminatory treatment – of a stigmatized quasi-caste in the United States, of 'Arab' and other 'coloured' migrants from the former colonies in France and Great Britain – and a class logic pushing the impoverished factions of the working class to rise up against economic deprivation and widening social inequalities with the most effective, if not the only, weapon at their disposal, namely direct confrontation with the authorities and forcible disruption of civil life".

The following extract is from the section titled: 'Violence from above: Deproletarianization, relegation, stigmatization'. *(The extensive notes have not been included.)*

This violence 'from above' has three main components:

1   Mass unemployment, both chronic and persistent, amounting, for entire segments of the working class, to deproletarianization and the diffusion of labour precariousness bringing in their wake a whole train of material deprivation, family hardship, and personal difficulties;
2   Relegation in decaying neighbourhoods in which public and private resources diminish just as the social fall of working-class households and the settlement of immigrant populations intensifies competition for access to scarce public goods;
3   Heightened stigmatization in daily life as well as in public discourse, increasingly linked not only to class and ethnic origins but also to the fact of residing in a degraded and degrading neighbourhood.

These three forces have proved all the more noxious for combining against the backdrop of a general upswing in inequality. Far from representing a peripheral by-product of a 'Thirdworldization' of rich countries or regressions towards pre-modern forms of socio-political conflict, this return of the repressed realities of poverty, collective violence, and ethno-racial divisions issued from the colonial past at the heart of the First World city must be understood as the result of the uneven, disarticulating development of the most advanced sectors of capitalist societies, whose manifestations are therefore quite unlikely to abate soon.

Unlike previous phases of economic growth, the uneven expansion of the 1980s, where it occurred at all, failed to 'lift all boats' and issued instead a deepening schism between rich and poor, and between those stably employed in the core, skilled sectors of the economy and individuals trapped at the margins of an increasingly insecure, low-skill, service labour market, and first among them the youths of neighbourhoods of relegation. In the United States, this gap has grown so pronouncedly that it is readily palpable on the streets of big cities, where beggars and the homeless became a common sight in the 1980s even in lavish business districts, and in the extremes of luxury and destitution, high society and dark ghetto, that have flourished and decayed side by side. Thus, while the share of national wealth owned by the richest one per cent of Americans doubled in a decade, jumping from 17.6 per cent in 1976 to 36.3 per cent in 1989, more people lived under the official 'poverty line' in 1992 than at any time since 1964: 36 million, including one of every three black or Latino households.

In France, income inequality grew for the first time in the postwar era in spite of a host of social transfer measures targeting deprived categories implemented by successive socialist governments. As the ranks of the 'Golden Boys' swelled at the Palais Brogniard along with the unprecedented appreciation in stocks and real estate values, so did those of the unemployed, the homeless and the destitute. Today, according to official estimates regularly broadcast by the media, over three million French people live in poverty, 300,000 are deprived of regular housing, and half-a-million are recipients of the national guaranteed minimum income plan (RMI) hastily instituted in 1988 in an effort to curb rising destitution. On the national news, reports on conflicts between 'bosses' and 'workers' going on strike to defend their wages and social rights have been replaced by stories about delinquency and sombre assessments of the predicament of 'Rmistes' (recipients of the RMI, a term coined to capture the new reality of quasi-permanent rejection from the wage labour sphere). In Great Britain supply-side economics and rollbacks in social expenditures by the state have likewise caused a redistribution of wealth upwards and a sharp divergence of living standards between working class and upper class as well as between provinces. The northern sections of the country have been dramatically impoverished, as the regional economies of major industrial centres such as Manchester, Liverpool and Glasgow crumbled. So much so that some analysts took to comparing the provinces of the north of England to the Italian mezziogiorno to highlight the growing national dualism. Employment shifts from manufacturing to education-intensive jobs, on the one side, and to deskilled services positions on the other, the impact of electronic and automation technologies in factories and even in white-collar sectors such as insurance and banking, and the erosion of unions and social protection have combined to produce a simultaneous destruction, casualization, and degradation of work for the residents of the dispossessed districts of the large cities. For many of them, economic restructuring has brought not simply loss of income or erratic employment: it has meant outright denial of access to wage-earning activities, that is, deproletarianization. Thus, most West European countries have witnessed a steady rise not only in unemployment – the average rate in the European Community increased from 2.9 per cent in 1974 to nearly 11 per cent in 1987 – but, more significantly, in the number of the long-term unemployed who come overwhelmingly from the lower class. By the early 1990s, the proportion of jobless without employ for a year or more exceeded three-fourths in Belgium, one-half in the Netherlands, and 45 per cent in France and the United Kingdom. The comparable figure of 8 per cent for the United States is misleading because its measurement is different (it suffices to work one hour in a month to be counted as 'employed') and it hides enormous variations across categories and locations: in many inner-city areas, effective jobless rates among adults hover well above 50 per cent and for many, exclusion from formal employment lasts for years and even decades. Survival based on a mix of casual labour, welfare support and illegal activities trumps regular wage labour participation.

The persistent, nay permanent, exclusion from wage labour of a segment of the working class and the correlative growth of the informal economy in declining urban areas are two converging indicators of the formation, at the core of First World cities, of what Fernando Henríque Cardoso and Enzo Faletto (1979) called an 'excess reserve army of labour', for whom economic advancement translates into a regression of material conditions and a curtailment of life chances. Witness the spread of hunger or malnutrition (attested to by the prosperity of 'soup kitchens' and assorted food banks) and the reappearance of bygone contagious diseases such as tuberculosis in the flagging neighbourhoods of relegation of New York, Paris and London.

Just as their economies underwent deindustrialization and globalization, advanced countries have absorbed a fresh influx (or the definitive settlement) of immigrants from the Third World who are typically channelled into those very neighbourhoods where economic opportunities and collective resources are steadily diminishing. The formation of a worldwide space of circulation of capital over the past three decades has led to the knitting of a global network of labour that has reshaped the population and brought in large numbers of fresh migrants from the big cities of Europe and North America (Fassman and Rainer 1996; Portes 1999). These 'new immigrants', as they are often called to distinguish them from the transatlantic migration chains that primarily connected the Old and the New Worlds until the middle of the twentieth century, originate mainly in former colonies of Western Europe or in the economic and political satellite countries of the United States. They tend to congregate in the poorer neighbourhoods of large urban centres, those where housing is cheaper,

where they can more easily gain a foothold in the informal and entrepreneurial
sectors of the economy, and where networks of compatriots or coethnics provide
critical assistance in the process of adaptation to life in the new country (Portes
and Rumbaut 1990; Castles 1993).

Whether or not the arrival of the new immigrants has accelerated the partial
deproletarianization of the native working classes by providing a substitute
pool of pliable labour needed by the expanding deskilled service sectors is
unclear. What is beyond doubt is that their concentration in the segregated
and degraded lower-income neighbourhoods has accentuated the social and
spatial polarization in the city because it occurred at a time when, thanks
largely to state support of individual housing through urban planning and
fiscal policy, the middle classes were fleeing mixed urban areas and relocating
in protected territories where they benefit from: a higher level of public services (France), provision of their basic household needs on the private market
(United States), or a mix of superior public and private goods (England).
Spatial segregation intensifies hardship by accumulating in isolated urban
enclaves, downwardly mobile families of the native working-class and immigrant populations of mixed nationalities who are young, economically fragile,
and equally deprived of readily marketable skills in the core of the new economy. Thus, over half of Vaulx-en-Velin's 45,000 residents in 1990 lived in
large, cheerless public housing projects, and one in four were of foreign origin;
over 40 per cent were under age 20 and one-third of all adults could not find
employment. Government programs of training and job search assistance are
unable to help youths gain a firm foothold in the shrinking and fragmenting
labour market, and sports and cultural activities can provide only so much
diversion. Similarly, joblessness among inhabitants of South Bristol aged 16 to
25 at the time of the riots stood at 50 per cent and had risen with the increased
presence of foreign families. The crime rate in Hartcliffe – among the highest in England at the time – was in no small part due to the severe dearth
of community resources and of recreational facilities needed to keep youths
occupied when trapped in the social void between school and work. Turning
to the United States, between 1978 and 1990, the County of Los Angeles lost
200,000 jobs, most of them high-wage unionized positions in industry, just
as it received an infusion of nearly one million immigrants.

Many of these jobs were lost to minority residents of South Central and to
inner-city communities where public investment and programs were being
aggressively curtailed (Johnson et al. 1992). As a consequence, in 1992 unemployment in South Central exceeded 60 per cent among young Latinos and
blacks and the illegal drug economy had become the most reliable source of
employment for many of them. Such cumulating of social ills and the nar-
rowing of the economic horizon explain the atmosphere of drabness, ennui,
and despair that pervades poor communities in large Western cities and the
oppressive climate of insecurity and fear that poisons daily life in the black
American ghetto (Wacquant 1992). Residents of these neighbourhoods feel

that they and their children have little chance to know a future other than the poverty and exclusion to which they are consigned at present. Added to this sense of social closure is the rage felt by unemployed urban youths due to the taint befalling residents of decaying urban areas as their neighbourhoods become denigrated as hellish breeding grounds of 'social pathologies'. Youths of Maghrebine origins in the northern district of Marseilles, their counterparts issued from Jamaica and Pakistan in London's Brixton, and blacks trapped on Chicago's South Side do not suffer only from material deprivation – shared, in the ethnically mixed areas of urban Europe, with their white neighbours – and from the ambient ethno-racial or ethno-national enmity: they must also bear the weight of the public scorn that is now everywhere attached to living in locales widely labelled as 'no-go areas', fearsome redoubts rife with crime, lawlessness and moral degeneracy where only the rejects of society would bear to dwell.

The reality and potency of the territorial stigma imposed upon the new 'urban outcasts' of advanced society should not be underestimated (Wacquant 1993). First, the sense of personal indignity it carries is a highly salient dimension of everyday life that colours interpersonal relations and negatively affects opportunities in social circles, the school, and the labour market. Second, one notes a strong correlation between the symbolic degradation and the ecological disrepair of urban neighbourhoods: areas commonly perceived as dumpsters for the poor, the deviant, and the misfit tend to be avoided by outsiders, 'redlined' by banks and real estate investors, shunned by commercial firms, all of which accelerates decline and abandonment. They can be overlooked at little cost by politicians except, precisely, when they become the site of visible unrest and street confrontations. Third, territorial stigmatization encourages amongst residents socio-fugal strategies of mutual avoidance and distancing which exacerbate processes of social fission, feed interpersonal trust, and undermine the sense of collectivity necessary to engage in community building and collective action. Last, there is the curse of being poor in the midst of a rich society in which participation in the sphere of consumption has become a *sine qua non* of social dignity – a passport to personhood if not citizenship (especially among the most dispossessed, who have nothing else at disposal to signal membership). As testified by the proliferation of 'mugging' in the British inner city, *dépouille* (the stripping of fancy clothes under threat of force) in the estates of the French *banlieue*, and gold-chain snatching and drug dealing on the streets of the black American ghetto, violence and crime are often the only means that youths of proletarian background with no employment prospects have of acquiring the money and the consumer goods indispensable for acceding to socially recognized existence.

Political alienation and the dilemmas of penalization

If direct and spontaneous forms of infra-political protest by way of popular disruption of public order, outright seizure of goods, and destruction of property have spread in the declining urban boroughs of advanced society, it is also that formal means of pressure on the state have declined along with the disruption and then decomposition of traditional machineries of political representation of the poor. In France, the crumbling of the Communist Party and the centrist turn of the successive socialist governments have left the working class in deep political disarray – a disarray upon which the extreme right-wing party of Le Pen was quick to capitalize with an ideology scapegoating immigrants that, for lack of something better, has the virtue of offering a crystal-clear picture of society, a coherent diagnosis of its main ills, and a radical cure that promises to restore workers' sense of dignity as citizens (redefined as 'nationals'). In Great Britain, a decade-and-a-half of Thatcherism prolonged by the neoliberal policy of Tony Blair has speeded up the long-term decline of trade unions and the ideological revamping of the Labour Party, while the breakup of working-class communities undercut the local mobilizing capacity of their grassroots organizations. In the United States, where the lower class has never had much of a political voice, the mass exodus of whites and the middle class to the urban periphery, the nationalization of political campaigns, the demise of big-city electoral 'machines', and the administrative fragmentation of the metropolis have converged to marginalize poor minorities in the political field (Weir 1993). Stripped of the institutional means to formulate collective demands in a language comprehensible by state managers, what are poor urban youths to do if not take to the streets? A teenage rioter from Bristol speaks for many of his peers in East Harlem, the Red Belt boroughs of Paris, and of Toxteth in Liverpool when he exclaims:

> I don't have a job and I'll never have one. Nobody wants to help us get out of this shit. If the government can spend so much money to build a nuclear submarine, why not for the inner cities? If fighting cops is the only way to get heard, then we'll fight them.

The widening gulf between rich and poor, the increased closure of political elites onto themselves and the media, the increasing distance between the lower class and the dominant institutions of society all breed disaffection and distrust. They converge to undermine the legitimacy of the social order and to redirect hostility towards the one institution that has come to symbolize its unresponsiveness and naked repressiveness: the police. In the vacuum created by the lack of political linkages and the absence of recognized mediations between marginalized urban populations and a society from which they feel rejected, it is no wonder that relations with the police have everywhere become both salient and bellicose, and that incidents with the 'forces of order' are invariably the detonator of the explosions of popular violence that have rocked poor urban neighbourhoods over the past two decades in the city (Cashmore and McLaughlin 1992; *Cultures et Conflits* 1992).

In the French working-class *banlieues*, the police are regarded by the youths of the housing projects (of Arab and French origins alike) as an undesirable presence sent for the express purpose of intimidating and harassing them, and nearly all instances of collective unrest over the past decade have been triggered by an incident opposing them to local law enforcement. It is not a coincidence that the police invented the bureaucratic category of 'urban violence' in those years, based on a pseudo-scientific scale of levels of aggression (of which the gathering of youngsters in the building stairways was the first stage!), in order to better de-politicize these confrontations and to make them liable to a strictly penal treatment (Bonelli 2001). The Scarman report on the riots that rocked British cities in the early 1980s notes likewise that inner-city youths are "hostile and vindictive towards the police and no longer have any confidence in them" (Benyon 1984: 126). But it is in the segregated black and Latino areas of the American urban core that relations with the police are the most antagonistic and the most virulent. Residents of the ghetto are torn between their need for protection from rampant crime and their fear that police intervention will add to the violence, not diminish it, due to their discriminatory and brutal behaviour. In the desolate districts of the Los Angeles ghetto, the forces of order act as if they were waging a trench war with the residents, treating them as an army of occupation would its enemies (Davis 1992; Herbert 1997). In June of 1992, Amnesty International released a report (1992) compiling evidence of a deep-seated pattern of routine police brutality against poor African-Americans and Hispanics in Los Angeles which had gone unchecked for years in near-complete impunity from local and federal authorities. The 60-page report details heinous incidents of excessive use of force, often "amounting to torture or other cruel, inhuman or degrading treatment", that involved the unwarranted use of firearms "in violation of international standards", shootings or beatings of compliant suspects and even innocent bystanders, the routine overuse of electric taser guns, and the unleashing of attack dogs on suspects (including juveniles and minor offenders, some of them already in custody) who had surrendered and posed no threat.

For the disaffected youths of declining urban districts, then, the police constitutes the last 'buffer' between them and a society that rejects them, and which they therefore view as 'the enemy'. They regard the police as trespassers in a territory where their rule is often openly contested, inciting defiance and hostility that can extend to verbal and physical aggression – as illustrated by the controversial song *Cop Killer* by the Afro-American rap singer Ice T [with the band Body Count – eds]. In all advanced countries, whenever the police comes to be considered as an alien force by the community it is supposed to protect, it becomes unable to fulfil any role other than a purely repressive one and, under such circumstances, it can only add to discord and disorder, often fuelling the very violence it is entrusted to curb (Wacquant 1993). Political responses to the return of urban marginality and collective violence have varied significantly from country to country depending on national ideologies of citizenship, state structures and capacities, and political conjuncture. They span a wide spectrum between the criminalization of poverty and dispossessed populations identified at one end, and politicization of the problem via the collective renegotiation of social and economic rights at the other. The two tendencies, symbolized by the prison and the ballot box, can be observed to operate simultaneously in all three societies considered here, albeit in different combinations and trained on different categories, as various factions of their respective ruling classes manage to steer state policy towards one or the other pole. No country has fully avoided increased recourse to the criminal justice apparatus (irrespective of the evolution of crime) and all have had to reconsider some citizenship rights and range of social entitlements, whether to restrict or expand them selectively. Yet it remains that, overall, the question has been most fully politicized in France and most completely depoliticized in the United States, with the United Kingdom occupying a sort of median ground between these two paths.

Through a decade of urban strife, the French government has passed legislation creating a guaranteed minimum income for those who have fallen through the cracks of the work and welfare grid; it has expanded unemployment benefits and training schemes for unskilled youths; it has established a mechanism to transfer wealth from rich to poor cities (albeit a very limited one), and deployed a comprehensive urban redevelopment program officially designed to improve conditions in 400 'sensitive neighbourhoods' throughout the country. Renewed state activism was officialized by the nomination, at the end of 1990, of a Minister of the City (with rank of state minister, highest in the French administrative hierarchy) and by the political engagement of both President and Prime Minister to win the battle of 'urban renewal'. Yet, over the ensuing years, urban disturbances have continued, if in a somewhat muffled fashion, and ferments of unrest remain, as testified by incidents in the declining public housing estates of Argenteuil, Sartrouville, and Mantes-la-Jolie in the Parisian Red Belt in 1994. The 'social treatment' of urban marginality by means of an 'urban policy' may alleviate its symptoms; it does nothing to attack its root causes.

The response of the United States government to the Los Angeles upheaval was in sharp contrast: once open rioting was checked by the immediate proclamation of a state of emergency and massive military presence, the first priority of the Bush administration was to send a team of special prosecutors and to boost funds available to bring the full force of the law to bear on the thousands arrested during the disturbance. Unlike in cases of meteorological disasters (such as the hurricanes and floods that periodically ravage the coastal areas of the South or the plains of the Midwest), in which the federal government extends prompt and generous material and financial assistance to victims (who are essentially property owners of the middle and upper classes), Washington was content to coordinate charity relief and to encourage private rebuilding and reinvestment efforts. And, although the riot had broken out at the very start of the 1992 presidential campaign, the fate of the urban poor was not deemed worthy of mention by any of the three major candidates to the White House. Stubborn refusal to acknowledge the structural mooring and political import of the uprising gave warrant to continue the policy of state neglect that helped cause it in the first place (Johnson *et al.* 1993) and all but guarantees that the human toll – in terms of crime, incarceration, fear and excess mortality – exacted by urban marginalization will continue to mount unchecked.

The United Kingdom is positioned about midway between these two poles of politicization and criminalization. The inclination to attribute disorder to a 'black criminal minority' is always strong; yet even the staunchly laissez-faire governments of Thatcher and Major had to reestablish a degree of state oversight of urban zoning and housing improvement. At the local level, many British cities have opted for a two-pronged approach, elaborating more effective policing techniques in order to regain control of the streets at the very outset of a putative riot on the one hand, and engaging in establishing connections and building trust between the forces of order and the resident populations (under the aegis of 'community policing'), on the other. After the Handsworth riots, for instance, the Birmingham police developed a series of indicators of tension designed to pre-empt the outbreak of violence and they were able, in collaboration with neighbourhood leaders, to keep young men off the streets when incidents threatened again. But one wonders how long such policies of 'papering over' widening social cleavages can be expected to dampen discontent, especially given that the state policy of 'urban regeneration' fostering market mechanisms deepens inequalities within as well as between cities (Le Galès and Parkinson 1993).

Coda: A challenge to citizenship

The popular disorders and urban protests that have shaken the advanced societies of the capitalist West over the past two decades find their roots in the epochal transformation of their economy (deregulation of financial markets, desocialization of wage work, revamping of labour to impose 'flexibility'), the social polarization of their cities, and in state policies that have more or less overtly promoted corporate expansion over social redistribution and commodification to the detriment of social protection. The ruling classes and governments of rich nations have, to varying degrees, proved unable or unwilling to stem the rise of inequality. And they have failed to curb the social and spatial cumulation of economic hardship, social marginality, and stigmatization in the deteriorating working-class neighbourhoods of the dual metropolis.

The conjugation of (real or perceived) ethnic divisions and deproletarianization in declining urban districts deprived of the organizational means needed to forge an emergent identity and formulate collective demands in political space promises to produce more unrest and to pose a daunting challenge to the institution of modern citizenship for the decades to come. Citizenship, in T.H. Marshall's (1964) famous formulation, serves essentially to mitigate the class divisions generated by the marketplace: it is its extension from the civil to the political to the socio-economic realm that has 'altered the pattern of social inequality' and helped make advanced society relatively pacified and democratic. During the postwar era of steady and protected growth, well-bounded and sovereign nation states were able to establish a clear separation between members and non-members and to guarantee a relatively high degree of congruence between the basic dimensions of membership – with the spectacular exception of African Americans in US society. Today, that ability and congruence are both deeply reduced so that the hitherto hidden fractures of the space of citizenship are appearing in full light. As the external boundaries and the (real or imagined) internal homogeneity of advanced societies are eroded, from above by high-velocity capital flows and from below by the confluence of the decomposition of the industrial working class and increased immigrant inflows, it becomes increasingly clear that citizenship is not a status achieved or granted once and equally for all, but a contentious and uneven "instituted process" (to use the language of Karl Polanyi) that must continually be struggled for and secured anew. Thus, the question facing First World countries at the threshold of the new millennium is whether their polities have the capacity to prevent the further contraction and fragmentation of the sphere of citizenship fuelled by the desocialization of labour and, correspondingly, what new mediating institutions they need to invent to provide full access to and active participation in it. Failing which, we may witness not only continued urban disorder, collective violence, and ethno-racial conflict (actual or imagined) at the heart of the advanced societies, but a protracted process of societal fission and a capillary ramification of inequalities and insecurities akin to a 'Brazilianization' of the metropolis of Europe and North America.

References

Amnesty International (1992) "united States of America: toruture, ill-treatment and excessive force by Police in Los Angeles, California". Report, June.

Benyon, J. (Dir.) (1984) *Scarman and After*. Oxford: Pergamon Press.

Bonelli, L. (2001) 'Les renseignements généraux et les violences urbaines'. *Actes de la Recherche en Sciences Sociales*, March, 136–7.

Cashmore, E. and McLaughlin, E. (eds) (1992) *Out of Order: Policing black people*. London: Routledge.

Castles, S. (1993) *The Age of Migration: International population movements in the modern world*. New York: Guilford.

Cultures et Conflits (1992) 'Thematic issue on "Emeutes urbaines: Le retour du politique"', n. 5,

Spring. Paris: L'Harmattan. http://www.conflits.org/index64.html (accessed August 15, 2009).

Cardoso, F.E. and Faletto, E. (1979) *Dependency and Development in Latin America*. Berkeley: University of California Press.

Fassmann, H. and Rainer M. (eds) (1996) *Migration in Europa: Historische entwicklung, aktuelle trends, politische reaktionen*. Francfort: Campus Verlag.

Davis, M. (1992) 'L.A. Intifada: An interview with Mike Davis', *Social Text*, 33, December, 19–33.

Herbert, S. (1997) *Policing Space: Territoriality and the Los Angeles Police Department*. Minneapolis: University of Minnesota Press.

Johnson, James H. Jr, Jones, Cloyzelle K., Farrell, Walter C. Jr and Oliver, Melvin L. (1992) 'The Los Angeles rebellion: A retrospective view'. *Economic Development Quarterly*, 6, 4, November, 356–72.

Johnson, James H. Jr, Farrell, Walter C. Jr and Oliver, Melvin L. (1993) 'Seeds of the Los Angeles rebellion of 1992', *International Journal of Urban and Regional Research*, 17, 11, March, 115–19.

LeGalès, Patrick and Parkinson, Michael. (1993) 'Inner city policy en Grande-Bretagne: Origine et principaux programmes', *Revue française d'administration publique*, 74, 483–98.

Marshall, T.H. (1964) *Class, Citizenship, and Social Development*. New York: Doubleday.

Portes, A. (1999) 'La mondialisation par le bas: l'Émergence des communautés transnationales', *Actes de la recherche en sciences sociales*, 129, September, 15–25.

Portes, A. and Rumbaut R.G. (1990) *Immigrant America: A portrait* (2nd edition). Berkeley: University of California Press.

Wacquant, Loïc. (1992) 'Décivilisation et démonisation: La mutation du ghetto noir américain', pp. 103–25 in Christine Fauré and Tom Bishop (Dir.), *L'Amérique des Français*. Paris: Editions François Bourin [revised English trans. 2004: 'Decivilizing and demonizing: The remaking of the Black American ghetto', in Steven Loyal and Stephen Quilley (eds.), *The Sociology of Norbert Elias*. New York: Cambridge University Press, pp. 95–121.]

Wacquant, Loïc. (1993) 'Urban outcasts: Stigma and division in the black American ghetto and the French urban periphery'. *International Journal of Urban and Regional Research*, 17, 13, September, 366–83. (Trad. fr. chapitre 6 dans ce volume.)

Weir, Margaret. (1993) 'Race and urban poverty: Comparing Europe and America', *The Brookings Review*, 11, 13, Summer, 23–7.

Reflections on Wacquant's chapter

Wacquant explores the "spectacular outbursts of public unrest, rising ethnic tensions and mounting destitution and distress at the heart of large cities" that have 'shattered' the image of peaceful development in the Western world since the Second World War. The exploration takes an in-depth look at three particular incidents (one in France, one in the UK and one in America) of "a violence from below". Two logics emerged: one of "a protest against ethno-racial injustice" and one of "a class logic pushing the impoverished factions of the working classes to rise up against economic deprivation and widening social inequalities" (see p. 159). This violence 'from below' is a direct response to a violence 'from above' that takes its form in three ways: 1) mass unemployment that is both chronic and persistent and that deproleterianizes; 2) "relegation in decaying neighbourhoods in which public and private resources diminish"; and 3) "heightened stigmatization in daily life as well as in public discourse" (see p. 159). To varying degrees, governments and ruling classes of rich nation-states have either proved unable or unwilling to stem the escalation of such inequalities.

"As the external boundaries and the (real or imagined) internal homogeneity of advanced societies are eroded, from above by high-velocity capital flows and from below by the confluence of the decomposition of the industrial working class and increased immigrant inflows, it becomes increasingly clear that citizenship is not a status achieved or granted once and equally for all, but a contentious and uneven 'instituted process' (to use the language of Karl Polanyi) that must continually be struggled for and secured anew".

There is then a challenge to citizenship and the challenge to find the appropriate institutions, organizations and practices through which voices may truly be heard and taken into account. Thus, to research the concept of citizenship in various ways demands unpicking or deconstructing of the complex interconnections between theory, policy and practice.

Research questions

The crisis points where social order and the meaning of 'community' and 'citizenship' are thrown into question are the points where research can reveal what is at stake for different groups.

- In the context of citizenship, whose voices and demands are repressed? For what purposes and in whose interests are they repressed?
- How and in whose interests is citizenship defined? Who is excluded and why?
- What does citizenship mean to different individuals and groups?
- What is the 'violence from above' that leads to 'violence from below'; and vice versa?
- What new institutions, organizations and practices are needed to bring about full access and inclusion in the public arenas that define citizenship?

Methodological discussion section *iii*

Places — visible, invisible and their 'dis/contents'

Jill Schostak and John F. Schostak

There is an intimate relationship between a given society and the schools and educational institutions it designs. As children bear society's hope and fears concerning the future, so schools bear the demands to prepare children for the future. But what kind of future? Or, whose future is at stake if children represent the potential for change? Do children become the battleground, the contested space, with schools as the instruments of war? In order to think this through, a distinction can be made between schools and research designed under the key principles of democracy and those that are designed for non-democratic political orders. Appropriate schooling in, say, a 'leadership democracy' (see Chapter 1) would involve celebrating elite forms of organization, with a pedagogy instilling respect for and obedience to hierarchies of management and control. On the other hand, a democracy based upon principles of equality and freedom for all would require all institutions, particularly schools, to employ such principles for preparing young people in the values, principles, procedures and practices of voicing viewpoints in public spaces as fundamental to engaging with others in the creation of community. The pedagogy underlying 'leadership democracy' has to do with compliance, the manufacture of consent and the moulding and fashioning of the public mind; the second has to do with having a voice that counts in all public matters. In each case the notion of the 'public' is fundamental to who has access to public space and thus who is rendered visible and audible or invisible and inaudible. In each case, power is organized differently for different purposes, whether it is organized as a force by one person or group to ensure compliance by others or whether it is about the use of powers as a force for freedom for all. If children are the bearers of contested futures, when does force become enabling or constraining? When is it violence?

As described in Chapter 1, the necessary relationship between public relations and leadership, or elite-managed democracies, was explicitly seen by its early theorists and practitioners like Lippmann and Bernays. The media and its relation to school, as discussed by Paraskeva in Chapter 7, then, provides a significant focus for research and discussion. The subject of violence as its meaning plays out between the media and schools is highly complex, thus

Paraskeva explores the contested spaces between the media and schools in the context of the struggle for meaning over 'violence'. How are such meanings made, are they circulated and in whose interests? In a strategy similar to the case of the bandana that transformed into a religious symbol, Paraskeva enlarges the meaning of 'genocide' to incorporate: mass killing, the erasure of cultural meanings and the suppression of knowledge. Where the media manages representations of violence in the interests of elites, Paraskeva points to and identifies a violent silence in schools. This school violence arises from "teachers' voices, outdated textbooks, and methodologies (no matter how state of the art, technologically speaking, they are)" that foster "cognitive passivity" (private communication to editors by Paraskeva). The teachers do the talking, they give orders and they occupy the classroom spaces with their agendas, exercising their power of what they deem to be relevant, whilst the pupils are expected to be docile and passively receptive to these agendas enforced upon them. In short, the powers of children are being placed into suspension as a precondition for the organization of Power as a structure and process of hierarchical command and control necessary for elite-managed leadership democracies. On a global scale, as Harber (2004) argues, schooling is itself a violence, a mechanism for the organization of violence where in many cases military-style discipline and school discipline merge (see also, for universities, Giroux in Chapter 12).

If schools provide the direct mechanisms for the organization of the powers of young people for the purposes of social control, the media provides the contextual mechanisms through which, as Lippmann (1922) described, the 'pictures in the mind' are managed. Inasmuch as the media constructs it, describes it, inscribes it and codes it, the media propagates and controls a form of cultural politics. Its tactics include, for example, glamorization in creating the megaspectacle, and selectivity in focusing on say Israel/Gaza, Rwanda or the Congo TO (see p. 121). According to Freire, the act of excluding individuals from decision making makes them begin to reject any truths that do not originate from the radio, TV or newspapers. This act of "distorting reality intentionally, [...] changes the (real) issue" (see p. 120), and thereby engages in creating and reproducing Derridean (2002) 'artifactualities' a term that emphasizes the artificial and the factual in the production and projection of a sense of the 'real'. The media is itself a form of violence, engaged as it is in constructing and manipulating how "individuals perceive reality and truth" (see p. 120).

What are the possible educational responses? Paraskeva proposes making the curriculum relevant through 'open education' in which students have a say. They can add their voices through engaging in negotiation, or collaboration, or even through formulating democratic practices. Such practices provide a "flexibility of spaces", and generate "a radical break from the existing status quo" (see p. 122). Paraskeva's approach agrees with Blanco that "the real battle for social justice should be fought in schools" (see p. 122) such that, in

Freire-like terms, individuals "increase their capacity to enter into a dialogue" between each other and "with their world" (see p. 123). There is a real need to "understand both the media and schooling *as* violence, [where avoiding] "such understanding is clearly 'changing the subject'" (see p. 124). In order to counter the dominant forms of 'knowledge' produced and disseminated through the media and schooling, Paraskeva draws on Sousa Santos, in saying we need "to engage in a battle against the monoculture of scientific knowledge and fight for an ecology of knowledges, which is "an invitation to the promotion of non-relativistic dialogues among knowledges, granting equality of opportunities to the different kinds of knowledge" (see p. 125). This would challenge "notions, concepts and practices of mulitculturism which are profoundly Eurocentric" (see p. 125) and begin a move towards "a democratization of knowledge" and "a commitment to emancipatory non-relativistic and cosmopolitan knowledge" (see p. 125).

For such a democratization of knowledge to be accomplished, every voice has to have access to the spaces of public debate where views can be taken into account (cf. Schostak 2006). Haw illustrates in Chapter 8 how, in generalized terms, the use of some research methodologies can give a 'voice' to young people of ethnic minority communities, living in deprived areas of the United Kingdom. In particular, she tells the story of how a project based on a social action participatory research perspective using video as a community consultation tool unfolds when it is used in Urbanfields, an area which "is considered one of the top four most dangerous British places to live in terms of gun crime" (see p. 129). This is a story of contested spaces.

Urbanfields and its counterparts typically attract the gaze of criminologists and of research that focuses on risk and resilience. In criminology, the prevailing models of research are biological and psychological ones that posit that if "risk and protective factors" can be identified they "could be affected by interventions prior to offending and [be used] to guide 'treatments' afterwards" (see p. 130). Through her story, Haw aims to critique such models of risk-factor research by showing that they failed to "generate sufficient sophisticated models to show how key factors interact" (see p. 130) because they neither take into account adequate conceptualization of different forms of agency, whether individual or collective, nor structural factors such as class, ethnicity or gender. Their lack of power to generate sophisticated models stems also from their use of statistical analysis, their reliance on discussion of probabilities and correlation, alongside a language of causality, all of which distance the community, the individuals within it and the interplay between them and their social contexts. In short, these models, when used to inform the research process, whether it is at the stage of collecting data or analyzing that data, are so removed from the reality of what it means, as an individual or as a collective, to live and operate in such social environments that they pertain to the academic alone and lack insight, reflection and critique even in that function.

What constitutes data? 'Did you get what you wanted?' is a typical question asked of researchers by participants who believe the research process consists entirely of hypothesis testing. They hold to a sense of rightness and wrongness, of black and white in terms of both their responses to the interviewers' questions and what they seek to show the researcher. In selecting a methodological framework, the gaze of the researcher[s] is directed in particular ways, and these ways might easily contest other ways of seeing what is going on in terms of what is data and what is not. Similarly, contested spaces for analysis will emerge and affect project outcomes and how it informs. Haw's methodological gaze is to be located "somewhere between the discursive and the cultural" in an attempt "to understand the connections between the external lived worlds of individuals and their internal 'felt' worlds" (see p. 131). An analytic approach that focuses on "a narrative moment" during the analysis allows the individual to relate their internal felt world back to their external worlds through "linking thinking, feeling and action" (see p. 131). The kinds of 'knowledge' produced and represented thus are more inclusive and connected with life experience from the points of view of the young people themselves. There is a more complex understanding of violence that results which concerns how the young people built up "pictures in the mind" (Lippmann 1922) to create a holistic grasp of their world(s) through the 'myths' that functioned to rationalize, normalize and bring people together by providing causal explanations and resolving contradictions presented to them by living in Urbanfields. The methodological issue then is how to open up such narrative spaces. Reflections upon the videos made by the young people provided such a method. The feedback between the video representation, interpretations and reflections upon multiple interpretations opens critical space. This method has long been used in classrooms to explore how emancipatory changes may be made (e.g. Richmond 1982; Schostak 1988–9) by generating reflective dialogue between participants that reveals how options are either opened up or closed off (Schostak and Davies 1991; Schostak 2006). The experience that the youth of Urbanfields had of being involved versus that of being 'done to' is a stark contested space that shows the issues involved in making decisions. The former opens up spaces in which emotions with their various energies and forces are able to appear, in, for example, forms of 'risky behaviour' that are practised in 'play-acting' and in 'play-fighting' yet which sometimes spill over into reality if one's 'protective' reputation requires it. The latter cannot accommodate such complexities. A methodological space, however, that is open to "the 'fine grained' choices of young people, living as they do in a world of ontological insecurity where emotional distance from its problems is being replaced by emotional engagement with them cannot be fully explained by decision-making models or behaviour repertoires because their choices are value laden and evolve out of a series of generative dynamic loops connecting thinking, feeling and practice" (see p. 142–3) begins to point the way to political change.

Politics and violence are intimately connected to space as 'territory' to be mastered and as 'place' where protagonists struggle to appropriate a given place as *their* place. Place is intimately connected to one's existence, both physically and symbolically. Pearce asks in Chapter 9 what it means to *have* a place, be *in* a place or even be *out of* place. She makes a move into a philosophically informed discussion of 'place' in order to explore what is conceptually at stake through what she names 'violency', a term she uses to illustrate how violence can be better assembled "in its various senses rather than its exterior dimensions" (see also Blanco's discussion of 'secure spaces' in Chapter 6). She employs a Deleuzian approach alongside a reworking of the philosophical concept of the 'sublime' to avoid reducing violence to being either an object or a subject. The focus is on spaces, the subtle spaces between subject and object that generate violence. A space in this sense is something like the bee in relation to a flower. There are two distinct beings but the relationship between the two is more than the fact that they just happen to be near each other. The flower is not merely an object of the bee, nor is it a subjective production. Rather there is a configuration, a kind of gestalt that is bee-flower. Or, think of a scene such as a beach on a sunny day. The beach is not the sand, nor is it the sea, but it is a kind of space produced in relation to both.

Think now of the myths described by Haw, or Normand's bandana that becomes a religious symbol, or Burman's discussion of becoming 'other'. In each case there is a reconfiguration of the spaces in which people appear: from school girl to religious advocate/troublemaker, or from legal resident to illegal immigrant, or from housing estate to gang territory. In each case the configuration of all the elements produces a kind of unity that is a spatial territorialization that is not reducible to any easy relation between particulars and universals. The question then is, can acts of configuring and reconfiguring spaces generate new understandings from working with both 'the spaces between the subject and the object' and with "the unknown and the unthought" (see p. 147)? Captured by the logic of a myth, is there a way of seeing potentialities for change that are as yet unthought, unknown? Change is perhaps unthinkable if the conditions of everyday life are marked as 'real', as the way things have to be. However each viewpoint from each participant in an event may provide a different 'mark of reality' (Schostak 1985) to what has taken place. The story can be told in different ways with different potential outcomes from each point of view. If these views can be placed into dialogue then what has been unthought and unknown from one point of view may be raised as thinkable and knowable from another point of view. Every space has its limits. Reconfiguring a space, say from wasteland to sports site, transforms the ways in which people act towards it. However, although a newly configured space may open up possibilities, it is also an enclosure, a framing that limits the possibilities of its use. A large corporation, for example, can impose its conditions, demanding consensus concerning the function of the space before allowing its construction. And once constructed, the space is governed by the rules of its use: all activities have to be appropriate for the given space. Where the appropriate use is a use desired by people, then the people themselves become self-governing. The space itself is, in that sense, an instrument of social order. However, what happens when two very different views collide with each other?

Pearce draws upon Rancière's distinction between politics of the state and the political moment. The politics of the State is about 'policing', that is, the construction of the conditions under which consensus can be engineered or conformity and compliance enforced. For Rancière the political moment that leads to real, large-scale change occurs but rarely. It is the time when the aura of Power is dispelled and possible futures open up, where new forms of social organization can be created. It is at such a time when the old order crumbles, making way for a new order, as in the French Revolution, the American War of Independence and the fall of the Soviet bloc. The danger, of course, following such moments is that the old forms of coercion, social injustice and other forms of violence are simply replaced with new variants as the new order seeks to assert its Power to control – or police – all spaces within society. In order to 'save' the dynamic opening of possibilities, to keep alive the potential for inclusion of new views and new voices, Rancière proposes the principle of being 'faithful to the disagreement' rather than attempting to engineer – or police – consensus (Rancière 1995). This, he considers, is a principle fundamental to democracy. Democracy offers a space within which protagonists who may never agree with each other may at least find a political space where they can coexist and where they must always seek creative forms of social, political, cultural and economic organization in order to deal with their differences in ways that are socially just. Democracy then, is the political instrument through which spaces are deterritorialized, opened up and reterritorialized to meet new demands, needs and interests. There is no final resting point. As Mouffe (1993) has said, democracy is the unfinished and indeed, unfinishable revolution. Methodologically, as Pearce points out, this involves a continual 'letting go' of ways of seeing, ways of representing 'reality' whilst also seeking out logics of spaces in order to find ways of navigating. She looks to a reconfiguration akin to the 'politics of emergence' of the theorists of radical democracy and proposes 'an ethics of discord' to render visible different ways of being.

The scale of the political task is made clear in Wacquant's analysis of Power in its 'violence from above' (Chapter 10). In the worlds of mass unemployment, both chronic and persistent, the working classes find themselves inadvertently and helplessly facing up to homelessness, destitution, and being regarded as the 'dregs of society' and as 'spongers' and in other such stigmatized ways. Forced, by their deprivation, to live in decaying neighbourhoods, their struggles against destitution contribute to the further decline of the area, starved, as it thus becomes, of resources. Furthermore, incoming immigrant populations settle in such deprived areas due to cheaper housing, and because they can "more easily gain a foothold in the informal and entrepreneurial sectors of the economy" (see p. 162). With the swelling of numbers, the competition for access to scarce public goods is intensified. The stigmatization of the individual in daily life as well as in public discourse is not linked to class and ethnic origin alone, but is generated from the fact of having to reside in such "a degraded and degrading neighbourhood" (see p. 160).

The uneven growth expansion of the 1980s issued "a deepening schism between rich and poor, and between those stably employed in the core, skilled sectors of the economy and individuals trapped at the margins of an increasingly insecure, low-skill, service labour market" (see p. 160). Youths were often the first in the neighbourhoods to be affected. For the poor, this "excess reserve army of labour" (Cardoso and Faletto 1979, cited on p. 161), "economic advancement translates into a regression of material conditions and a curtailment of life chances" (see p. 161).

On the one hand are the destitute poor and on the other, "the middle classes [...] fleeing mixed urban areas and relocating in protected territories where they benefit from: a higher level of public services (France), provision of their basic household needs on the private market (United States), or enjoy a mix of superior public and private goods (England)" (see p. 162). Collision and violence lurk at the boundaries dividing the two sides. "Government programs of training and job-search assistance are unable to help youths gain a firm foothold in the shrinking and fragmenting labour market, and sports and cultural activities can provide only so much diversion" (see p. 162). Forces to ensure containment, forces aimed at displacement, strategies that pacify, approaches to enclose and limit are all brought to bear on what effectively are 'social pathologies' to those who hold the power. "The widening gulf between rich and poor, the increased closure of political elites onto themselves and the media, the increasing distance between the lower class and the dominant institutions of society all breed disaffection and distrust" (see p. 164). Something has to 'give' at this precarious boundary of 'discontents' between the two sides in "the vacuum created by the lack of political linkages and the absence of recognized mediations between marginalized urban populations and a society from which they feel rejected" (see p. 165). This is the province of the 'forces of order', in the form of the police who become the target for society's "unresponsiveness and naked repressiveness" in the eyes of the marginalized (see p. 165). The police no longer constitute the buffer between law and disorder, but are reconfigured into 'the enemy' by those who are disadvantaged and dispossessed of rights, of power, of identity, of 'life'. Writing of the *banlieues* – housing estates or housing projects – in France and of the 'uprisings' of 2005, Balibar (2007) writes in similar vein of 'two worlds' and the boundaries between them "often geographically very close to one another but separated by a social abyss and a permanent antagonism (which feeds the policies of territorial management and municipal and local power struggles" (Balibar 2007: 48). Again, it recalls Murray's cynical call for a 'custodial democracy' (2005), that is, democracy for the well off and strict policing to contain the poor. Riots are, as in Wacquant's title, in this context a return of the repressed. In the politics of Mouffe, Laclau and Rancière discussed by

Pearce, these are what might be called the 'nearly moments' of the political when Power is shaken.

References

Balibar, E. (2007) 'Uprisings in the banlieues', *Constellations*, 14, 1, 47–71.

Harber, C. (2004) *Schooling as Violence: How schools harm pupils and societies*. London: Routledge Falmer.

Lippmann, W. (1922) *Public Opinion*. New York: Harcourt Brace and Company.

Mouffe, C. (1993) *The Return of the Political*. London and New York: Verso.

Murray, C. (2005) 'The advantages of social apartheid. US experience shows Britain what to do with its underclass – get it off the streets', *Sunday Times*, 3 April; American Enterprise for Public Policy Research. Available at: http://www.aei.org/publications/filter.all, pubID.22252/ pub_detail.asp (accessed August 15, 2009).

Rancière, J. (1995) *La Mésentente: Politique et philosophie*. Paris: Galilée.

Richmond, J. (1982) *Becoming Our Own Experts*. London: Talk Workshop Group, ILEA English Centre.

Schostak, J.F. (1985) 'Creating the narrative case record', *Curriculum Perspectives*, 5, 1, 7–13.

Schostak J.F. (1988–9) *Children's Listening and Talking Project*. Funded by GRIST, Norfolk, UK. Available at: http://www.enquirylearning.net/ELU/Issues/Education/archivesEarlyyears.html (accessed August 15, 2009).

Schostak, J.F. (2006) *Interviewing and Representation in Qualitative Research Projects*. Maidenhead, UK: Open University Press.

Schostak, J.F. and Davies, R. (1991) 'Narratives of lives: Accounting for experience', in J.F. Schostak (ed.), *Youth in Trouble*. London: Kogan Page.

Chapter 11

Manufacturing fear

The violence of anti-politics

Panayota Gounari

Introduction

We live in dark times where the rhetoric of fear, terror and evil has reached a new level. From apocalyptic talk, Messianic calls for salvation and eschatological cries for the doomsday of our planet by religious ultra-right and fundamentalist Christians, to the 'war on terror' and the 'axis of evil'; the neoconservatives of the Bush administration aided by the Christian right and a docile media have carefully crafted a reactionary capitalist neoconservative administration centred around a rising authoritarianism and militarism. At the same time, they also positioned the United States in the midst of a self-constructed (while at the same time destructive) political and ideological Dark Age – a catastrophic legacy that is going to take tremendous effort to reverse and deconstruct. Public servants leave the affairs of the *polis* in the 'hands of God' as evidenced in former President Bush's initial rationale for the pre-emptive war against Iraq and Sarah Palin's use of God as a justification for the war in Iraq: "our leaders – our national leaders – are sending [the troops] out on a task that is from God. That's what we have to make sure that we're praying for, that there is a plan and that plan is God's plan", she asserted at the Wasilla Assembly of God in June of 2008. In addition, the assault on secularism with 'faith-based' social services seriously challenges the separation of church and state, the debate on evolution vs. 'intelligent design' still wages, alongside debate on school prayer, abortion, divorce and same-sex marriage. These are hot social issues and they have been used by reactionaries as a moral justification to invoke the 'supernatural' that now acquires new power over politics.[1]

This chapter explores the construction and/or manufacturing of danger and threat, and the ensuing fear in US society, and argues that the rhetoric around fear and danger has generated not only a 'culture of fear' but also a 'politics of fear' that is necessarily anti-political, since it erases politics in order to be. Within this framework of heteronomy[2] in US society, it is not the people who decide on the instauration of laws. Rather, the creation of desirable institutions is dictated from outside (God, nature, the markets, fear of evil and repressive apparatuses). These neoconservative and neoliberal constructs that suffocate human agency through the blind embrace of fatalism ('God knows best') are generated by a deterministic view of history. This deterministic view of history, according to Paulo Freire, "which exalts imposed silence and which results in the immobility of the silenced, the discourse of praise to adaptation, taken to mean fate in destiny, is one that negates the humanization we cannot escape responsibility for" (Freire 2004: 59). Thus, in heteronomy, human agency is reduced to accepting the social order as is, even to considering it inevitable, to the extent that questioning or asking for explanations would mean aligning ourselves with something unacceptable. For example, questioning civil liberties' containment in the name of homeland security is considered 'unpatriotic'. This move signals a retreat from the political realm, a retreat that is now largely due to a culture of fear that, in turn, produces an 'anti-politics' of fear. Here anti-politics refers to a process and a regime that closes down the universe of politics, supports a state of heteronomy and enforces civic disengagement, while promoting a conservative agenda that in reality erases politics.

I contend that the Dark Age we currently live in, similar in many of its features to the one that followed the fall of the Roman Empire, holds at least the seeds of regeneration, of change. Granted, since we are steeped in a culture of fear, anxiety and darkness, it is difficult not to project these into the future and fall into gloomy prognostics. However, a dynamic critical analysis of the contemporary state of terror, fear and violence finds fissures in the already-cracked wall of a hawkish neoconservative authoritarianism. It is in these weaknesses, these fissures, that we are able to articulate new political projects as we break away from anti-politics. According to Herbert Marcuse:

> The fissures are deep enough. The internal contradictions of the system are more acute than ever: first, the contradiction between the immense social wealth on the one hand and its repressive and destructive use on the other; second, the tendency toward automation, which capitalism is forced to if it wants to maintain expanded reproduction.
>
> (Marcuse 1967a)

A critical understanding of these fissures will enable us to envision a new age through which we "will witness deterioration and demolition, but [it] will also generate amidst the wreckage new values and new institutions heralding a new epoch in human history" (Stavrianos 1976: 3).

The culture of fear and the 'personal safety state' in the United States: The anti-politics of fear

The 'culture of fear' is not a new concept in US history. However, the advent of digital visual media,[3] the apotheosis of the culture of the image, the advances in warfare technology coupled with a rise of authoritarianism and the changing character in US politics, among other things, have redefined both the manufacturing of fear and its 'implements'. The latter have now become much more sophisticated, turning fear into a perfect ideological, discursive, and material machine. Much has been written about the culture of fear (see Glassner 2000), especially after 9/11, and the ways it has been rooted in the construction of an imminent danger/threat that looms over a US society now under siege. The fight against a manufactured phantom enemy, smartly termed as the 'war on terror', has produced more insecurity than security. Despite proclamations that "we are now safer", according to the July 2007 National Intelligence Estimate, "Al Qaeda has fully reconstituted itself in Pakistan's northern border region. Terrorist attacks worldwide have grown dramatically in frequency and lethality since 2001. New terrorist groups, from Al Qaeda in Mesopotamia to the small groups of young men who bombed subways and buses in London and Madrid, have multiplied since 9/11" (Cole and Lobel 2007). These numbers hardly make the case that people are safer.

Obviously, fears and dangers are not only deeply rooted in anti-politics, they also produce it. Hence, the present historical conjuncture points to what Žižek calls "post-political bio-politics" (Žižek 2008: 40). The post-political aspect denotes the claim to "leave behind old ideological struggles and to focus on expert management and administration" (2008: 40). The post-political is necessarily depoliticized since it strips politics from ideology and history; it rationalizes it and restricts its function to 'management'. On the other hand, bio-politics designates the regulation of the security and welfare of human lives as its primary goal. "With the depoliticized, socially objective, expert administration and coordination of interests as the zero level of politics, the only way to introduce passion into the field, to actively mobilize people, is through fear, a basic constituent of today's subjectivity" (2008: 40). For this reason, concludes Žižek, "bio-politics is ultimately a politics of fear; it focuses on defense from potential victimization or harassment" (2008: 40).

Post-political bio-politics as politics of fear finds fertile ground in a "personal safety state" (Bauman 2006: 154). The state switches from a state of social welfare to become a garrison state and a guarantor of private interests. This is a reduced state in terms of the civilizing and welfare functions and social provisions, a largely antisocial state that functions as crisis manager, provides only symptomatic solutions; it has no long-term social vision and exercises ephemeral politics. In this sense, it only asserts its role as "the handmaiden for the global economy" (Bauman 2006: 134). Accordingly, "society is no longer adequately protected by the state; it is now exposed to the rapacity of forces the state does not control and no longer hopes or intends to recapture and subdue – not singly, not even in combination with several other similarly hapless states" (Bauman 2006: 147) where states have, more and more, acquiesced power to global corporations within the designs of neoliberalism. The personal safety state is not known for being particularly democracy friendly, since at its core lies the management of responses to citizens' individual fears. Therefore, consensus in this scenario is built around fear. A central strategy of the anti-politics of fear is to switch attention from the collective to the individual, from collective security to individual safety. Personal safety becomes a central concern, diverting attention from real and important issues such as the root causes of increasing violence, poverty, unemployment, and deterioration of everything public, among others. State authority switches focus to the eradication of terrorism, reducing economic, social, and political issues to the concept of 'protection'. Repressive apparatuses, such as the army or the police, now take central stage on an ideological and material level.

At the same time, we can also observe a redefinition of real and symbolic space, within the framework of the state. As Bauman (2002) notes, the events of September 11 have signalled, in the most dramatic and spectacular way, the symbolic end to the era of space, where events become truly global and interdependent. September 11 challenged the security of the traditionally established 'territory' as a shelter and a hideout: "Places no longer protect, however strongly they are armed and fortified. Strength and weakness, threat and security have now become essentially *extraterritorial* (and diffuse) *issues that evade territorial* (and focused) *solutions*" (Bauman 2002: 88). The materialization of that threat through a violent act also "allowed for the translation from the language of global insecurity (difficult to master and awkward to use – a semantically impoverished language with few if any syntactic rules) into the all-too-familiar, daily deployed and easily understood language of personal safety" (Bauman 2006: 89).

Manufactured dangers crack the imaginary individual and collective sense of security/safety promoted by institutional and commercial sources such as the army, private security companies, security experts, police, intelligence briefings leaked to the press (which are uncritically disseminated verbatim by the media), and, of course, the US Department of Homeland Security. This department, according to its official website is: "responsible for assessing the nation's vulnerabilities. It takes the lead in evaluating vulnerabilities and coordinating with other federal, state, local, and private entities to ensure the most effective response". It comes as a new addition, since 2003, to a wealth of institutions now in charge of manufacturing threats and dangers in order to justify their existence and that of a booming military and warfare industry and private security companies. For the concerned citizen (who has access to the Web) the US Department of Homeland Security provides a daily colour-coded 'National Threat Advisory' (low, guarded, elevated, high and severe). Nine out of ten times, the threat level is 'elevated', which translates into 'significant risk of terrorist attacks', while the indicator for all domestic and international flights is always 'high'. The colour-coded threat level system is used to "communicate with public safety officials and the public at-large ... so that protective measures can be implemented to reduce the likelihood or impact of an attack. Raising the threat condition has economic, physical, and psychological effects on the nation" and the experts at Homeland Security are well aware of how to manipulate these effects. Americans are advised to "continue to be vigilant, take notice of their surroundings, and report suspicious items or activities to local authorities immediately". The anti-politics of fear creates a climate where everybody becomes a potential suspect and, in the process, people lose their individual and collective autonomy.

Increased fear can be linked to reliance on the individual and the disappearing social provisions and solidarity. People retreat from the affairs of the *polis* into their own individual space where all that matters is to remain safe and to keep their possessions safe. Fear generates an uncritical acceptance of anything and makes people deterministic and cynical about the future. It promotes apathy about politics and the function of the political system. Horror of violence prevents us from thinking and therefore it is used to paralyze thinking. It mobilizes feelings of fear, but one would have difficulty connecting the feeling with a theory that is able to explain its underlying cause.

If politics is, in a sense, the "ongoing critique of reality" (Bauman 2002: 56), questioning this reality and its practices would be the first step against anti-politics. Politics here should be understood as a project in the making, unfinished and open, a "mechanism of change, not of preservation or conservation". Politics, according to Cornelius Castoriadis is an "explicit and lucid activity that concerns the instauration of desirable institutions and democracy as the regime of explicit and lucid self-institution as far as is possible, of the social institutions that depend on explicit collective activity" (in Bauman 1999: 84). In a substantial democracy, politics should always aim at establishing and safeguarding democratic practices as these evolve historically to characterize and shape different societies in space and time. Politics constitutes a unique public sphere, a type of *agora* in which people come together, interact, make decisions, forge citizen bonds, carry out the imperatives of social change, and ultimately search for the good society insofar as "justice belongs to the polis" (Boggs 2000: 7).

It is difficult to imagine how fearful and panicked citizens, locked in a one-dimensional ideological framework, could engage in democratic practices. Anti-politics tends to promote a conservative agenda that makes participation in collective decision making irrelevant, shrinks the public sphere, reinforces individuality over the collective, offers pre-packaged answers to pressing social and political problems, and, ultimately, supports containment and repression. Anti-politics marks a retreat from civic engagement, a deepening feeling of powerlessness, the embrace of a culture of cynicism that builds a wall of apathy and indifference to the *koina*, that is, the affairs of the *polis*. Amidst all the economic, cultural and social changes in an age of globalized extraterritorial power, individuals find themselves unable to make sense of their own existence both as individuals and as members of a community. This mood of confusion and apathy can be observed in almost every aspect of private and public life in the United States. In the absence of a serious counter-discourse to the ongoing belligerent rhetoric on war, the discourse of terror, the sacrifice of civil rights to the altar of 'homeland security', the apocalyptic discourse around the future of human societies and the TINA (There Is No Alternative) notion, the call for more consumption, more privatization, and less state control, we are witnessing an imprisonment of people in individualities that block out any notion of dissent and struggle for the collective.

The anti-politics of violence and authoritarianism

In an almost prophetic response to students after one of his lectures in Berlin in 1967, Herbert Marcuse poignantly described the always-present tendencies toward fascism when he wrote:

> The new fascism – if it comes – will be very different from the old fascism. History does not repeat itself so easily. When I speak of the rise of fascism I mean, with regard to America, for example, that the strength of those who support the cutback of existing civil and political liberties will grow to the point where the Congress can institute repressive legislation that is very effective. That is, the mass basis does not have to consist of masses of people going out into the streets and beating people up, it can also mean that the masses support increasingly actively a tendency that confines whatever scope still exists in democracy, thus increasingly weakening the opposition.
>
> (Marcuse 1967a)

Over 40 years later, his assessment cannot be closer to reality. Repressive legislation such as the Patriot Act has been promulgated with bipartisan support behind the masquerade of security and democracy, which is, in reality, a dangerous retreat of democracy given its abolition of habeas corpus, licence for widespread surveillance, and an increasing curtailment of both civil and civic rights. In a similar manner, we loosely use the term 'foreign policy' as a cover for military invasions, pre-emptive wars, and international aggression. In the new authoritarian vocabulary 'our' aggression is legitimized protection, while 'their' mere existence is considered aggression.

Aggression finds new ground both at home and abroad. The war on terror is waged on two fronts. Terror is domestically constructed, and internationally disseminated. At home it helps keep the citizenry in a state of uncertainty while boosting a militarized economy. Under the auspices of neoconservative ideology that divests any responsibility of the state for social provisions (as evidenced in the elimination of welfare for the poor, degradation of anything public, including education and universal health care, rollbacks of affirmative action, cutbacks in housing), the weakened social and welfare state resorts more and more to material and symbolic violence (as illustrated in increased militarization, booming of the prison industry, which makes the United States the country with the highest number of prisoners, most of whom are blacks or Latinos which, in turn, exponentially increases the police forces and the presence of police in public schools). The dangerous shift from substantive democratic practices to more authoritarian statism was accurately observed in the 1970s by Nicos Poulantzas in his writings about the state within the framework of internationalization. He pointed to a steady shift in the state from its 'popular democratic' features to its more authoritarian elements. As noted by Stanley Aronowitz, Poulantzas' analysis is a dual or parallel theory that argues: "the authoritarian and democratic states exist in the same social space. That is, the formal popular democratic features of the modern state do not disappear in advanced capitalist societies even as its authoritarian features emerge, as perhaps, dominant" (Aronowitz 2001: 168). Poulantzas notes "the widening gap between political democracy and socio-economic democracy, in particular the rise of poverty in advanced capitalist states, the increasing role of the national state in favoring transnational rather than domestic capital, especially smaller businesses and the agricultural sector". The gradual erasure of democratic life and the widening gap between the rich and the poor is also taking hold in the United States as Aronowitz (2001) clearly points to "the rising of authoritarianism of the ideological apparatuses, particularly education and the fierce politicization of the so-called private sphere, notably the family, which is now subject to the intervention of courts and other repressive authorities" (2001: 168).

As the state gives up social provisions in favour of 'protection', "real and symbolic violence combine with a number of anti-democratic tendencies to make the world more dangerous and the promise of global democracy difficult to imagine in the current historical moment" (Giroux 2008: 17). According to Mikhail Bakhtin, the constitutive moment of all earthly powers is "violence, suppression, falsehood" pointing to the "dominion of the state and the 'trepidation and fear of the subjected' as primarily, or even exclusively, the subjects' fear *of* the state, oozing from the perpetual practice and even more constant threat of the state's violence" (in Bauman 2006: 155).

Fascism, authoritarianism, totalitarianism and militarization are some of the terms invoked to talk about the current state of affairs in the United States. Obviously these terms are deeply historical and, indeed, nuanced in meaning and ideological register. Giroux's (2008) discussion of proto-fascism and the emerging authoritarianism in the United States in the redefinition of power, control and rule, particularly after 9/11, is especially illuminating at this point. In his account, fascism as a mass movement that emerges out of a failed democracy and as a social order is characterized by a system of terror directed against perceived enemies of the state. He opts for the term "proto-fascism" not only because it provides a more nuanced account of the phenomenon but also because "in many cases it reveals a deliberate attempt to make fascism relevant in new conditions" (Giroux 2008: 19). Giroux presents and analyzes six characteristic features inherent in the development of proto-fascism in the United States: (1) traditionalism that is manifested in egregious inequality, corporate greed, hyper-commercialism, political corruption, and utter disdain for economic and political democracy; (2) corporatization of civil society and the diminishment of public space; (3) rampant nationalism and a selective populism bolstered by the relationship between the construction of an ongoing culture of fear and a form of patriotic correctness; (4) attempts to control the mass media through government regulation, consolidated corporate ownership, or sympathetic media moguls and spokespersons; (5) the rise of the language of eternal fascism that diminishes people's capacity to think critically; and, finally, (6) the growing collapse of the separation between church and state and increased use of religious rhetoric (Giroux 2008: 21–2, 24). All six elements create the mosaic of a state that, instead of mitigating fears and agonies and diffusing anxieties, increasingly removes power for politics and invests it in transnational capital movement, militarized economy, and repressive apparatuses (army, police, prison). They also point to the gradual disappearance of the political where containment, fear and punishment take central stage over quality public education, healthcare, and social services.

The ongoing war on terrorism is, according to Jean Baudrillard, nothing but a continuation of the *absence of politics* by other means[5] through which state terrorism is seldom discussed and retail terrorism is always used to legitimize perpetrated state terror as evidenced by the pre-emptive attack on Iraq under the guise of preventing or fighting terror.

> In the absence of global politics and global political authority, violent clashes are only to be expected. And there will be always someone eager to decry the act of violence as terrorist, that is, an illegitimate, criminal and punishable act. The expressions 'terrorism' and 'war on terrorism' will remain hotly, essentially contested concepts, and the actions they prompt will remain as inconclusive as they are self-perpetuating and mutually reinvigorating (Bauman 2002: 94).

Violence and aggression are justified and legitimized only at our end, yet we are quick to condemn forms of violence not manifested yet as terrorism, unless the events of 9/11 have provided a carte blanche for US worldwide aggression for past, present, future, possible and imagined acts of terror. In the ongoing war on terror the enemy is not outside: the enemy is being built into the system as a cohesive power that holds together a highly unstable and uncertain social net. Former National Security Advisor to President Jimmy Carter, Zbigniew Brzezinski, notes that "constant reference to a war on terror did accomplish one major objective: It stimulated the emergence of a culture of fear. Fear obscures reason, intensifies emotions and makes it easier for demagogic politicians to mobilize the public on behalf of the policies they want to pursue" (Brzezinski 2007).

Against an exponential increase of violence generated by the so-called war on terror with its wanton killing of innocent civilians by smart bombs delivered with precision by unmanned drones, it is important to situate any analysis of violence within a typology of violence as proposed by Žižek (2008) where he differentiates between what he calls subjective, objective (symbolic) and systemic forms. Subjective violence is the most visible (crime, mass murder, terror, etc.) and is enacted by social agents, evil individuals, disciplined repressive apparatuses, and fanatical crowds. Unfortunately, current liberal attitudes (the humanitarian jump to action) promote a reaction to subjective violence making all other more subtle forms invisible. Objective violence that is invisible (racism, hate-speech, discrimination, and other forms of dehumanization) is inherent to the normal state of things and it includes symbolic violence. Objective violence is embodied in forms of language (discourses). Finally, *systemic* violence, is inherent to a system and it is sustained not only through direct physical violence but it is also manifested through more subtle forms of coercion that sustain relations of domination and exploitation, including the threat of violence (Žižek 2008: 9).

The successful manufacturing of fears in the United States is mostly dependent on subjective violence. This is a pragmatic society that lives in the here and now; immediacy is at its core. In subjective violence, it can name perpetrators and victims and represent/illustrate the atrocities to elicit the desired reaction. With respect to its own violent acts worldwide, those play out mostly at the objective and systemic level, and they succeed in maintaining and expanding relations of domination and exploitation.

Subjective violence always stands in need of spectators since it is through their gaze that it takes on meaning and importance, and it is the spectators' interpretations that make it what it is. At the same time this type of violence uses material implements while objective and systemic violence rely on discursive, ideological, and symbolic means that nevertheless can have very real (material) manifestations as exemplified by the relentless attacks on illegal immigrants and the institutional racism that gives rises to these attacks in the first place.

In this sense, visible or invisible violence (that is, both symbolic and real) is another prolific source of contemporary fears. I now want to turn my discussion to violence as anti-politics. In order to do this, I will rely on Hannah Arendt's classic discussion *On Violence* (1969) where she makes it possible to capture nuances and understandings of violence in the age of terror and warfare. Arendt's seminal work makes a very interesting distinction between violence and power. Beyond the simplistic notion that power is nothing but a façade for violence – where violence is seen as a flagrant manifestation of power and deemed absolutely necessary to maintain it – she inverts Weber's famous formulation that modern states have been constituted through the gradual process of attaining a monopoly over the means of violence, "the rule of men over men based on the means of legitimate, that is allegedly legitimate, violence" (Arendt 1969: 35). Arendt claims that violence is distinct from power because force or strength always needs implements and that "the very substance of violence is ruled by the end-means category whose chief characteristic is that the end is in danger of being overwhelmed by the means which it justifies and which are needed to reach it" (Arendt 1969: 4). On the contrary, power is an end in itself in the sense that it is the condition enabling a group to think and act in terms of the means-end category (Arendt 1969: 51). She cautions that abuse of violence could result in the means overwhelming the end.

According to Arendt, "one of the most obvious distinctions between power and violence is that power always stands in need of numbers", that is, a solid human basis, whereas "violence up to a point can manage without them because it relies on implements" (1969, 41–2). Violence can always destroy power: "out of the barrel of a gun grows the most effective command, resulting in the most instant and perfect obedience" (Arendt 1969: 53). However, power can never grow out of raw violence. Rule by sheer violence comes into play where power is being lost, as is the case, for instance, with totalitarian regimes since "no government exclusively based on the means of violence has ever existed. Even the totalitarian ruler, whose chief instrument of rule is torture, needs a power basis – the secret police and its net of informers ... even slavery was based on superior organization of power (that is, on the organized solidarity of the masters) and not on superior means of coercion" (Arendt 1969: 50). Arendt is not claiming that there is no violence inherent to power, but rather that violence always seeks legitimization or justification (rightly or wrongly) in power. That is, there is no such thing as raw violence. In her view, the implements of violence alone won't succeed. Individuals without others to support them do not seem to have enough power even to use violence successfully.

Arendt further insists that power and violence are opposites: where one rules absolutely, the other is absent. The opposite of violence is not nonviolence, since to speak of nonviolent power is redundant (Arendt 1969: 56) and violence does not constitute a means to power: it is the people's support, she claims, that "lends power to the institutions of a country, and this support is but the continuation of the consent that brought the laws into existence to begin with. Under conditions of representative government the people are supposed to rule those who govern them. All political institutions are manifestations and materializations of power; they petrify and decay as soon as the living power of the people ceases to uphold them" (Arendt 1969: 41).

These nuanced distinctions are important to the degree that today boundaries between them are blurred as power is gradually removed from politics. Power is no longer the essence of the state and violence takes central stage, especially as instrumental rationality intrudes in every sector of public life. Violence today seems to have found Arendt's prerequisites, that is, "guidance and justification through the end it pursues" (Arendt 1969: 41).

Arendt's analysis begs an important question: who is the perpetrator of violence? The state has a legal monopoly on violence and the right to use it to defend its interests. This positions all other forms of violence as 'illegal', since institutionalized violence is the norm/law that legitimizes the perpetration of violence. For example, by naming anyone as 'enemy combatant' the United States is free to torture them, to deny them their rights to habeas corpus, and to incarcerate them without ever being charged with a crime, as with prisoners in Guantanamo Bay. Therefore, we have here two concepts of violence: institutionalized state violence and oppositional violence that is necessarily illegal (Marcuse 1967b; Benjamin 1996). Or, as Walter Benjamin asserts, it is not possible to separate violence from law since all violence is either law-making or law-preserving, and all law, however remote it may seem from its origins and from the forces that maintain it, is latent violence (1996).

Along the lines of what constitutes legality Marcuse accurately notes that "it is meaningless to speak of the legality of resistance: no social system, even the freest, can constitutionally legalize violence directed against itself. Each of these forms has functions that conflict with those of the other. There is violence of suppression and violence of liberation; there is violence for the defense of life and violence of aggression. And both forms have been and will remain historical forces" (Marcuse 1967b). He gives the example of the Bolshevik Revolution where, at the beginning, "there was no cruelty, no brutality, no terror going beyond resistance against those still in power. Where in a revolution this sort of terror changes into acts of cruelty, brutality, and torture, then we are already talking about a perversion of the revolution". Benjamin seems to be on the same page when in his *Critique of Violence* he wonders whether violence in the social and political realms could be justified as pure means in itself, independent of whether it was applied to fair or unfair ends. He posits that an acceptable form of revolutionary violence is the one exercised by the proletariat, not only in the form of strikes, but in the form of the general class war that was to bring down the bourgeoisie and the state (Benjamin 1996).

Through these theoretical accounts we can testify to the many faces of violence through terror and the politics of fear as they take on new dimensions, semioses, significations and functions. Violence as it manifests in the war on terror is deeply anti-political. In this case, we can attest the self-defeating factor in the victory of violence over power, when terror is used to maintain domination. Reiterating Arendt's illuminating analysis regarding the constitutive elements of violence, terror is not the same as violence; "it is rather, the form of government that comes into being when violence, having destroyed all power, does not abdicate but, on the contrary, remains in full control" (Arendt 1969: 55). Another important element attesting to the 'success' of terror is the 'degree of social atomization', which, as I have amply demonstrated in the previous section, has become more and more the very fabric of US society.

Conclusion: Anti-politics of fear and violence as examples *par excellence* of heteronomy

Against a state apparatus bent on ideological manipulations, distortions and the inherent violence in the abuse of power, human beings remain agents of history who "even in the darkest of times [...] have the right to expect some illumination [that] may well come less from theories and concepts than from the uncertain, flickering, and often weak light that some men and women in their lives and their works, will kindle under almost all circumstances and shed over the time span that was given to them on earth" (Arendt quoted in Bauman 2002: 51).

An understanding of power, violence, terror, authoritarianism and the construction of fear in the current US political landscape can provide insights about new forms of control in the neoliberal era of 'affluenza', as well as new forms of resistance and democratic politics. Concepts such as fascism, totalitarianism and authoritarianism that have been historically linked with other situations now take on new meanings. For example, 'totalitarian', is not only a terroristic political coordination of society, but also a nonterroristic economic-technical coordination that operates through the manipulation of needs by vested interests (Marcuse 1967b). Within this framework, fear and violence do nothing less than create a state of heteronomy. Here, heteronomy refers to the condition where it is believed that the laws and institutions of a society have been inevitably put in place by somebody or something that lies outside the civil society ('heteros': different; 'nomos': law). According to Cornelius Castoriadis (1991), societies should be autonomous, that is, self-instituted historically through the dynamics and politics that exist inside them with the actual and active participation of people. However, in the case of heteronomy, society is seen as a creation given by somebody else: the ancestors, gods, the God, the 'laws of history' (in a Marxist sense), or by capital and the markets (as is the case with neoliberalism and capitalism).

In the current state of affairs, by and large, laws are instituted and dictated by fear and implemented through symbolic and material violence. The institution of society is perceived as being given by a metaphysical entity, something that exists outside civil societies, something that is stronger than people. For example, the hegemonic US government plays the insecurity and fear card to implement largely antisocial policies, to eradicate its civilizing and welfare functions. At the same time, heteronomy obliterates questioning and dissent, because its institutions are reduced to common sense that is naturalized in people's minds. Heteronomy functions, therefore, in conditions of closure of meaning and the shrinking political universe. In a capitalist neoconservative authoritarian reality, heteronomy works to establish and perpetuate the myths of naturalness of the markets and restriction of state controls, equal access, equal opportunities, work ethic (if one works hard s/he will succeed), illusion of freedom of choice, patriotism linked to cultural superiority, and so forth. Through manufactured fear, people lose both their individual and collective autonomy. By autonomy, I refer to a person who is truly in a position to consciously change society, not somebody who is paralyzed by fear and subject to constant symbolic and material violence that numbs his/her critical faculty. Autonomous thinking that is about denouncing any and all authority, including the authority of one's own proper thought, cannot develop in conditions of repression and authoritarianism. In the personal safety state, freedom is redefined as freedom to consume or freedom from government. However, according to Castoriadis, I can say that I am free in a society where there are laws, if I have had the effective possibility (and not only on paper) to participate in the discussion, deliberation, formation and implementation of these laws. What that means is that the legislative power should belong effectively to the collective, to the people. However, as Marcuse cynically notes:

> The loss of the economic and political liberties which were the real achievement of the preceding two centuries may seem slight damage in a state capable of making the administered life secure and comfortable. If the individuals are satisfied to the point of happiness with the goods and services handed down to them by the administration, why should they insist on different institutions for a different production of different goods and services? And if the individuals are pre-conditioned so that the satisfying goods also include thoughts, feelings, aspirations, why should they wish to think, feel, and imagine for themselves?
>
> (Marcuse 1964: 50)

As I have attempted to demonstrate in this chapter, both manufactured fear and violence cancel out politics and produce an anti-politics that supports a state of heteronomy, since "neither violence nor power is a natural phenomenon, that is, a manifestation of the life process" but "they belong to the political realm of human affairs whose essential human quality is guaranteed by man's faculty of action, the ability to begin something new" (Arendt 1969: 82).

Given that politics must always find its point of departure in the concrete situation, it is important to identify the ideological and material conditions perpetrated through fear that block individuals from developing pertinent subjective positions. Redefining politics raises questions of ethical responsibility about the degree to which individuals concerned with public affairs are promoting their own special interests. It is this ethical responsibility that moves people to subjective positions since, according to Alain Badiou, "a person is composed into a subject in a given moment, mobilized in order for a truth to proceed" (Badiou 2002: 26). Ultimately, the "difference between radical-emancipatory politics and such outbursts of impotent violence is that an authentic political gesture is active, it imposes, enforces a vision, while outbursts of impotent violence are fundamentally reactive, a reaction to some disturbing intruder" (Žižek 2008: 212–13).

When we raise questions about the space politics inhabits and the ways it neutralizes itself through fear, thereby depoliticizing politics, we are also exposing the various types of agency that this process produces or suppresses. Questioning the anti-politics of fear and the institutions that produce and maintain it is a first step towards reinventing politics, revealing subjective positions that would enable people to assume ethical responsibility and to act upon it. In other words, the ethical responsibility to question must invariably lead to the comprehension of the constellation of factors that lead to violence, including violence as an act against an *a priori* violence as accurately understood by Freire:

> Violence is initiated by those who oppress, who exploit, who fail to recognize others as persons – not by those who are oppressed, exploited, and unrecognized. It is not the unloved who initiate disaffection, but those who cannot love because they love only themselves. It is not the helpless, subject to terror, who initiate terror, but the violent, who with their power create the concrete situation which begets the "rejects of life". It is not the tyrannized who initiate despotism, but the tyrants. It is not the despised who initiate hatred, but those who despise. It is not those whose humanity is denied them who negate humankind, but those who denied that humanity (thus negating their own as well). Force is used not by those who have become weak under the preponderance of the strong, but by the strong who have emasculated them.
>
> (Freire 2000: 55)

References

Arendt, H. (1969) *On Violence*. New York: Harcourt Brace & Company.

Aronowitz, S. (2001) *The Last Good Job in America*. Lanham, MD: Rowman & Littlefield.

Badiou, A. (2002) *Ethics: An essay on the understanding of evil*. London: Verso.

Bauman, Z. (1999) *In Search of Politics*. Stanford, CA: Stanford University Press.

Bauman, Z. (2002) *Society under Siege*. Cambridge UK: Polity.

Bauman, Z. (2006) *Liquid Fear*. Cambridge, UK: Polity.

Benjamin, W. (1996) 'Critique of violence', in Marcus Bullock and Michael W. Jennings (eds), *Selected Writings: Volume 1, 1913–26*. Cambridge, MA and London: Belknap Press, pp. 236–53.

Boggs, C. (2000) *The End of Politics*. New York: Guilford Press.

Brzezinski, Zbigniew. (2007) 'Terrorized by "war on terror": How a three-word mantra has undermined America'. *The Washington Post*, Sunday, March 25. Available at: http://www.washington post.com/wp-dyn/content/article/2007/03/23/AR2007032301613.html (accessed August 26, 2009).

Castoriadis, C. (1991) *Philosophy, Politics, Autonomy*. Edited by David Ames Curtis. New York/ Oxford: Oxford University Press.

Cole, D., Lobel, J. (2007) 'Why we're losing the war on terror', *The Nation*. September 24. Available at: http://www.thenation.com/doc/20070924/cole_lobel (accessed August 15, 2009).

Freire, P. (2000) *Pedagogy of the Oppressed* (2nd edition). New York: Continuum.

Freire, P. (2004) *Pedagogy of Indignation*. Boulder, CO: Paradigm Publishers.

Giroux, H. (2008) *Against the Terror of Neoliberalism: Politics beyond the age of greed*. Boulder, CO: Paradigm Publishers.

Glassner, B. (2000) *The Culture of Fear: Why Americans are afraid of the wrong things*. New York: Perseus.

Marcuse, H. (1964) *One Dimensional Man*. Boston: Beacon Press.

Marcuse, H. (1967a) *The Problem of Violence: Questions and answers*. Translated from *Das Ende der Utopie* (Berlin: Verlag Peter von Maikowski, 1967). Available at: http://www.marxists.org/reference/archive/marcuse/works/1967/questions-answers.htm (accessed August 15, 2009).

Marcuse, H. (1967b) *The Problem of Violence and the Radical Opposition*. Translated from *Das Ende der Utopie* (Berlin: Verlag Peter von Maikowski, 1967). Available at: http://www.marxists.org/reference/archive/marcuse/works/1967/violence.htm (accessed August 15, 2009).

Palin, S. on YouTube *Sarah Palin: War in Iraq is God's Plan*. Available at http://www.youtube.com/watch?v=9H-btXPfhGs (accessed 15 August, 2009).

Stavrianos L. S. (1976) *The Promise of the Coming Dark Age*. San Francisco: W. H. Freeman.

Žižek, S. (2008) *Violence*. New York: Picador.

Reflections on Gounari's chapter

Gounari argues that the United States is in the midst of a self-constructed political and ideological 'Dark Age' where "God, nature, the markets, fear of evil and repressive apparatuses" constitute the guiding forces for deciding on the law. The very act of questioning has almost become an unpatriotic act. Fear for oneself, for one's family, for one's country, and fear of others (within or without the nation's boundaries) is palpable. At present, it emanates not from the threat per se, but rather it precedes the threat and, by doing so, it has elided into "aggression [that is] legitimized protection", thereby fostering particular kinds of activities, that operate both on the international front, such as pre-emptive wars, and on the home front, such as the curtailing of civil liberties. In other words, political forces are engaged in manufacturing fear and danger with the result that "the welfare state makes way for the warfare state" and all the conditions of an 'anti-politics' are established. If politics is, in a sense, "the ongoing critique of reality" and if democracy is "the regime of explicit and lucid self-institution as far as is possible, of the social institutions that depend on explicit collective activity", the rhetoric of exclusion becomes not merely a reality, but *the* reality.

What can be done? Gounari sees the reinvention of politics as the first step. This entails questioning the anti-politics of fear and the institutions and policies accompanying it. As Arendt says, human beings have the ability to start something new: taking ethical responsibility and acting upon it would be a new start towards reclaiming politics.

Research questions

Research cannot duck the 'big issues' that arise when people are organized by those who have the power to manipulate and control through violence and the fear of violence. Nor can it duck the political thinking and practice that is required if change is to take place. Critical questions include:

- What forms of political philosophy are able to critique, resist and generate alternatives to the philosophies and institutions that are involved in violence and the manufacture of fear as a basis for social control?
- What are the ideological and material conditions brought about and sustained by fear that prevents the development of subjects and subject positions where action is possible?
- What cultural, social and organizational resources, practices and procedures are required to create the social forms that combat oppression and exploitation?
- What concrete situations in everyday life can provide the starting points for political renewal?
- What, in different circumstances, places and times, mobilizes action?

Chapter 12

Militarizing higher education

Resisting the pedagogy of violence

Henry Giroux

As part of his farewell address on 17 January 1961, President Dwight D. Eisenhower recognized that in the aftermath of World War II and at the dawn of the Cold War, the United States faced a dire menace abroad in the form of the Soviet Union and a less visible but equally dangerous threat within its own borders, which he memorably referred to as "the military-industrial complex".[1] Eisenhower viewed the military-industrial complex as an outgrowth of a growing and sinister relationship among government agencies, the military and the defence industries, and believed that it made a mockery out of democratic values while undermining the foundation of democratic institutions and civic society.[2]

Later in the decade, Senator William Fulbright took seriously Eisenhower's distrust of the military-industrial complex and extended its political and theoretical reach. He did so by coupling the emerging power of an overly strong military-industrial complex with the province of higher education, and its long-standing commitments to academic freedom, civic engagement and pure research guided by intellectual curiosity or social needs rather than commercial or military interests. Recognizing that major universities had become increasingly dependent on Pentagon contracts, grants and funds for their research laboratories, Fulbright retrieved Eisenhower's cast-off phrase, the "military-industrial-academic complex", to warn against the creeping influence of the federal government and a for-profit arms industry over America's major research universities.[3] Fulbright's comments were blunt and to the point: "In lending itself too much to the purposes of government, a university fails its higher purpose".[4]

Unfortunately, Eisenhower and Fulbright's predictions about the fundamentally anti-democratic nature of the military-industrial-complex and its efforts to annex the university went unheeded as the Cold War unfolded and the university's relationship with larger society underwent fundamental changes. As Rebecca S. Lowen points out in her brilliant study of Stanford as an exemplar of the new Cold War university, "The postwar university was a wholly new institution, one that was uniquely responsive to the society of which it was now very much a part".[5] During the 1960s, especially with the massive student resistance directed against the Vietnam War, the possibility of a powerful military state undermining the reality and promise of higher education as a democratic public sphere generated various protests on college campuses that aimed at keeping the military and intelligence agencies as far away from university campuses as possible.[6] Distrust of the military and government intelligence agencies reached a high point in 1975 when Senator Frank Church headed a Senate committee that investigated the Watergate break-in and uncovered numerous CIA abuses, including its secret funding of student organizations, the agency's attempts to overthrow the democratically elected government of Chile, and clandestine plots to assassinate Fidel Castro.[7] Once the Vietnam War ended, the dissenters went home and a fog of historical and social amnesia descended over the country, paving the way for an eventual return of the repressed, as the military-industrial-academic complex gained greater momentum from the late 1980s to the present – a momentum whose power, I suggest, now grows largely unchecked.[8]

While there has been an increasing concern among academics and progressives over the growing corporatization of the university, the transformation of academia into what John Armitage calls the "hypermodern militarized knowledge factory"[9] has been largely ignored as a subject of contemporary concern and critical debate.[10] Such silence has nothing to do with a lack of visibility or the covert attempts to inject a military and security presence into American higher education. Not only is the militarization of higher education made obvious by the presence of over 150 military-educational institutions in the United States designed to "train a youthful corps of tomorrow's military officers"[11] in the strategies, values, skills and knowledge of the warfare state, but also, as the American Association of Universities points out, in the existence of hundreds of colleges and universities that conduct Pentagon-funded research, provide classes to military personnel, and design programs specifically for future employment with various departments and agencies associated with the warfare state.[12]

Rather than being the object of massive individual and collective resistance, the militarization of higher education appears to be endorsed by liberals and conservatives alike. The National Research Council of the National Academies published a report called *Frameworks for Higher Education in Homeland Security*, which argued that the commitment to learning about homeland security is an essential part of the preparation for work and life in the twenty-first century, thus offering academics a thinly veiled legitimation for building into undergraduate and graduate curricula intellectual frameworks that mirror the interests and values of the warfare state. Similarly, in a report titled *National Defense Education and Innovation Initiative*, the Association of American Universities argued that winning the war on terrorism and expanding global markets were mutually informing goals, the success of which fell squarely on the performance of universities. This group argued, with a rather cheerful certainty, that every student should be trained to become a soldier in the war on terror and in the battle over global markets, and that the universities should do everything they can "to fill security-related positions in the defense industry, the military, the national laboratories, the Department of Defense and Homeland Security, the intelligence agencies, and other federal agencies".[13]

It gets worse. Faculties now flock to the Department of Defense, the Pentagon, and various intelligence agencies either to procure government jobs or to apply for grants to support individual research in the service of the national security state. As corporate money for research opportunities dwindles, the Pentagon fills the void with billions of dollars in available grants, stipends, scholarships, and other valuable financial rewards, for which college and university administrators actively and openly compete. Major universities have appointed former CIA officials as either faculty members, consultants or presidents. For instance, Michael Crow, a former agent, is now president of Arizona State University and Robert Gates, the former Director of the CIA, was the president of Texas A&M, until named in 2006 as the Secretary of Defense under the George W. Bush administration. Such collaboration seems to be in full swing at a number of universities. For example, Pennsylvania State University, Carnegie Mellon, the University of Pennsylvania, Johns Hopkins and a host of other universities have surprisingly expanded the reach and influence of the national security state by entering into formal agreements with the FBI in order to "create a link between leading research university and government agencies".[14] Graham Spanier, the president of Penn State, argues in a statement pregnant with irony, that the establishment of the National Security Higher Education Advisory Board, which he heads, "sends a positive message that leaders in higher education are willing to assist our nation during these challenging times".[15] FBI Director Robert S. Mueller III is more precise about what is expected from this partnership. He writes: "As we do our work, we wish to be sensitive to university concerns about international students, visas, technology export policy, and the special culture of colleges and universities. We also want to foster exchanges between academia and the FBI in order to develop curricula which will aid in attracting the best and brightest students to careers in the law enforcement and intelligence communities".[16] Behind such stated concerns, however, lies the harsh reality of a national security state that harasses foreign students, limits the ability of US scholars to work with colleagues in 'enemy' countries like Cuba and Iran, and denies visas to international graduate students and intellectuals getting work in the United States, particularly those individuals who are critical of US policies.

As militarization and the reality of extreme violence become central to both political and everyday life, it becomes all the more important for higher education to be defended as a vital public sphere crucial for both the education of critical citizens and the defence of democratic values and institutions. Given the current threat posed by the national security state to higher education's democratically informed civic mission, I want to engage the question of what the role of higher education might be when "the government has a free hand to do whatever it wants in the name of national security".[17] More specifically, I want to offer an alternative analysis of the fate of democracy and the role of higher education, one that refuses to simply serve the expressed needs of milit-arization, neoliberalism, and the national security state, all of which appear to be pushing the United States towards a new form of authoritarianism.[18] In what follows, I first want to situate the development of the university as a "hypermodern militarized knowledge factory" within the broader context of what I will call *the biopolitics of militarization* and its increased influence and power within American society after the tragic events of 11 September 2001. Second, I will highlight and critically engage the specific ways in which this militarization is shaping various aspects of university life, focusing primarily on the growth of militarized knowledge and research as well as the growing influence of the CIA on college campuses. Finally, I will offer some sugges-tions both for resisting the rising tide of militarization and for reclaiming the university as a democratic public sphere.

Biopolitics and the reworking of power and disposability

Within the last few decades, matters of state sovereignty in the new world order have been retheorized so as to provide a range of relevant insights about the relationship between power and politics, the political nature of social and cultural life, and the merging of life and politics as a new form of 'biopolitics'.[19] Biopolitical mediation of life and death takes on a heightened significance as the state not only consolidates its power over all spheres of life but also increas-ingly exercises its sovereignty "in the power and capacity to dictate who may live and who may die".[20]

The concept of biopolitics, while revealing different tensions for its major theorists, registers a number of distinctive characteristics that mark contem-porary politics in the United States. As both Giorgio Agamben and Michel Foucault argue, politics is no longer exclusively defined through a notion of sovereignty and power in which the spheres of the economic, social and political are viewed as separate and largely unrelated. That is, the traditional separation between the realm of politics and the complex set of relations that constitute what it means to be a living human being is no longer viable.[21] Politics must now be defined in more ample terms – as contributing to the "production of social relationships in all aspects of life".[22] Consequently, politics extends far beyond merely "legislating norms and preserving order in public affairs";[23] It is inextricably linked to matters of life and death, largely mediated through the prism of disposability, fear and "security as the sole task and source of [state] legitimacy".[24] State violence and totalitarian power, which historically have been deployed against marginalized populations – in the United States, prin-cipally black Americans – are now the rule for the entire population, as life is more ruthlessly regulated and placed in the hands of military and state power.

Like the consumer goods that flood American society, immigrant workers, refugees, the unemployed, the homeless, the poor and the disabled are increasingly viewed as utterly expendable, relegated to a frontier zone of invisibility created by a combination of economic inequality, racism, the collapse of social safety nets, and the brutality of a militarized society, all of which, according to Zygmunt Bauman, "designates and constitutes a production line of human waste or wasted humans".[25]

Examples of the exercise and abuse of sovereign power have been made visible at times, as when it was publicly disclosed that the American government had made torture integral to its military and clandestine operations at Abu Ghraib in Iraq, Guantanamo Bay in Cuba, Bagram Air Base in Afghanistan and numerous other detention centres around the world.[26] As Neil Smith points out, "these prisons are a global embarrassment for the United States",[27] particularly when a highly respected organization such as Amnesty International labels Guantanamo "the gulag of our times".[28] Further examples are shamelessly visible in the sickening massacre which took place in Haditha in Iraq;[29] and in a politics of 'disappearing' (reminiscent of the Latin American dictatorships of the 1970s) in which human beings are subjected to the outsourcing of torture by the United States government under a policy known as 'extraordinary rendition'. This policy, signed by President George W. Bush, authorizes the CIA not only to set up detention facilities outside of the United States in which to detain, interrogate and torture alleged terrorist suspects and sympathizers without any benefit of a court of law but also to abduct and transport such suspected terrorists to other countries such as Syria and Egypt that engage in human rights abuses, including torture.[30] Known innocent individuals who have been subjected to this barbaric policy include: Maher Arar, a Syrian-born Canadian citizen detained at JFK Airport in September 2002 and taken to Jordan and Syria where he was tortured;[31] and Khaled el-Masri, a Kuwait-born citizen with German nationality, who was abducted while vacationing in Macedonia and transported to an American-run prison where he was beaten and kept in solitary confinement for five months.[32] Both men were eventually released. Arar not only was completely cleared of any terrorist connections by the Canadian government but was eventually given a formal government apology and a compensation package worth millions.

A biopolitics of disposability and exclusion is also evident in the existence of secret CIA prisons known as "black sites"[33] and the abrogation of basic civil rights enacted by the passage of the Military Commissions Act of 2006, which allows people named as 'enemy combatants' to be imprisoned and charged with crimes without the benefit of a lawyer or the right of *habeas corpus*. Disposability works in a dual sense in this policy in that it not only legalizes acts of torture and abuse on those who are 'disappeared' from traditional legal protections, but it also disposes of the crime by granting immunity to is perpetrators.[34] The biopolitics of disposability was also on full display in the aftermath of Hurricane Katrina, which laid bare the racial and class fault lines that mark an increasingly damaged and withering democracy. Clearly, the Bush administration's response to the tragedy of Hurricane Katrina revealed a biopolitical mindset that disregards populations rendered 'at risk' by global neoliberal economies, embracing instead an emergent security state founded on fear, class privilege and updated notions of racial purity.[35]

The biopolitics of militarization in a post-9/11 world

As biopolitics is reduced to the imperatives of homeland security and war becomes the major structuring force of society – a source of pride rather than alarm – the discourse and values of militarization that spread throughout a society has shifted, as Hardt and Negri argue, from a "welfare state to [a] warfare state".[36] What is new about militarization in a post-9/11 world is that it has become normalized, serving as a powerful educational force that shapes our lives, memories, and daily experiences, while erasing everything we thought we knew about history, justice, solidarity and the meaning of democracy.[37]

An indication of how intensively the United States privileges the military over non-military sectors of society – a central dimension of the process of militarization – can be found in comparing federal expenditures on the military and education before and after 9/11. For example, in 2000, the US allocated approximately $24 billion to K-12 education and $280 billion to the Department of Defense; but in 2003, federal expenditures on all levels of schooling totalled $102.8 billion while $379.3 billion was designated for the military.[38] Such immense levels of defence spending by the federal government have grave implications for expanding a US war machine. The projection of US military force and power in the world can be seen in the fact that the US owns or rents 737 bases "in about 130 countries – over and above the 6,000 bases" at home.[39] Not only does the United States alone spend "approximately as much as the rest of the world combined on its military establishment"[40] – producing massive amounts of death-dealing weapons – it is also the world's biggest arms dealer, with sales in 2006 amounting to "about $20.9 billion, nearly double the $10.6 billion the previous year".[41]

Chalmers Johnson argues that US imperial ambitions are driven by what he calls "military Keynesianism, in which the domestic economy requires sustained military ambition in order to avoid recession or collapse".[42] One consequence of 'military Keynesianism' is massive waste, incompetence, and an egregious lack of oversight. For instance, in 2001 the Pentagon's own Inspector General admitted that the department could not account for $2.3 trillion in spending. At the same time, "a congressional investigation reported that inventory management in the army was so weak it has lost track of 56 airplanes, 32 tanks, and 36 missile launchers".[43] Besides spending that cannot be explained, the Pentagon has given priority to expensive weapons projects at the expense of providing "appropriate body armor for the troops, and plates for the Hummers in Baghdad".[44] In some cases, soldiers in Iraq and Afghanistan have purchased additional body armour with their personal funds. According to journalist George Monbiot, the US federal government "is now spending as much on war as it is on education, public health, housing, employment, pensions, food aid and welfare put together".[45] The result is a social state starved through tax cuts for the very rich, welfare schemes for major corporations, and the allocating of billions of dollars to fund a costly war in Iraq and an imperial foreign policy.

As democratic politics is neutralized and the state makes security its most cherished goal, state policy and terrorism begin to mimic each other, and in the end begin to "form a singly deadly system, in which they justify and legitimate each others actions".[46] Under such circumstances, the formation of a critical citizenry and the call for a genuine participatory democracy become unpatriotic and thus subject to charges of treason or dismissed as unchristian in an ideologically charged American political culture that defines the relationship of the United States to the rest of the world largely around a Manichean division between good and evil.[47] What happens when militarism provides the most legitimate framing mechanism for how we relate to ourselves, each other and the rest of the world? One consequence is the development of what C. Wright Mills once called "a military definition of reality",[48] which is now largely accepted as common sense by most people in American society. As Andrew J. Bacevich argues, too few have pondered what the consequences might be for American democracy when it accepts the possibility of a war on terrorism that has no foreseeable end, no geographical borders, and an ill-defined enemy. Similarly, too few people seem willing to ponder the question: what happens to civic virtue when armed force becomes the most important expression of state power, and military establishments become the most trusted and venerated institutions in American society?

The militarized knowledge factory: Research, credentials and the CIA

As in other spheres of American civic life, the institution of higher education is being militarized through a variety of government agencies, appeals and practices. War industries not only provide large grants to universities, but also offer job opportunities to their graduates while simultaneously exercising a subtle, though influential, pressure in shaping the priorities of the programs and departments crucial to their corporate interests. Companies that make huge profits on militarization and war, such as General Electric, Northrop Grumman and Halliburton, establish through their grants crucial ties with universities while promoting a philanthropic self-image to the larger society.[49] John Armitage has argued that as the university becomes militarized it becomes "a factory that is engaged in the militarization of knowledge, namely, in the militarization of the facts, information and abilities obtained through the experience of education".[50] The priority given to such knowledge is largely the result of the vast sums of research money now given to shape the curricula, programs and departments in universities across the country. In 2003, for example, Penn State received $149 million in research and development awards while the Universities of California, Carnegie Mellon, and Texas received $29.8 million, $59.8 million, and $86.6 million respectively, and they are not even the top beneficiaries of such funds.[51] Along with the money that comes with such defence-oriented funding is a particular set of assumptions about the importance of ideas, knowledge and information and their relevance to military technologies, objectives and purposes.

Of course, this is about more than how knowledge is obtained, shaped and used by different elements of the military-industrial complex; it is also about the kind of pressure that can be brought to bear by the power of the Department of Defense and the war industries on colleges and universities to orient themselves towards a society in which non-militarized knowledge and values play a minor role, thus removing from higher education its fundamental purpose in educating students to be ethical citizens, learn how to take risks, connect knowledge to power in the interest of social responsibility and justice, and defend vital democratic ideals, values and institutions. Fuelled by a desire for more students, more tuition money and a larger share of the market for online and off-campus programs, many universities and colleges are altering their curricula and delivery services to attract part of the lucrative education market for military personnel. The rush to cash in on such changes has been dramatic, particularly for any online, for-profit educational institution, such as the University of Phoenix, which has high visibility on the Internet. The incursion of the military presence in higher education furthers and deepens the ongoing privatization of education and knowledge itself. Most of the players in this market are for-profit institutions that are problematic not only for the quality of education they offer but also for their aggressive support of education less as a public good than as a private initiative, defined in this case through its service to the military in return for a considerable profit. And as this sector of higher education grows, it will not only become more privatized but also more instrumentalized, largely defined as a credentializing factory to serve the needs of the military, thus falling into the trap of confusing training with a broad-based education.

Given the present state of affairs, those in the academy must ask themselves uncomfortable questions: What role do intellectuals play in the conditions that allow theory and knowledge to be appropriated by military interests and what can they do politically to prevent theory, knowledge and information from being militarized in the first place? How does such opposition connect to their work and extend their sense of social and political responsibility to the world outside of the academy?

The CIA and higher education

One of the more disturbing indications of academe's willingness to accommodate the growing presence and legitimating ideologies of the national security state can be found in the increasing presence of the CIA and other spy agencies on American campuses. Daniel Golden, writing for the *Wall Street Journal* in 2002, noted that in the aftermath of 9/11 an increasing number of faculties and universities – capitalizing on both a new-found sense of patriotism and less politicized sense of self-interest – were turning to the 16 intelligence agencies and offering them their services and new recruitment opportunities.[52] Moreover, as universities recognize that the intelligence agencies have deep pockets for funding opportunities, the CIA has benefited from this new receptivity and is reciprocating by "turning more to universities ... to develop high-tech gadgets that track down terrorists and dictators".[53] In addition, it is developing more federal scholarship programs, grants and other initiatives in order to attract students for career opportunities and to involve faculty in various roles that address "security and intelligence goals".[54] The CIA's cosy relationship with academics has also been reinforced by the agency's increased presence at annual meetings held by academic groups such as the International Studies Association and the American Anthropological Association.

What seems to be forgotten in the new-found collaboration between the CIA and the academy is the history of the CIA secret funding of the activities of the National Student Association in the 1960s, its attempt to "destroy the career of University of California President Clark Kerr",[55] its harassment of John Lennon, and numerous students, faculty, and others critical of American domestic and foreign policy during the 1960s and 1970s, as well as its unsavoury efforts to interfere in and overthrow foreign governments that were at odds with American policies – for instance, Allende's elected socialist government in Chile and the August 1953 coup against Iranian Premier Mohammad Mossadeq.[56]

One of the most controversial post-9/11 programs sponsored by the CIA, based on the urging of Professor Moos, is the Pat Roberts Intelligence Scholars Program (PRISP). The program is named after Senator Pat Roberts,[57] who was the head of the Senate Select Committee on Intelligence under the Bush administration until the takeover of the Senate by the Democrats in 2006. There is a certain irony in recalling that Senator Roberts was well-known for siding with the Bush administration on warrantless domestic spying programs, blocking a vote to investigate the program, consistently stonewalling an investigation into Bush's use of pre-war intelligence to justify the war in Iraq, defending Guantanamo Bay Prison, and refusing to investigate the CIA's complicity in the abuse and torture of detainees. The *Los Angeles Times* claimed that "In a world without doublespeak, the panel, chaired by GOP Sen. Pat Roberts of Kansas, would be known by a more appropriate name – the Senate Cover-up Committee".[58]

The Roberts Program began as a two-year pilot program scheduled to run until the end of 2006. It was designed to train 150 analysts in anthropology, each of whom would receive a $25,000 stipend per year, with a maximum of $50,000 over the two-year period. The program also provided tuition support, loan paybacks and bonuses for immediate hiring of those candidates considered to have critical skills. In return, each participant in the program agreed to work for an intelligence agency for one-and-a-half times the period covered by the scholarship support. In this case, two years of support would demand that an analyst work for a government intelligence agency for three years. Students who receive such funding cannot reveal their funding source, are not obligated to inform their professors or fellow students that they are being funded by and will work for an intelligence agency, and are required to attend military intelligence camps.[59]

It gets worse. Government agencies have on occasion used academic scholarship not to promote a spirit of understanding complex cultural differences, critical reflection and self-critique, but to expand their own methods of torture and abuse. One such example recently surfaced at the 2006 American Anthropological Association's annual meeting. Scholars attending the meeting were appalled to discover that the work of some of their colleagues in the field of cultural anthropology had been used by the US Armed Services to develop certain interrogation tactics at Abu Ghraib prison as well as at other locations. Professor Roberto J. Gonzales, an anthropologist who opposes the use of social science knowledge to further the 'science of suffering' has pointed to the emergence of what he calls the "anthropology of insurgency".[60] Promoting this new area of study are the numerous intelligence agencies such as the CIA, the Defense Department, and new government offices such as the Cultural Operations Research Human Terrain that now actively recruit social scientists, including anthropologists, or simply expropriate their work in the interests of purely military functions.[61] This type of knowledge appropriation is particularly indicative of the increasing militarization of the field of anthropology and the emergence of anthropological counterinsurgents such as Dr David Kilcullen, an Australian anthropologist and lieutenant colonel, who unabashedly works (on loan) with the US State Department's counterterrorism office and refers, with no apologies, to counterinsurgency as "armed social work".[62]

Conclusion

The militarization of American society suggests more than a crisis in politics. It is also representative of a fundamental crisis in democracy and the critical educational foundation upon which it rests. Such a challenge requires taking seriously how knowledge production – our chief export – is still militarized in an 'information age'; which democratic institutions are under attack as a result; and what steps can be taken to resist the drift towards "perpetual war for perpetual peace".[63] As militarization spreads throughout the various pedagogical sites and circuits of power that animate the educational force of the culture, whether newspapers, talk radio, television, the Internet, public schools or higher education, it becomes all the more crucial to prevent war, violence and hyper-masculine aggression from becoming so embedded in what and how we learn, that the ideology and practices of militarization become a matter of common sense, and so invisible, unquestionable and much more dangerous.

Higher education should play a particularly important role in opposing its own transformation into a "militarized knowledge factory" as well as the growing impact of militarization in the larger society. One crucial step in this process is to reclaim higher education as a democratic public sphere, one that both provides the conditions for students to become critical agents who connect learning to expanding and deepening the conditions for the struggle for genuine democratization. As Jorge Mariscal points out, "Militarization and open democratic societies ... do not make a good match, the former producing pathologies at both the individual and collective levels. The face of militarization on the ground is perhaps most disturbing insofar as it reveals a disconnected hardening of individuals to human suffering".[64] In part, this means forging the tools to fight for the demilitarization of knowledge on college campuses – to resist complicity with the production of knowledge, information and technologies in classrooms and research labs that contribute to militarized goals and purposes.

There is also the crucial need for faculties, students, administrators and concerned citizens to develop alliances, and for long-term organizations to resist the growing ties among government agencies, corporations and higher-education facilities that engage in reproducing militarized knowledge, which might require severing all relationships between the university and intelligence agencies and war industries. It also means keeping military recruiters out of public and higher education. One such example can be found in People Against Militarization (PAMO) of the Ontario Institute for Studies in Education (OISE), which brought faculty, students and community activists together to protest a partnership between OISE and the Atlantis Systems Corp., a company that provides knowledge, training and simulation equipment for the militaries of a number of countries, including the United States and Saudi Arabia. PAMO provides a valuable model, proving that such protests can be used to make visible the ongoing militarization of higher education, while also providing strategies indicating how faculty, students and others can organize to oppose it.[65]

As the forces of militarization increasingly monopolize the dominant media, students, activists and educators must imagine ways to expand the limits of education in ways that enable the university to shape coming generations of cultural producers capable of not only negotiating the old media forms, such as broadcasting and reporting, but also generating new electronic media, which have come to play a crucial role in bypassing those forms of media concentrated in the hands of corporate and military interests. Examples extend from the incredible work of the Media Education Foundation, which produces a range of documentaries, many of which address topics such as war games and videos for youth and other topics related to the militarization of the culture[66] to the Global Network Against Weapons and Nuclear Power in Space, which consists of songwriters and singers who produce music protesting the militarization of space.[67] The central issue here is how the university and the liberal arts in particular can be re-imagined in the interests of producing critical discourses, practices, knowledges and counter-publics committed to enabling students to expand their capacities and skills as engaged citizens committed to the realization of a genuine, global democracy.

In the fight against the biopolitics of militarization, educators need a language of critique, but they also need a language that embraces a sense of hope and collective struggle. This means elaborating the meaning of politics through a language of critique *and* possibility, on the one hand, and a concerted effort to expand the space of politics by reclaiming "the public character of spaces, relations and institutions regarded as private," on the other.[68]

While it has become fashionable in the academy to talk about biopolitics through the language of 'bare life,' 'state of exception,' and the 'state of emergency,' this discourse often represents a very limited conception of agency, politics and sovereignty – one that misrepresents both the complexity of power and the multi-faceted nature of resistance. We need a more capacious understanding of biopolitics, one in which power is not reduced exclusively to domination and the citizen can achieve more than the limited role of consumer or a soldier. We live at a time when matters of life and death are central to political sovereignty. While registering the shift in power towards the large-scale production of death, disposability and exclusion, a new biopolitics must also point to notions of agency, power and responsibility that operate in the service of life, democratic struggles, and the expansion of human rights. Such struggles must be made visible, and can be found among AIDS workers in Africa, organized labour in Latin America, and Palestinians acting as human shields against Israeli tanks in the West Bank and Gaza. We can also see a biopolitics of resistance and hope at work in a long tradition of antimilitarist struggles in the United States, which have taken place not only in the wider public sphere but also in the military itself.[69] Efforts to end violence, speak out against war, and criticize acts of torture and abuse extend from the founding of the nation to the anti-war movements of the 1960s and the new millennium, including the emergence of groups fighting against global sweatshops, the arms race, global racism, wage slavery, child poverty, the rise of an imperial presidency, and the ongoing wars in Iraq, Afghanistan and the Middle East.

In addressing the militarization of the academy and everyday life, it is also crucial for educators to recognize that power works in myriad ways in the interest of both domination and struggle. In contemporary times, this suggests that educators should pay more attention to how different modes of domination inform each other so that strategies for resistance can be layered, complex, and yet held together by more generalized notions of hope and freedom. For example, any redemptive biopolitics of demilitarization would have to be understood in relation to an equally powerful biopolitics of capital, raising fundamental questions about how capital in its neoliberal incarnation and militarization in its various forms connect and inform each other on the level of the local, national and global. We might, for instance, raise the question of how neoliberalism with its fragmenting of democratic solidarities, privatized notions of agency, and eviscerated conception of politics paves the way for the production of militarized subjects, and the normalization of military mentalities and moralities, and how these practices affect generations of young people.

Finally, if higher education is to come to grips with the multilayered pathologies produced by militarization, it will have to rethink not merely the space of the university as a democratic public sphere, but also the global space in which intellectuals, academics, students, artists, labour unions and other social movements can form transnational alliances both to address the ongoing effects of militarization on the world – which include war, pollution, massive poverty, the arms trade, growth of privatized armies, civil conflict and child slavery – and to develop global organizations that can be mobilized in the effort to resist a culture of war with a culture of peace, whose elemental principles are grounded in the relations of economic, political, cultural and social democracy. As Andrew Bacevich has argued, we can no longer afford to live in a world in which soldiers are elevated to the status of national icons, military violence is mystified in a shroud of aesthetic respectability, force becomes the privileged mechanism for mediating conflicts, and military spending exceeds spending for schools, health and other social provisions combined.[70] Since militarization operates simultaneously on symbolic, material and institutional levels, strategies must be developed and waged that address all of the terrains on which it operates. Militarization poses a serious threat to higher education, but more importantly it poses a dangerous threat to the promise of democracy at home and abroad, and to the very meaning of democratic politics and the sustainability of human life. Surely it is time for educators to take a stand and oppose the death-dealing ideology of militarization and its distorting effects on higher education and everything else it touches outside of the university.

Reflections on Giroux's chapter

Giroux argues that within state borders, behind doors closed to public view, powerful alliances are formed between corporate bodies with like-minded goals. One such alliance, namely, between higher education institutions and what Eisenhower termed "the military-industrial complex", forms the focus for this chapter. In particular, he argues, there is an increasing anti-democratic influence by the military on universities. The increasing trend of all American universities, even the major ones, towards reliance upon "Pentagon contracts, grants and funds for research laboratories" is counter to the ideology of a university's commitment to academic freedom, civic engagement and "pure" research driven by intellectual curiosity or social needs. Whilst there is dissent about the increasing "corporatization" of universities, their development into a "hypermodern militarized knowledge factory", he argues, largely goes unnoticed, and appears not to be a political issue, although the infiltration is quite visible. It has now been deemed essential to the curriculum for undergraduates and postgraduates to learn about "homeland security" by The National Research Council of the National Academies. Not only are universities seeking contracts, grants and funds from the Pentagon, but former CIA agents are being appointed to senior faculty positions. With the transformation of the welfare state into a warfare state, a politics of disposability and exclusion has emerged. In this climate where a state makes security its main objective and neutralizes democratic politics, "state policy and terrorism begin to mimic each other" coming to see the world polarized in "a Manichean division between good and evil".

This heralds both "a crisis in politics" and "a fundamental crisis in democracy". Higher education needs to both resist being wittingly or unwittingly transformed into a "militarized knowledge factory" as well as organize opposition to its insidious infiltration. Furthermore, it needs to do so recognizing that "militarization operates simultaneously on symbolic, material, and institutional levels", and thus "strategies must be developed and waged that address all of the terrains on which it is operational".

Research questions

Research questions need to be asked that explore the extent and nature of a contemporary crisis of democracy. For example:

- What strategies need to be developed in order to create the conditions for the emergence of spaces for public debate, decision making and action in all the institutions, organisations and communities of everyday life?
- How may researchers contribute to the renewal, in particular, of universities as a democratic public sphere?
- How may research contribute to the emergence of a culture of peace as the basis for democracies?
- How may universities be re-configured as 'the global space in which intellectuals, academics, students, artists, labour unions, and other social movements can form transnational alliances' as a counter to the forces of anti-democracy?
- What institutions, as well as universities, are vital in the production of the public as a democratic sphere for debating, deciding, acting?

Methodological discussion section *iv*

The language of critical resistance, emancipatory practices, and the co-option of research by Power

Jill Schostak and John F. Schostak

In a sense, this final section returns to the opening themes covered in the introduction and in Chapter 1 in order to explore the extent to which research, researchers and the institutions that employ them have been co-opted by Power. Gounari writes of a retreat from the political, that is, the public space constructed by the co-principles of liberty and equality that are essential to democratic decision making and action by the people for the people. Such a theme is reminiscent of Fromm's (1942) *The Fear of Freedom* and more recently of Bernstein's (2005) discussion of the corruption of politics and Rancière's (2005) analysis of the contemporary hatred of democracy. In a language of critical resistance, Gounari paints a vivid picture of the 'anti-politics' of fear in America, and the first step in combating this requires a politics that is "an ongoing critique of reality" (Bauman 2002: 56) and is to be understood as "a project in the making, unfinished and open" (see p. 184). It is this picture that portrays how certain forms of power have been accrued by the state and how that power is put to use. Indeed, it has to be said that first and foremost of these powers is that the state is the sole legitimate user of violence whether through the police internally, or the military externally. Such a research-based picture provides a counter- or anti-picture to the regimenting of the public mind (Bernays 1928) through the pictures created by public relations in the manufacture of consent (Lippmann 1922).

What constitutes the public, then, is a contested space that Power seeks to dominate by reducing access to the public spaces of decision making and action. The neoliberal move has been to reduce government and the public sector provision of welfare while expanding the private sector control of space through the agency of the market where space is appropriated as private property dominated by corporations, sovereign wealth funds, the top 1 per cent of individuals who own 40 per cent and the richest 10 per cent who own 80 per cent of the world's wealth (WIDER 2006). In this struggle between private and public the role of property is pivotal. By designating corporations as legal – albeit fictional – persons, they can own property in their own right. By limiting the liability of shareholders, corporations can act as shields through which private decisions are made and risks are taken in the name of the corporation. In the name of the corporation and in the name of private individuals, space is enclosed and separated off from public access and control. By reducing the space within which democratic decisions are made and increasing the space for private ownership, democratic control over production and the allocation of resources is excluded. Therefore, space, as Pearce discusses in Chapter 9, becomes a framework for the production of violence through the strategies described by Gounari as an anti-politics of fear.

The role of research then is to explore the complexities and machinations of anti-politics, to avoid co-option by the state and to formulate strategies for resistance. Gounari argues that, quite simply, the public have been conditioned to accept political policies without question and have been persuaded that the very idea of questioning has come to be considered as bordering on an unpatriotic act. Fear is the tool and the weapon by which the population is held in check, as the 'elite few' exercises political power, wherever and whenever they choose. This fear that has been created has not arisen as a response to some specific threat; rather it precedes such a threat, anticipates it. It is a fear that is everywhere and nowhere, typified by the 'war on terror'. Rather than a public space defined as the space for democratic decision making and action, as argued in previous chapters, the public is reduced to being nothing but consumers in a marketplace, an audience for the entertainment and news media, taxpayers and citizens whose opinions are to be influenced and their votes competed for by party elites in periodic elections. More specifically, the public is a target.

This generalized fear creates uncertainty that, it can be argued, is intended to keep the people docile, their minds closed to any form of critical thinking so they remain willingly locked in their private domains, behind closed doors, isolated and therefore unlikely to engage in collective action. This public, its mindset both constructed by fear and constrained by fear, accepts, without questioning, pre-emptive strikes, pre-emptive wars and curtailed civil liberties in the name of 'homeland security'. Having manufactured this fear, there is an imperative to maintain it and political energies – for example, daily news feeds for the media – are devoted to doing precisely that. On the Homeland Security website[1] there is a gauge for assessing the vulnerability of the nation and people are encouraged to use it in order to keep themselves up to date with the level of threat to themselves and their country on a daily basis. The threat level is usually calibrated such that it translates into something akin to a significant likelihood of terrorist attacks. A 'culture of fear' enables a 'politics of fear'. Faced with such apparent danger, the state is justified in further privileging the militarized economy and privatized corporate business whilst reducing spending in the public sector on social welfare including healthcare, education and unemployment. This is combined with the political spin that unemployment is no longer a social issue to be addressed by public community strategies. Rather, under the political and economic philosophy of neoliberalism, it is a problem for the individual who is now categorized as lazy, or having no work ethic, as in Murray's 'underclass' (1990, 2000). Thus, the foundations are laid for 'custodial democracy' (Murray 2005).

Researching issues of violence, involves radically opening up spaces to formulate a language of critical resistance and identifying methodological strategies for action. If neoliberalism claims universality and truth, then the critical methodological strategy has to focus on the limiting cases that undermine its claims, the contradictions in its conceptualization and its practice and the alternatives that it claims to have supplanted. In doing this, neoliberalism will be subjected to a questioning that reveals its implication in the very problems it claims to address. Indeed, citing Arendt's distinction between violence and power, Gounari shows just how far democracy has been undermined and diminished by neoliberalism. Arendt states that violence can destroy power, but power cannot arise from violence. Power in this sense refers to the powers of individuals who together are constitutive of the powers of government. It is in this sense that the political emerges as an ever-present framework for the articulation of the demands, interests and values of people. Anti-politics then includes all the practices and mechanisms required to neutralize the constituting powers of people. These derive, in effect, from the constituted powers of the state that have been organized in terms of laws, the institutions of government and the organizations – such as police, social services and the military – involved in surveillance and control. Thus the powers accrued by the state are progressively alienated from the constituting powers of the people until, perhaps, they seem to have arisen from elsewhere as in Castoriadis' notion of 'heteronomy' discussed by Gounari. The processes of the market in a sense exemplify this 'elsewhere' since its operations escape full control by any given state. The financial crisis that led to the collapse of banks in 2008 and 2009 showed the extent to which such power is external to states and to public democratic management. Neoliberalism, in equating 'democracy' with the operations of the market, and in conflating private property with the freedom of the individual, has naturalized the exclusion of democratic forms of management from the domain of the private organization of power. Such private power is organized through the use of business corporations that are, in legal terms, private persons as well as through the accumulation of vast wealth by the relative few.

Walking through any city, there are few if any genuine spaces that can be called public in the sense of the public being able to enter freely into associations to organize that space. Space is predominantly privately owned and managed. Entering any space is on the conditions formulated by the private owner. On the streets, the public has to keep moving, stopping only to buy a bit of time in a café or restaurant, a place of entertainment, or to purchase goods and services. Resting in a park or chatting with friends in the street is permissible so long as people eventually return to their homes. Otherwise they are soon spotted as troublemakers or 'down-and-outs'. The agencies of the state are there to protect the civil liberties of owners, dealing with troublemakers and managing signs of collective protest. Due to the lack of direct access to the mechanisms of 'democratic' decision making, exhibiting concerns or making demands publicly has few other forms than 'strikes', 'demonstrations' or 'protests' – all of which are defined as a potential danger to public order and security which enables the police to be brought in to supervise and control the crowds. Take, for example, the G20 protests of 2009 in London. The public as 'taxpayers' through the agency of government had subsidized and underwritten the debts of private financial corporations whose directors then proceeded to pay themselves bonuses and pensions and shore up their 'profit margins' that had been depleted by the crisis. The global implications of corporate greed, unregulated financial markets and the continual attacks on public services and welfare need to be drawn into democratic forms of debate, decision making and action. The only meeting space is reserved, of course, for the 'world leaders' of the 20 nations that compose the summit. Thus, there are no equivalent spaces available to people to voice demands and engage in decision-making procedures; hence the only space that is available is outside those places designated for the G20 meeting or other spaces outside the symbols of financial power. These spaces become spaces of struggle where the police and the protestors are framed into battle lines,[2] the police in their riot gear, the protestors in their ordinary clothes or dressed in caricature, ghoulishly or clownishly. A manikin symbolizing a 'banker' is hung and burnt at a traffic light, later a man – Ian Tomlinson – dies from the shock of being beaten by the police. He was a bystander, not a protester.[3] Such beatings were, according to protesters, not isolated incidents. Several were subsequently confirmed by CCTV, mobile phones and camcorders.[4] The expectation of violence had been "talked up for weeks in advance" by the police.[5] However, although Power is revealed in such headline-grabbing moments, it is underpinned by the more pervasive mechanisms of surveillance whether through CCTV, the storing of personal information in public and private databases, the identity papers, travel permits and everyday inspection procedures to enter, leave or travel that provide the backdrop to mass management of populations whether for public order or for the purposes of making money and protecting private property.

The state reserves to itself alone the legitimate exercise of violence to maintain order within its boundaries and to protect its boundaries from external threat. In such images and accounts of the battle lines that are drawn between the police and the citizens who protest in the only way available to them is concretely revealed as the structural violence that underpins Power. That is to say, the exercise of violence to enforce order, compliance to laws and obedience to those who hold the offices of Power is always available to the state and only the state can legitimately exercise such force through the police, the courts and the military. It is vital, therefore, that the State and its use of violence internally or externally is subject to democratic scrutiny and control. Hence freedom of speech, whether through investigative journalism, academic publication or the use of the Internet to broadcast video recordings of incidents like the events leading up to Ian Tomlinson's death, acts to monitor the use of violence and to contribute to creating the conditions for legal sanctions against the abuse of force. If Power depends on 'regimenting the minds of the public' (Bernays 1928) through the use of the media for public relations then Power can be deconstructed by the same means in order to open up democratic spaces and generate the conditions for democratic practice in the arenas of public decision making.

Schools, colleges and universities represent the major potential, if not actualized, spaces for systematic critical reflection upon the ways in which local and global structures and processes impact on people in their everyday lives. Historical and sociological research has long explored the extent to which schooling reinforces and reproduces social class, gender, cultural and ethnic-based inequalities (see, for example: Simon 1974; Willis 1977; Schostak 1983). Indeed, Simon reported an English senior civil servant in the then Department of Education and Science commenting on education policy for UK schools saying "people must be educated once more to know their place" (1985: 223). At the time there was a considerable media campaign against progressive or child-centred, comprehensive schools (where children from all backgrounds and abilities were taught in the same school in mixed-ability classes) and democratic approaches to teaching and learning. The media demand was for a return to 'basics' – that is, a core curriculum, in particular, the basics of numeracy and literacy – and teacher-centric teaching and learning with students segregated according to ability (see Schostak 1993). Mechanisms brought in focused around a tightly defined national curriculum, standard achievement tests (SATs), regular inspection, the publication of league tables based on inspections and examination results and finally the devolving of budgets to schools in order to undermine the power of local education authorities. Alongside a manufacturing of consent through the media campaign, there were thus clear legislative and resourcing mechanisms set in place to engineer compliance. Consistent with the managerial approach to schooling, research was evaluated in policy terms to the extent that it was able to supply evidenced-based findings, modelled explicitly on medical models of research employing randomized control trials, systematic reviews and what Reynolds called 'high reliability organizations' such as air traffic control and nuclear power stations (see Reynolds 1996; Reynolds and Stringfield 1996: Hammersley 2007). There has, of course, been criticism (MacLure 2005; Torrance 2004, 2006, Stronach 2006; Hammersley 2007; Schostak and Schostak 2008; Schostak in press). However, the demand for the utility of research continues alongside an aggressive concentration of research into elite, research-intensive universities and large units of research excellence on the one hand and teaching universities on the other. Whether it is the mass teaching of students for employment needs, the funding of research by big business, government and defence or the increasing managerialism of universities, the independence of universities as places for free democratic scholarship and research is under threat. The UK research councils are under pressure to produce research that is 'useful' that has a commercial spin-off (e.g. Barry 2009; Corbyn 2009). In general, then, education and research are structured to produce elites and be productive for them in creating the employees, products and services of the future.

Giroux's chapter provides a closer focus on what Eisenhower called 'the military-industrial complex' formed by powerful alliances between government agencies, the military and defence industries with the prime objective of promoting, marketing and implementing their particular vision for what constitutes a better world. Since the Cold War, the military complex has gained considerable ground in infiltrating higher education institutions although it ran into resistance during the demonstrations on university campuses against the Vietnam War. Once the demonstrations ceased, the infiltration gathered pace and has gone ahead largely unchecked. More recently, it is argued, not only is the university becoming corporatized, but it is becoming a "hypermodern militarized knowledge factory". Although the infiltration is visible, neither the Republicans nor the Democrats find it a problematic issue to put on their political agendas. How visible is the infiltration? A report called *Frameworks for Higher Education in Homeland Security* (NRC 2005) argues that a commitment to learning about homeland security is an essential part of preparing for work and life in the twenty-first century. In other words, intellectual frameworks incorporating the interests and values of the warfare state have become part of both undergraduate and postgraduate curricula. The typical former funding resources for university research programmes are drying up and the Pentagon is stepping in, whilst former CIA agents are being appointed to senior faculty positions in universities.

This bleak picture for higher education institutions, Giroux argues, has gathered momentum since the events of September 11 2001. In effect, there has been a retheorization of matters of state sovereignty, and its transformation into a biopolitics, that is, an exclusion and disposability of individuals, where if you do not fit in then the state pronounces you 'human waste' as Bauman so graphically describes it. Activities such as Guantanamo Bay were legitimated until President Obama, as one of his first acts of becoming president, suspended the military tribunals that were taking place (21 January 2009). As Hardt and Negri point out, the 'welfare state' has become a 'warfare state' as democracy becomes neutralized. Since September 11 2001, a mutual support system has developed between universities and the CIA. Universities offer openings for recruitment and services, whilst the CIA offers funding for research and scholarships. The price universities pay is that the research is co-opted towards a culture of warfare. Universities are no longer places and spaces that encourage "a spirit of understanding complex cultural differences, critical reflection and self-critique" (see p. 205). In Giroux's view, this militarization of Americans heralds "a crisis in politics" and "a fundamental crisis in democracy" (see p. 205). Giroux's argument is an argument about and for critical action and since "… militarization operates simultaneously on symbolic, material and institutional levels, strategies must be developed and waged that address all of the terrains on which it is operational" (see p. 208). To this end, he suggests that strategies of resistance should be organized around a two-pronged attack. Firstly, there is a need to develop "a language of critique", "a sense of hope and collective struggle" in order that the meaning of politics can be re-imagined through "a language of critique *and* possibility" (see p. 207). Secondly, a concerted effort to expand the spaces of politics by reclaiming "the public character of spaces, relations and institutions regarded as private" (see p. 207) is imperative.

If research methodology, as so far argued, is essential to creating the conditions for people to develop and employ their powers in free association publicly for the creation of community with each other, then all institutions must necessarily be democratic in their operational principles and practices, otherwise freedoms and thus democracy will be corrupted by elites who control institutions for their own purposes. The research task, then, is to explore the ways in which such principles and practices can be embedded.

References

Barry, P. (2009) 'These directions map out a one-way road into service, not open inquiry', *Times Higher Education*, June 5. Available at http://www.timeshighereducation.co.uk/story.asp?section code=26&storycode=406175 (accessed August 15, 2009).

Bauman, Z. (2002) *Society under Siege*. Cambridge, UK: Polity.

Bernays, E.L. (1928) *Propaganda*. New York: Horace Liveright.

Bernstein, R.J. (2005) *The Abuse of Evil: The corruption of politics and religion since 9/11*. Cambridge, UK and Malden, MA: Polity.

Corbyn, Z. (2009) 'Research councils unveil 'future vision', *Times Higher Education*, April 9. Available at http://www.timeshighereducation.co.uk/story.asp?sectioncode=26&storycode= 406112 (accessed August 15, 2009).

Fromm, E. (1942) *The Fear of Freedom*. London: Routledge and Kegan Paul.

Hammersley, M. (Ed.) (2007) *Educational Research and Evidence-based Practice*. Los Angeles, London: Sage.

Lippmann, W. (1922) *Public Opinion*. New York: Macmillan.

MacLure, M. (2005) 'Clarity bordering on stupidity': Where's the quality in systematic review? *Journal of Education Policy*, 20, 4, July, 393–416.

Murray, C. (1990, 2000) 'The underclass revisited', American Enterprise for Public Policy Research, posted 1 January 2000. Available at http://www.aei.org/publications/pubID.14891/ pub_detail.asp (accessed August 15, 2009). The book version is available at http://www.aei. org/books/bookID.268,filter.all/book_detail.asp (accessed August 15, 2009).

Murray, C. (2005) 'The advantages of social apartheid: U.S. experience shows Britain what to do with its underclass – Get it off the streets', *Sunday Times* 3 April; American Enterprise for Public Policy Research, posted 4 April. Available at http://www.aei.org/publications/filter. all, pubID.22252/pub_detail.asp (accessed August 15, 2009).

National Research Council (NRC), Committee on Educational Paradigms for Homeland

Security (2005) *Frameworks for Higher Education in Homeland Security*. Washington DC: National Academies Press.

Rancière, J. (2005) *La Haine de la Democratie*. Paris: La Fabrique editions.

Reynolds, D. (1996) *Making Good Schools: Linking school effectiveness and school improvement*. London: Routledge.

Reynolds, D. and Stringfield, S. (1996) 'Failure-free schooling is ready for take off', *Times Education Supplement*, 19 January, p. 10.

Schostak, J.F. (1983) *Maladjusted Schooling: Deviance, social control and individuality in secondary schooling*, London, Philadelphia: Falmer.

Schostak, J.F. (1993) *Dirty Marks: The education of self, media and popular culture*. London: Pluto Press.

Schostak, J.F. (2009) 'Researching and representing wrongs, injuries and disagreements: Exploring strategies for radical research', *Power and Education*, 1, 1, 2–14. Available at http://www.wwwords.co.uk/power/content/pdfs/1/issue1_1.asp (accessed August 15, 2009).

Schostak, J.F. (in press) 'Historical trends and contemporary issues in representing research in education', in Reid A. *et al.*, *Companion to Research in Education*. London: Sage.

Schostak, J.F. and Schostak J.R. (2008) *Radical Research: Designing, developing and writing research to make a difference*. London: Routledge.

Simon, B. (1974) *The Two Nations and the Educational Structure 1780–1870*. London: Lawrence & Wishart.

Simon, B. (1985) *Does Education Matter?* London: Lawrence & Wishart.

Stronach, I. (2006) 'On promoting rigour in educational research: The example of the RAE', BERA conference, Warwick September.

Torrance, H. (2004) 'Systematic reviewing – the "call centre" version of research synthesis: Time for a more flexible approach', invited presentation to ESRC/RCBN seminar on Systematic Reviewing 24 June, University of Sheffield. Available at http://www.esri.mmu.ac.uk/respapers/papers-pdf/seminar-systematicreviewing.pdf (accessed August 15, 2009).

Torrance, H (2006) 'Globalising empiricism: What if anything can be learned from international comparisons of educational achievement', in H. Lauder, P. Brown, J.-A. Dillabough, and A.H. Halsey (eds), *Education, Globalisation and Social Change*. Oxford: Oxford University Press. pp. 824–34.

WIDER (2006) 'Pioneering study shows richest two percent own half world wealth'. Launch of WIDER Study on The World Distribution of Household Wealth, 5 December 2006, in London at the Foreign Press Association, and in New York at the UN Secretariat, press release. Available at http://website1.wider.unu.edu/pressrelease/pressrelease.htm (accessed August 15, 2009).

Willis, P. (1977) *Learning to Labour*. Farnborough: Saxon House.

Part C

Framing the design and writing up

Chapter 13

Writing for emancipatory research

Jill Schostak and John F. Schostak

In writing up research for an audience, what – or who – is it that research is supposed to 'underwrite', for what purposes and to what effect? And in the process, who or what is threatened? Although Power may seek to define the limits of research writing through its impositions on what counts as appropriate, writing is a dynamic composition of powers though which public, private and intimate meanings are articulated by individuals in the course of their everyday lives. Writing research is meaningful only when it is inscribed in the many conversations, arguments and fantasies that compose the prosaic and poetic dimensions of personal and social life underwriting the decisions and actions of individuals.

As such, writing goes well beyond any simple, consciously rational engineering of the control of its meanings or 'intentions'. It will not keep its place. It is not so much, as Lacan would say, that the unconscious is structured like a language, but that writing is structured like an unconscious that plays with and plays at being the conscious tool of Power. Its surface may 'say' one thing while at the same time underwriting the forbidden discourse(s) audible and visible only in puns, slips of the tongue, the graffiti, the ghostly faces in the shadows at the margins of the eye where the denied, unmet and unvoiced 'goods', 'desires', 'needs' and unutterable injuries, complaints and disappointments have their subaltern existence. Writing is a complex, even dangerous, affair. It can be used to seduce, offend and confuse as much as clarify and educate. Yet, it is a vehicle – the only vehicle – through which our worlds are both represented and composed, whether in the sounds, the smells, the splashes of light, the touch of the finger or the mark of a bruise. A world is always a space of inscriptions where people stitch together ideas in relation to the phenomena of consciousness, and where ideas are composed consciously and unconsciously into sensible, intelligible, communicable and contestable worlds or beliefs about worlds. It is in these constructed 'worlds' that research writing plays its critical role.

Each world is ideologically distinct, that is, it has its own logic of ideas formed of beliefs, values and facts that connect with hopes, desires and fears to produce what is known or can be made knowable and "relies on narratives, metaphor and myths that persuade, praise, condemn, cajole, convince, and separate the 'good' from the 'bad'" (Steger 2008: 3–4). Ideology, then, is complexly inscribed through all the rhetorical, poetic, mythic, rational and theoretic methods by which the otherwise discrete elements of life can be composed into meaningful unities. In short, ideologies are embedded in the ways in which people perceive their worlds and imagine them as wholes. Hughes (1976) wrote of the significance of key words in stories to bring to life the whole of a narrative such as, for Christians the mention of the word 'cradle' or the 'three wise men' evokes the whole Christmas story. Similarly, key symbols like a flag evoke 'national pride', the story of Britishness, what it means to be American or French. Or, a person such as Ghandi or Mandela stands as a symbol evoking liberation and the birth of a nation. In everyday life, such part-whole relationships subsume the individual under a greater totality that gives an order, a structure a meaning, a purpose to existence transforming the finitude and the triviality of the individual into something that contributes or belongs to something significant and eternal. In order to explore such relationships, ethnographies of everyday life begin with the accounts that people tell of their lives. When writing up, these accounts can be explored for their part-whole resonances in constructing community imaginaries. In such imaginaries each anecdote connects with others that constitute the key organizing narratives or mythologies that comprise the narrative case records of ethnographies (Schostak 2006). Haw's chapter, for example, uses its title as the part that sparks to life the stories that can be told, that in the 'telling space' (Schostak 2005; Schostak and Schostak 2008) the conditions are created for the mythic unity of the territory of a gang. Each group, each community has its own reservoir of stories, of myths that compose the unities of their ways of seeing and sharing a world. But no myth, no story, no symbol fully captures the experience, the sense of being, the lived singularity of the individual. And no individual quite fits or lives up to the expectation of the idealized character, the universalized principle, the spectacular nature of the events recounted. It is the space between the individual and the story or myth that is told to give meaning, to provide justification, to demand recognition for the individual and the group or community that provides the possibility of movement, of making a difference, of creating changes. It is here that potentially there are deep conflicts between the particularity of individuals and the universal(s) meant to contain them (cf. Normand's account of the bandana that becomes a religious symbol, Chapter 4). Any territory is covered by the laws that can be enforced through violence. This is a principle as true for a gang as for a corporation or for a state. Although the state reserves all legitimate use of violence to itself, its capacity to police all its territory all the time is limited to available technologies and resources for surveillance and control. The lapses, the gaps, the ambiguous spaces are then available for exploitation.

The opportunities for critical writing emerge from the analysis of the tensions, and the conflicts between universalizing claims between protagonists or competing groups, institutions, communities and the particularities of the circumstances lived by individuals. Research methodology is thus a political practice. There are three critically distinct positions to be explored that the writing of research can underwrite. The first adopts the position of the state and its need for absolute mastery of a given territory and the individuals that belong as citizen-subjects of that territory. This can be accomplished through governing elites with the elites being the 'public' in terms of debate, decision making and control. The organization of the elites can take many forms. The elites themselves can be governed by a monarchy, priesthood or dictatorship or, indeed, be elected by 'citizens' as a defined subgroup of a population, as in leadership democracies. Research in this position is undertaken to enhance surveillance and control or the regimenting of minds and behaviour through the manufacture or engineering of consent.

The second position is adopted when what has been engineered becomes taken for granted and naturalized as the only true, real, good form of social order and its governance. That is, its constructed, arbitrary nature is repressed, forgotten and overwritten by a discourse of naturalness. It is the position of followers and cheerleaders of the status quo. Research takes on the role of surveys of compliance and deviance, studies of the robustness, the effectiveness and the reliability of machineries of management to bring about proper outcomes.

The third position radically questions the basis for all belief, knowledge and practice. This questioning may come to rest if a claim can be made that there is a limit to questioning founded upon the certainty found through rejecting everything that cannot withstand the questioning and retaining everything that survives. For Descartes, this place of certainty was the 'I think, therefore I am', the place of the doubting 'I' that itself could not doubt that it was doubting! Thus, like a geometrician, one could use reason to build rational structures of thinking starting from this place. Although Descartes' method has been criticized, it contributed and still contributes to methodical ways of thinking about how knowledge can be constructed and the limits to doing so. Rather than the establishment of knowledge about the world, for people to make a difference to their lives requires thinking about the nature of the 'good life' and the 'good society' that would sustain it. Here, there are no simple answers, no geometrical constructions. Different people have different views. For some it is based upon faith in a deity. For others it is faith in the essential nature of humanity. For others, there are such differences that no single resting place is possible. This, as Critchley (2007) argues, can lead to a passive nihilistic attitude where, since there are no stable values upon which to build the good society for all, the focus centres on the self and perfecting one's own life in total disregard for those outside. Or, it can lead to an active nihilism epotimized in Critchley's view by al-Qaeda which he sees as "the quintessence of active nihilism" since it is a "covert and utterly postmodern rhizomatic quasi-corporation outside of any state control". For him its "legitimating logic" is that:

The modern world, the world of capitalism, liberal democracy and secular humanism, is meaningless and that the only way to remake meaning is through acts of spectacular destruction, acts which it is no exaggeration to say have redefined the contemporary political situation and made the pre-9/11 world seem remote and oddly quaint. We are living through a chronic re-theologization of politics.

(Critchley 2008: 3)

Alternatively, rather than a return to religious values that are held unquestioningly, a politics can be focused on issues of social justice that take seriously the question of how to create the conditions of freedom and equality for all. For Critchley this requires a need for an ethics that is founded in ethical experience and the acts of ethical subjects. How this is to take place is still an open question. Neither freedom nor equality are finished or indeed finishable states of affairs that can be assured by a final system complete in all its details. Nor can one privileged group – however enlightened and well intentioned – be the bearer of all the universal laws, values and ethical principles that are to be imposed on all others, even if it is considered to be 'in their best interests' without resort to the threat or practice of violence to enforce their will. In revolutionary practice, the limit between one political system and another is then erected as a critical boundary that can admit no deviation, no ambiguity (cf. Žižek 2007). The 'other' is clear and must be eliminated (cf. Paraskeva's use of the term 'genocide').

It is the logic of the end of history, the final political order whether it is the socialist dream of Marxism, the domination of the world by the 'pure race', or the 'true faith' or the triumph of globalized liberal democracies (Fukuyama 1992). Without a serious political alternative, there is in that sense no further history of the battles between competing world systems, merely little local troubles to be dealt with. The issue, of course, is whether this is illusion, and whether what has been repressed by the dominant Power(s) will be – or are being – re-asserted. Research then needs a form of writing that can explore, critique and deconstruct the sense of certainty, of finality, and in so doing, it can either point out the weaknesses in the social, cultural, political and economic organizational structures and processes in order to offer solutions that reinforce the dominant Power(s); or, alternatives that include the repressed, marginalized, excluded views can be embedded in the research and writing process in order to enfranchise voices within the processes and structures of public debate and decision making. In either case, it is a choice that has political and ethical consequences. It is at this point that the methodologies employed in claims concerning 'knowledge' are shown to be unavoidably political and ethical in their essence. According to the choices made by a researcher, the interests of individuals are either enhanced or exploited, marginalized, repressed and excluded. That is, decisions are made that are strategically aligned by the decisions of the researcher or by readers of a research report to the interests of a class, a gender, a nation or a race or religious or cultural grouping or community. The disinterested researcher or research report is not a viable option in these circumstances. A choice necessarily has to be made in terms of whether the research is on the side of Power or the powers of individuals as the basis for the constitution of public debate, judgement, decision and action. 'Objectivity' thus differs according to the decision made, whether this is done consciously or unwittingly. Objectivity under Power takes its legitimacy from policy requirements concerning the acceptable criteria governing research methodology and research agendas. It is elite and 'expert' driven and the 'object' of research is treated as materials to be measured, shaped, controlled to fit with policy agendas. In short, it picks up on the strategy of 'engineering consent' and 'regimenting the minds of the public' as formulated in the public relations approach of Bernays (1928) and Lippmann (1922) and exemplified in research focused on making schools effective in terms of delivering on policy requirements (see, for example, Bloom 1987) and the resource material provided by Hammersley 2007). In contemporary terms it is driven by a neoliberal agenda where individuals are free and equal only in the sense of being stripped of individualizing qualities and reduced to elements in a system of demand and supply, free and equal to enter into contracts of exchange only on the basis that they are both willing and *able* to do so. We are all free to compete – but not equal. Ability to enter into an exchange in the marketplace is based upon the talent and the hard work that has allowed them to build the necessary wealth to pay for purchases in the marketplace. This then becomes the justification for inequality derived from a presumed initial position of freedom, a freedom that is simply the freedom to compete. Inequality occurs naturally solely because there are differences in talent and in people's willingness to undertake hard work. People are poor because they are either inferior in talent or because they are lazy. Hence, a distinction is typically made between the 'deserving poor' (those who might work hard but simply do not have the talent) and the 'undeserving poor' (those who are lazy).

Alternatively, objectivity can be defined in terms of the inclusion of the *effective* voices of all individuals. That is to say, effectiveness is grounded in the recognition of the powers of all individuals to be counted in the whole public process of debate, the informing of judgement, decision making and undertaking action. A closed political order defined by elites and the research methodologies it legitimizes cannot encompass such a system. Rather, a system open to new viewpoints and dynamically changing interests requires what Laclau and Mouffe refer to as 'radical democracy', where in Rancière's terms rather than consensus there is a 'faithfulness to the disagreement' (1995). That is, political solutions have to be found that permit differences. Rather than objectivity based only upon standardization, commonalities and invariance, objectivity as a public commitment requires the inclusion of difference, incommensurability and variation if freedom and equality are to be the basis of the production of new forms of social realities.

How then, to write the research? If it is to be radical, then it is a kind of disobedient writing that draws upon the realms, voices, objects, structures and processes that are ignored, denied, repressed, outlawed and forbidden by Power. As discussed in Section *i*, research and writing research, if it is to be radical, engages in a project of writing both in the context of and outside of the contemporary forms of capitalism. The criteria of critique employed by the researcher-writer returns then to the fundamental question of how freedom and equality are to be practised, resourced and institutionalized in everyday life. In the context of 'free-market' capitalism, the freedom in question is that of buyers and sellers to agree an exchange where all differences are reduced to being calculated by the same unit of measurement, that is, monetary value that determines the price of all things. On the large scale, it is argued by proponents of capitalism, all individuals acting in their own self-interest will, through the mechanisms of the free market, bring about the best distribution of resources. The modern-day formulations of this kind of view Kaletski (2009) saw as a key reason for the financial crisis of the time. A critical writing strategy thus involves making explicit the fundamental assumptions of dominant views and then testing these. For example, two critical assumptions of classical competitive markets included the rationality of economic decision makers and perfect knowledge. Such assumptions facilitate a mathematization of economic behaviour:

> … and this mathematical tractability soon came to be viewed as a more important academic objective than correspondence to reality or predictive power. Models based on rational expectations, insofar as they could be checked against reality, usually failed statistical tests. But this was not a deterrent to the economics profession. In other words, if the theory doesn't fit the facts, ignore the facts.
>
> (Kaletski 2009)

Such models provide a picture in the mind of 'reality' and the mathematical representations of 'reality' can be taken apart – or deconstructed – by comparing them to more complex descriptions of what actually happens from the multiple points of view of economic actors. In Kaletski's view, the contemporary models held by policy makers were far from providing a plausible representation of the realities of market behaviour and thus argued for a 'paradigm' shift. But where should such a shift take place?

Such a shift in ways of seeing, describing and accounting for what happens in the world as a basis for decision making and action returns us yet again to the critical role of conceptions of freedom, equality in relation to the powers of individuals as the constituting force of their own futures. That is to say, the key focus has returned to Power and the powers of individuals and their collective powers to create, modify and transform all social, cultural, political and economic forms of organization and the laws under which they agree to live.

However, in elite-driven 'leadership democracies' dominated by private corporate wealth and power, people do not currently have the appropriate structures, resources, organizational mechanisms or procedures to engage in public debate, decision making and action concerning the allocation of resources in relation to contributions made by individuals to the production of social 'goods'. And the cultures of mutual and collective practice where they exist are continually eroded, or, in Bauman's terms, liquified by contemporary market globalizing processes where everything is in flux. Thus, there is little scope for collective action except through demonstrations, protests and riots which in turn lead to repressive and even violent state responses to 'protect' society by a return to social order. How then can the radical be inscribed in the critical places of everyday life? La Boetie, as discussed in the introduction, proposed a simple solution to the commands of Power: disobey.

Disobedient w/ri(gh)ting for democracy and social justice

Rather than the deep surveillance and the deep regimentation of minds so typical of contemporary everyday life, the vital programme for critical and radical research has to be the creation of the conditions for the emergence of public space as the precondition for deep democracy. This means that research needs to engage directly with the conditions under which public space is continually created and sustained in every social interaction involved in the formation of desire, demand, judgement, decision and the will to action. If radical forms of research are always directed towards freedom and thus towards equality it is therefore always disobedient to all forms of hierarchical control and unequal social, economic, political and cultural arrangements. How may such disobedience be inscribed or written into everyday practices through the engagement of research?

Writing, of course, can be heard as righting and as well includes a subliminal echo of the word 'rite'. It is more than a play on words. It evokes the shiftiness implicit in ways of perceiving images as a basis for the interpretation of sensory phenomena and indicates the co-presence of multiple possible levels of reading signs that have been embedded in the world(s) of perceivable objects. When does a possible meaning become something that has 'traction' in a given social world? Take again, for example, Normand's (Chapter 4) description of the bandana that progressively transformed into a religious symbol. The school is a well-defined territory governed by rules of behaviour and dress codes. The bodies of the individuals who come under its jurisdiction are like texts to be read in terms of their conformity to expectations. The cloth worn on the head was initially read as a fashion item. The student, however, muddied its legibility, progressively using it to inscribe a religious symbol on her body, openly displayed – defiantly and provocatively? – during the ritual performances of everyday school life. In the writing was the presumption of a democratic right to present herself as she chose. However, every territory has its ritual performances (cf. Goffman 1967, 1969) that construct and maintain the boundaries of what is permissible in the presentation of a 'self' or 'identity'. And there are the taken-for-granted or tacit understandings, ways of behaving, ways of talking, ways of 'being' and of 'becoming' that are often only revealed when there is a disturbance to the typical or normal practices of everyday life (cf. Garfinkel 1967). In this case, the disturbance to the normal practices sanctioned by Power came from an allegiance to an alternative Power. It is a rebellious writing, but it is a writing on behalf of this alternative Power. The powers of the individual are in each case subsumed under some greater Power. The question in democratic practice is how powers are to be organized in ways that are just for all.

This question of justice can be explored further by recalling Burman's chapter where the wife of a legal immigrant becomes an illegal immigrant as a result of a loss of married status following domestic abuse (Chapter 3). Where the student in Normand's chapter calls upon her rights as a citizen, the victim of domestic abuse is not a citizen, loses her rights as a spouse and thus loses her right to residence. In brief, the issue focuses attention upon gender, physical violence, the strategic role of immigration status by Power to define 'identity' and raises questions concerning a more universal notion of 'right' and 'justice'. At this point, therefore, an appeal to theory, or rather debate about theory, must be made in order to generate understandings on how to respond to claims about harm, wrongdoing and thus the need for justice. In engaging in theoretical debate, the key issue for emancipatory forms of research is what is at stake for individuals by choosing one theoretical framework rather than another. In a sense, a bet is made that *this* theory will hold better consequences for people than *that* theory. It is a bet because the long-term political, social, economic, cultural and personal consequences of any theory cannot be assured with certainty. Much critical writing concerns identifying, exploring, analyzing and deconstructing the assumptions, the certainties, the 'facts' upon which theories, explanations, interpretations and 'evidence' are founded. In research on violence, writing becomes further concerned with the potential of theorizing for violence. Thus Burman, for example, discusses the principles that can be adopted so as not to violate those who are the subjects of research (Chapter 3). Without the debate that stimulates such principles to guide methodology for research in psychology (Parker 2005) and more generally in social and cultural research (Schostak and Schostak 2008), research itself can reinforce inequalities, the harm and the lack of freedom it seeks to overcome.

Recalling the chapter by Derouet, justice was explored in terms of multiple distinct spheres. For Walzer (1985), discussed in Chapter 1, each sphere is to be kept distinct so that, for example, success in business does not leak over to buy success in politics. However, it does. How should contemporary politics be arranged in order to attain justice? Such principles as Rawls' (1971) – that if there is to be inequality, it should be to the benefit of the least privileged – remains nothing other than an ideal hope to be realized only in some forever postponed future. If there is to be change, it has to be realizable in ordinary, everyday terms. Following the research of Thévenot and Boltanski (2006) and Boltanski and Chiapello (2002), to understand how this may be accomplished we need to explore the deeper changes taking place in contemporary forms of capitalism (see Section *i*) and counter them with a disobedience that both speaks truth to Power through research findings and also withdraws power from Power. That is, as discussed in the introduction, in La Boetie's (1550s) terms, it is only through the collective giving of power to the institutions of state and corporate organized Power that elites are able to govern the mass. Refusing to give that power would then, in practical terms, mean that the institutions of Power could not operate. Arendt (1963) in her studies of the violence sustained by ordinary everyday forms of behaviour in the context of Nazi war crimes wrote of the banality of violence. Milgram (1974), in his experimental study of obedience, showed how far many ordinary people were willing to go under the authority of 'experts' – even to the point of administering an apparently lethal voltage of electricity to 'learners' in a learning experiment. In a repeat of the experiment, Burger (2009) still found that surprisingly high percentages of people would go the whole way. What is it in everyday life that creates the conditions for such obedience to authority; or, what needs to be established in everyday life that creates the conditions for critical debate and the use of the collective powers of individuals to act humanely and justly towards each other?

Writing disobediently involves exploring and creating the conditions through which people communicate, signify, narrativize and imagine their lives together. The wealthy cannot make their wealth without the systematic global cooperation of individuals working together collectively in the various organizations of everyday life. Thus in Fraser's (2007) words:

> Justice requires social arrangements that permit all members to participate in social interaction on a par with one another. So that means they must be able to participate as peers in all the major forms of social interaction: whether it's politics, whether it's the labour market, whether it's family life and so on.

In the radical democracy of Laclau and Mouffe (1985) this means that democracy must be inscribed into the day-to-day action of people as they engage with each other to compose the conditions of their lives. In this sense, democracy is an unfinished and indeed unfinishable revolution (Mouffe 1993). The key power of people is that through talking together they continually compose and recompose the conditions of their lives. They tell it in their biographies, their gossip, their anecdotes of what happened where, how, when, to whom and why, and they formalize it in their official histories, their laws and their organizational policies and public relations texts. Such a key power from the point of view of Power has to be regulated as discussed in Chapter 1. Indeed, in Rancière's terms (2005), there is a hatred of democracy at the back of Power. It keeps people at a distance from decision making and collective democratic action by inscribing deference to elite discourses into everyday life and obedience under the elite control and command structures of privately owned or state-controlled organizations. The chapters of this book have variously shown the nature of that Power, drawing upon the experiences of vulnerable, angry, fearful people in their struggles, describing the harm that has been done and continues to be done to them. Whether such Power is that of the gang controlling its territory, or the militarization of universities, or, more generally, the corporatization of everyday life globally through market capitalism, the critical battle between the powers of individuals and the organizations of Power is over territory, the bodies and minds of the people within those territories, the boundaries that can be created and enforced and their rule. Where are the limits of public and private rule over territories to be defined? Whose force matters in deciding the question: the public as composed of all individuals or of their representatives; or the private as composed of property owners? If a corporation – as a legal 'person' – owns the malls, the shops, the places of entertainment and the places of work, then there is no opportunity for public decision making within those spaces except as protest, rebellion or through strikes which in turn can be legally controlled, policed or put down by government.

How public space is to be inscribed into all collective organizations, then, is critical to the development of democracy and social justice. Public space is the space of democratic becoming and of being for all individuals in a common world, that is, a world where the talk and the actions of one cannot have meaning or existence without taking into account the being and the potentials of all who live in it. This common space defines itself through the interactions of talking beings – that is, beings who inscribe and organize their powers through language – and can be described in terms of the 'chora' which "is amorphously thought of as the space of being and becoming, the real place that a body in particular, and more generally a society, a globe, or a cosmos inhabits" (Maybury 2005).

The space of being and becoming is the place where the experience, the demands and the powers of individuals are mediated and contested in relation to a triangulation of views concerning the real or imagined necessities of local and global circumstances. This triangulation places people in relation to each other in their mutually composed – whether consensually or antagonistically – spatial realities. Since triangulation depends upon multiple views obtained through multiple methods, there is a struggle to fix, to solidify, to embed in a space that is always decomposing and recomposing with every new viewpoint that is drawn into it or with every new child born and that demands to be included (cf. Arendt 1998). That is, space is always in the process of going awry (cf. Žižek 1991). It is the space where otherness always threatens the comfort of stable forms and calls into being the hard boundaries of policed borders, the status of legal and illegal and the rejection of those who do not fit.

Disobedient writing is a strategy of exploiting the slippage, the 'awryness', the space between what Adorno (1973) calls the non-conceptualities, that is, the reality of things, or in Kantian terms the thing-in-itself as distinct from its appearance in consciousness. It produces alternative forms of representing the phenomena that appear to consciousness that then enables the glimpsing of a radical methodology of inscription. It has its echoes in Derrida's notion of *écriture* which refers to and opens up a radical space:

> *Écriture* is writing in a broader sense than the script produced on paper by whatever means, hand or other. It is a metaphor, a figure for "an entire structure of investigation, not merely 'writing in the narrow sense,' graphic notation on a tangible material" (Spivak 1976: ix–lxxxix). Rather it is "the constitution of a thick space where the play of hiding/revealing may take place" (Lyotard 1971: 75 as cited in Readings 1991: 6). Neither irreducible to a series of rules on the investigations of graphic systems nor a simple opposition to speech in order to invert a binary opposition, it announces a rhetoric of identity situated in some physical context (Wolfreys 1998). Not only does the notion of writing refer to speech and thought as forms of writing, but it is also expanded along further horizons to include the writing, the written-ness, of the subject's identity (Wolfreys 1998).
>
> (Schostak 2005, Vol. II: 1–2)

Écriture as a structure of investigation and as a spacing for hiding/revealing is a play that is rather like the play of tensions resulting when a bridge or skyscraper oscillates in high winds, or the play of a fishing rod used to reel in its catch that fights all the way:

> The act of writing, reading and thinking is "always in some sense a response", to the other (Wolfreys. 1998: 5). The otherness of non-correspondence, of the manifestation of the other in the same, haunts identity and thereby splits it, bringing about a transformation between a certain act of looking or gazing and a certain event in writing.
>
> (Schostak 2005, Vol. II: 55)

This question of the 'real' that is to be revealed, reeled in and grasped in concepts is central to any methodology that seeks to base action upon knowledge. But, the real (the non-conceptuality), in some radical way, always seems to slip from the grasp. Thus, it calls again upon the powers of individuals to engage with each other in the destruction of constraining forms and the creation and recreation of alternative forms of social organization to meet the multiplicities of demands of people. It is here, where rebellious writing identifies the fissures, the places of strain, the looseness of the knotting, where movement and change are possible because there are pent-up demands to make a difference.

It is here too, where radical methodologies can drive democracy to every point of interaction. What can be developed in terms of a paradigm shift by research in everyday practice in all the institutions of life?

Researching violence drives attention and practice to the critical political issues of how power is to be collectively managed in living together. The features of disobedient writing that opens public space to the powers of individuals that can be drawn from readings of the chapters include:

1   a creative engagement with the experience of freedom in the sense of Balibar's (1994) *égaliberté*, that is, the coextensiveness of equality and liberty as it arises when people make demands for social justice. Its frustration can be seen to motivate explosions of violence (see, for example, Chapter 10) and its repression opens the possibilities for exploitation and bullying (see, for example, Chapter 6) and the formation of Power (see, for example, Chapters 1,7,11 and 12);

2   conceptual analysis and critique of the language or discursive forms of everyday language as employed in the stories, the biographical accounts, the anecdotes, the local myths (see Chapter 8) or the discourses of immigration (Chapter 3) and institutional racial discrimination (see Chapter 5) are essential to the critique of the language of Power and its leakage across different discursive regimes from business, to the military to the university as discussed by Giroux in Chapter 12. This opens the way to strategies for:

   a.   deconstructive analysis of concepts, theories, arguments and practices that allow the possibilities of displacing and reconfiguring the ways in which the unities – for example, neighbourhoods, faith communities, cultural identities, cities, nations and so on – of the world are imagined and opened up to contestation (see, for example, Chapter 4);

   b.   temporal and spatial analysis and critique in order to reconfigure the social construction and use of space (see, for example, Chapter 9);

   c.   analysis and critique of the place of the subject, subjectivity and the production or incarnation of the objective as a 'real' of the subject. That is to say, for example, the market is at once a subjective production in terms of subjects interacting with each other to exchange goods and services and an objective reality that can be observed and analyzed. As an objective form it can be naturalized as something 'given', 'thing-like' in its objectivity and thus that all things have their price become 'natural'. Only by showing how the 'natural' has been artificially produced by multiplicities of decisions and kept in play by everyday practices can the possibility of doing something different be conceptualized;

3   dialogical analysis and critique that sets alternative views into debate and challenge. This opens the way to the creation of the conditions for public space where people engage together in the creation of forms of social

organization to handle their differences and identify commonalities. This is fundamental to the production of public space as an effective limit on private exploitation. Through the discourse that takes place in dialogue, subjects are continually repositioned and identities modified in order to take account of changed circumstances (see, in particular, Torfing 1999). Each view, each repositioning, creates the sense of the spaces between views, spaces that are as yet open to reconceptualization, open to being the ground of a new commitment that enables change as views reconfigure to encompass the new (Schostak 2006);

4   and finally, (see for example Derouet's chapter) an engagement with those social, cultural, economic and political circumstances through which collective community action can be organized to create democratically inclusive spaces for debate, the formation of judgement, making decisions and undertaking action.

Disobedient writing – like the bandana that becomes a headscarf – inscribes the forbidden within the scenes of Power. Emancipatory research explores the possibilities for the powers of individuals in their everyday practices to engage democratically. Finally, then, it may be asked: when, as children during their school years; and when, as young adults, individuals leave school, what has been the sum of their experiences about the range of democratic practices they have been involved in? How has research contributed and how will it continue to contribute to those experiences? As adults throughout the different phases of their lives, in order to address the deep-seated social justice issues and the violence through which everyday life is structured, how may democratic practice be directly employed? Under what circumstances and in which scenes of action can individuals actually use their powers to employ reason freely in public in the creation of appropriate social forms to meet their many demands?

References

Adorno, T.W. (1973) *Negative Dialectics*. Trans. E.B. Ashton. London and New York: Routledge.

Arendt, H. (1963) *Eichman in Jerusalem: A report on the banality of evil*. London: Faber and Faber.

Arendt, A. (1998) *The Human Condition*. Introduction by Margaret Canovan. Chicago: University of Chicago Press; first published 1958.

Balibar, E. (1994) '"Rights of man" and "rights of the citizen": The modern dialectic of equality and freedom', in Etienne Balibar, *Masses, Classes, Ideas: Studies on politics and philosophy before and after Marx*. New York: Routledge. The original is: "La proposition de l'égaliberté", in Les Conférences du Perroquet, n° 22, Paris novembre 1989.

Bernays, E.L. (1928) *Propaganda*. New York: Horace Liveright.

Bloom, A. (1987) *The Closing of the American Mind: How higher education has failed democracy and impoverished the souls of today's students*. New York: Simon and Schuster.

Boltanski, L. and Chiapello, E. (2002) 'The new spirit of capitalism', paper presented to the Conference of Europeanists, March, 14–16, 2002, Chicago.

Burger, J.M. (2009) 'Replicating Milgram: Would people still obey today?' *American Psychologist*, 64, 1–11.

Critchley, S. (2007) *Infinitely Demanding: Ethics of commitment, politics of resistance*. New York: Verso.

Fraser, N. (2007) 'Emancipation is not an all or nothing affair', interview by Marina Liakova. Available at http://www.eurozine.com/articles/2008–08-01-fraser-en.html (accessed August 15, 2009).

Fukuyama, F. (1992) *The End of History and the Last Man*. New York: Free Press. Second paperback edition with a new Afterword: Simon and Schuster, 2006.

Garfinkel, H. (1967) *Studies in Ethnomethodology*. Englewood Cliffs, NJ: Prentice-Hall.

Goffman, E. (1967). *Interaction Ritual: Essays on face-to-face behavior*. Garden City, New York: Doubleday.

Goffman, E. (1969) *The Presentation of Self in Everyday Life*. London: Allen Lane; Harmondsworth: Penguin.

Hammersley, M. (ed.) (2007) *Educational Research and Evidence-based Practice*. Los Angeles, London: Sage.

Hughes, T. (1976) 'Myth and education', in G. Fox *et al.* (eds), *Writers, Critics and Children*. New York: Agathon Press; London: Heinemann.

Kaletski, A. (2009) 'Goodbye, homo economicus', *Prospect*, Issue 157, April. Available at http://www.prospect-magazine.co.uk/article_details.php?id=10683 (accessed August 15, 2009).

La Boetie, E. (1550s) 'The politics of obedience: The discourse of voluntary servitude'. Available at http://tmh.floonet.net/articles/laboetie.html (accessed August 15, 2009).

Laclau, E. and Mouffe, C. (1985) *Hegemony and Socialist Strategy: Towards a radical democratic politics*. London: Verso.

Lippmann, W. (1922) *Public Opinion*. Harcourt Brace and Company.

Maybury, T. (2005) 'Rethinking regionality [Captain Cook):(re-births):(Byron Bay]', *Transformations*, Issue 12, December. Available at http://transformations.cqu.edu.au/journal/issue_12/article_02.shtml (accessed August 15, 2009).

Milgram, S. (1974) *Obedience to Authority: An experimental view*. London, Tavistock.

Mouffe, C. (1993) *The Return of the Political*. London and New York: Verso.

Parker, I. (forthcoming, 2005) *Qualitative Psychology: Introducing radical research*. Buckingham: Open University Press.

Rawls, R. (1971) *A Theory of Justice*. Cambridge, MA: Harvard University Press.

Rancière, J. (1995) *La Mésentete: Politique et philosophie*. Paris: Galilée.

Rancière, J. (2005) *La Haine de la Democratie*. Paris: La Fabrique editions; English edition, translated by Steve Corcoran, 2007, 2009, *Hatred of Democracy*, London: Verso.

Schostak, J.R. (2005) *{Ad}dressing Methodologies: Tracing the self in significant slips: Shadow dancing*. Unpublished PhD: University of East Anglia. Available at http://imaginativespaces.net/thesis/contentsthesis.html (accessed August 15, 2009).

Schostak, J.F. (2006) *Interviewing and Representation in Qualitative Research Projects*. Open University Press.

Schostak, J.F and Schostak J.R. (2008) *Radical Research: Designing, developing and writing research to make a difference*. London: Routledge.

Steger, M.B. (2008) *The Rise of the Global Imaginary: Political ideologies from the French Revolution to the global war on terror*. Oxford: Oxford University Press.

Thévenot, L. and Boltanski, L. (2006) *On Justification: Economies of worth*. Trans. Catherine Porter. Princeton NJ: Princeton University Press.

Torfing, J. (1999) *New Theories of Discourse: Laclau, Mouffe and Zizek*. Oxford: Wiley-Blackwell.

Walzer M. (1985) *Spheres of Justice: A defence of pluralism and equality*. Oxford: Blackwell.

Žižek, S. (1991) *Looking Awry: An introduction to Jacques Lacan through popular culture*. Cambridge, MA and London: MIT Press.

Žižek, S. (2007) *Slavoj Žižek Presents Robespierre: Virtue and terror*. Introduction by S. Žižek; text selected and annotated by Jean Ducange; translated by John Howe. London, New York: Verso.

Critical conclusions for new beginnings

Violence is both a global and a local issue. Is there a political solution to violence? Can research contribute to creating the conditions for a culture and practice of nonviolence? The overarching – or underwriting – research question, then, is how research methodology can be applied to reframe the key social institutions that both constrain and enable the expression and development of our powers as individuals in association with each other. Power, then, is not the problem. The problem is how it is configured to produce the spaces in which we live our lives with others. It is the long-recognized distinction in political theory between *constituting* powers and *constituted* power that is at stake. In face-to-face terms, in the local circumstances of our lives, what enables or prevents us from forming whatever associations we want in order to accomplish whatever we want?

In the Hobbesian view, people left to their own devices will engage in a war of all against all. Thus, to prevent this, Hobbes proposes a strong central government imagined as the Leviathan so awesome in Power that people are frightened into compliant obedience to order. In opposite terms, Rousseau imagined people as essentially good by nature but corrupted by society. Who is right? Probably neither. Rather than either/or, there is the coexistence of a plurality of views, values, ambitions, practices and social forms and thus of disagreements. Rancière, as discussed in Chapter 13, sees disagreement as inescapable and as fundamental to politics. Democracy is the political form through which people engage with each other, not to reach consensus but to create social forms that are faithful to the disagreements between people. In that way, people do not lose their distinctiveness, nor are they forced to submit their individuality to a greater dominating Power. In order to sustain such a democratic space of tolerance for the differences that lead to disagreements, some way of distinguishing between powers used for mutual support and those for purposes of domination must be identified. As Eagleton points out, turning to Hegel we can:

> ... discover there is a set of criteria for distinguishing between powers which should be fulfilled and those that should not. This is the case when

we should exercise only those powers, and in only those ways, that help us to create the conditions for others to exercise their own powers just as fully and freely. The paradigm of this process is that reciprocity of self-fulfilling powers, in which your self-realisation becomes the very means and condition of my own and vice versa, which we know as love. Or as Marx puts it rather less idyllically in the *Communist Manifesto*, formulating what one might call the notion of political love: a situation in which the free development of each becomes the condition of the free development of all.

(Eagleton 2009:10)

This 'political love', if it can be called that, refers to the constituting powers of individuals in free association with each other to create forms of social organization that guarantee that freedom, in all equality. However, the forms of social organization that have been produced to assure free development formalize as constituted forms of power. In the Marxist perspective, the constituted form of freedom is the state of communism as 'whatever set of political arrangements would allow this to happen' (Eagleton 2009: 10). In the perspective of Bernays and Lippmann discussed in chapter 1, leadership democracies run by elites who represent the 'public' are the preferred form of constituted power. The contemporary neoliberal market democracies that have in various ways been discussed throughout the book, proclaim to be the 'natural' outcome of a long history of struggle and development and indeed, to be – barring the details – essentially the final socio-political form of constituted powers that guarantee freedom, a freedom privileged above equality. For Balibar, as described in Chapter 1, freedom for all can only exist when there is also equality. Inequality produces 'unfreedom'. Hence, the arguments variously presented throughout the book lead to a view of social justice as grounded in both freedom and equality. Where these conditions are denied for people, they are experienced as a form of violation. Where the social institutions and organizations that have been constituted are employed to restrict and regiment access to resources and to the spaces where decision making and action is undertaken, then they are experienced as Power. Power can be experienced as legitimate where it protects the rights, the property and the ways of life of people. Where Power uses force to maintain inequality, to exclude voices and demands, to undermine and set barriers to the freedom of movement it can be experienced as violence.

Each of the chapters has contributed to a critique of the prevailing conditions under which violence occurs in contemporary life. And each provides examples of the kinds of research that can be undertaken in response to and in the context of violence. However, critique cannot take place unless there are some principles, some framework of understanding – or indeed, some convictions – that alternatives are not only possible, but better. Each author, in their different ways, calls upon a concept of social justice that appeals to notions of 'freedom' and 'equality' and of the collective action underpinned by 'democracy' as the political vehicle through which justice and the 'good society' may be obtained.

Particular forms of social organization are not 'natural'. They have to be thought about and constructed through everyday interaction – that is to say, they are artificial. Such constructions can come to seem natural and as some-how essential to a particular 'way of life' and social identity. In this way they become above critique, immune to change. And when challenges are offered to particular practices, institutions and organizations, they can be experienced as threats to a whole way of life and thus motivate violence. In the interests of Power, people, nations and faith communities may become 'other' and labelled as friend or foe, good or evil. Each chapter provides its examples of the binary construction of the world into camps, zones or territories.

All it takes to resist and undermine Power, La Boetie in the early 1550s says, is disobedience. As described in Chapter 1, Power derives its force from the collective powers given to it by individuals. Refusal to obey immediately sucks its strength dry. However, Power distributes its rewards and incentives differ-entially, seducing and shaping allegiance by the privileges it provides, promises or takes away. How then, can the conditions for resistance, disobedience and the re-creation of the conditions for 'political love', for the mutual constructions of freedom and equality, be set in motion? The radical democratic theory and practice of Laclau, Mouffe, Rancière, and others discussed in different chapters is grounded in what Balibar calls *égaliberté* – the coextensiveness of freedom and equality – and thus provides a starting point for research that seeks to make a difference in the lives of people. It has been argued that if research is to contrib-ute to creating the conditions for openness, public debate, decision making and action, then the aspiration is to employ critical methods that are participatory, inclusive of voices and viewpoints and democratic in principle and practice. The practical question is then, how far can – and should – democratic princi-ples and procedures be driven down into the procedures and practices of every stage and dimension of research into every aspect and institution of everyday life? If research is to be emancipatory, there can be no uncritical conclusion, no final resting place at the end of history. Each change in circumstances, each new viewpoint, demands a creative response for new beginnings.

Reference

Eagleton, T. (2009) 'Loving Power', in J. Satterthwiate, H. Piper and P. Sikes (eds.) *Power in the Academy*. Stoke-on-Trent: Trentham Books.

Notes

1 Values, violence and rights

1 Kant, An Answer to the Question: What is enlightenment? (1784) – full text at: http://theliterarylink.com/kant.html
2 Margaret Thatcher, interview for *Woman's Own* ('No such thing as society'): http://www.margaretthatcher.org/speeches/displaydocument.asp?docid=106689
3 State of the Union Address, 29 January 2002.
4 See: http://www.youtube.com/watch?v=m2yy3XLeS7U

2 Rethinking justice in education and training

1 The SMIC is the minimum wage guaranteed by the state to all those who have a job. This is an important part of the welfare state. It is often criticized for being too low. Here 'smic culturel' means that cultural teachings would be neglected to the benefit of more practical, job-related skills.
2 The Langevin-Wallon plan was presented in 1947 with the purpose of reforming education in France. It argued that regardless of their family, social and ethnic origins, all children had an equal right to the full development of their abilities and "the introduction of 'social justice' in school through the democratization of teaching will place each in the place assigned to them by their aptitudes for the greatest benefit of all." Source: http://pagesperso-orange.fr/claude.rochet/ecole/docs/langevin.pdf (accessed August 15, 2009)
3 Hirschman, A.O (1970) Exit, Voice and Loyalty: Responses to Decline in Firms, Organizations and States, Cambridge, MA: Harvard University Press.

3 Between justice and pathologization

1 These five principles have been extracted from the originally submitted much longer version of the chapter. The chapter was shortened to meet word length requirements.
2 The Women Asylum Seekers from Pakistan Project was funded by the Big Lottery Fund, and owned by South Manchester Law Centre.
3 It is beyond the scope of this chapter to address the debates surrounding: (1) the terminological issues and complexities surrounding domestic violence ('domestic violence' vs. 'abuse'; 'familial' vs. 'wife' battering – remembering that perpetrators are not only spouses, but often include other family members); (2) discourses of interpersonal violence, and intimate violence/abuse; (3) how this also usually includes sexual violence; (4) how non-physical abuse is often overlooked – giving rise to an underemphasis on mental health issues and trauma; and (5) the ways in which domestic violence is already framed within a 'private' discourse of the family, such that it is rarely understood politically as a form of torture (see

e.g. Hanmer and Itzin, 2000). Such framings also bring to the fore the public/private legal and cultural divide dealt with later in this chapter.

4 This colonial relationship was particularly evident when the UK suspended Pakistan's membership of the British Commonwealth during Musharraf's imposition of 'emergency' (i.e. military) rule in autumn 2007, which was only reinstated once the date for democratic elections was announced in early 2008.

5 At this point I want to acknowledge the Project Advisory Group whose insights and discussions form the basis of my arguments here. Hence my thanks to: Meg Allen, Khatidja Chantler, Andrea Grogan, Sajida Ismail, Vera Martins, Philomena Harrison, Yvonne Prendergast and Nadia Siddiqui.

6 An early attempt to reflect upon these assumptions as guiding principles can be found in Burman et al. (2006).

7 Indeed, it should also be acknowledged that these dangers were not only symbolic, as indicated by the fact that the final dissemination visit to Pakistan was delayed by several months owing to political instability in the region, and was only authorized by the project advisory team by a narrow majority. The commitment and engagement of Nadia Siddiqui, as the principal investigator on the project, deserves particular acknowledgement here, in researching at a moment and in a context of very considerable political violence and instability.

8 We use the term 'minoritized', rather than 'minority' or minority ethnic' to draw attention to the processes by which cultural, religious and racialized minority groups are rendered into a minority, rather than presuming this as some kind of prior or essential identity (see Batsleer et al. 2002; Burman and Chantler 2004, 2005; Burman et al. 2004). Of course, this use of the binary 'minoritized'/'majoritized' should be distinguished from the way it functions in some development-studies contexts, where 'minority' typically means the rich, often white, peoples and countries whose power dominates the world's majority, notwithstanding their numerical paucity.

9 In a joint, patrilocal family context, i.e. where the daughter/wife would join the husband's household, she is particularly under the critical scrutiny of her mother-in-law.

10 This is politically ambiguous because it is unclear how almost half a national population (sex ratios in Pakistan being slightly under 50 per cent) could be understood to be a persecuted 'minority' group, but at the very least this designation illustrates the conceptually anomalous character of the evaluation of gendered oppression.

11 These include such practices as providing legal and counselling services on site and at admission to women's shelters.

12 This was often unsuccessful because of the way media interviews about the research would be edited in order to confirm the dominant narrative – thus making us even more cautious about discussing this work in public arenas.

13 The study also documented bizarre evaluations on the part of judges that revealed the cultural and gendered limits of what they could comprehend. We documented accounts from service providers and legal representatives of judges disbelieving a woman's account not on the basis of problems of corroboration but because they simply could not believe a woman could endure so much and still survive.

Methodological discussion section *i*

1 In the speech, President Bush talked of preventing "regimes that sponsor terror from threatening America or our friends and allies with weapons of mass destruction". Such regimes included North Korea, Iran and Iraq and "States like these, and their terrorist allies, constitute an axis of evil, arming to threaten the peace of the world". For full text see: http://stateoftheunionaddress.org/2002-george-w-bush (accessed August 10, 2009).

4 The scarf unveiled

1 Within the framework of autonomy granted to secondary schools in teaching and education, school rules, which are adopted by school boards, define the 'rights and duties of each
member of the educative community' and the rules related to discipline in conformity with
article 3 of the French Act of 30 August 1985. This measure sets the list and the scale
of disciplinary sanctions to be pronounced against pupils as provided for by legal texts:
admonition, blame and temporary or definitive exclusion from school. The school has
total freedom to appreciate the measures of prevention, care, reparation and school punish-
ments. However, they must be mentioned in the school rules in order to be pronounced. In
addition, the circular of 11 July 2000 specifies the rules of life related to the relationships
between the members of the educative community, notably the use of some personal goods
(mobile phone, laptop computer, walkman, etc.) and, in the name of safety, the outfits which
are incompatible with some lessons or which are likely to put the safety of individuals and
hygiene rules at risk or to cause troubles in school management. Within the framework
of duties related to the 'respect of others and of the environment', each one has to adopt
a tolerant and respectful attitude related to others and their convictions, to respect others
and the whole staff, politeness being one duty written in school rules.

2 In 1992, the Council of the State cancelled school rules which prohibited pupils from "wearing any conspicuous signs, whether they are clothing, religious, political or philosophical
signs". According to the Council, such regulations disregarded the terms of Article 10 of
the Education Act of 10 July 1989, taken up in Article L 511–12 of the Education Code
under which "in secondary schools, pupils have, in the respect of pluralism and neutrality, the freedom of information and of speech" (Kherouaa case). Furthermore, the Bayrou
circular requested that school rules should provide that "discrete signs worn by pupils as
proof of their personal attachment to convictions, notably religious ones, are allowed in
schools. However, conspicuous signs which are per se proselytizing or discrimination tools
are banned. Provocative attitudes, breaches of attendance and of safety duties, behaviours
likely to exert pressure upon other pupils or to disturb the progress of teaching activities
or to trouble school order are also forbidden".

3 The bill by Jacques Myard, a French MP, served, among others, to explain the motives of
the protagonists. His bill mentioned the rise in Islamic activism in favour of a strict Islam,
as the sole cultural reference, in the shape of networks of radical activists. He called for a
reaction to avoid the development of ethnic and community-centred behaviours, to stop
intifadas within school spaces in defiance of the founding values of the republic. Quoting
Samuel Huntington and his 'shock of civilizations' thesis, the text considered that schools
should not be turned into "a place of confrontations between communities" while incidents
multiplied in schools. He assimilated the veil, "a symbol of sexual discrimination against
the movement of societies towards women's emancipation", to the 'tchadri' imposed on
Afghan girls by the Taliban and "against the dignity and the liberty of women".

4 A poster proclaiming the school as a 'sanctuary' read in a 'notice to the population': "you are
entering a space of listening, dialogue and mutual understanding. Leave your weapons and
your invective, your headdress and your diatribes, your verses and suras at the doorkeeper's.
She will give them back to you as you exit the school. Here only being natural and smiling
are compulsory".

5 Social research and 'race'

1 This chapter draws upon and revises a previously published chapter: Singh, G., and Johnson,
M.R.D. (1998) 'Research with ethnic minority groups in health and social welfare', in C.
Williams, H. Soydan and M.R.D. Johnson (eds) *Social Work and Minorities: European perspec-
tives*, London: Routledge, pp. 231–46.

9 Passionate places and fragmented spaces

1 This is a word that I have drawn from the OED online to mean violence in various senses.
2 In 2003 an artist, Jill Magid, used the surveillance camera system in Liverpool for a project that was to explore identity formation. To access each film data set that had been recorded, she needed to complete five forms every time. She did this by composing and transforming them into a series of love letters to the security survellaince team. She was then given the relevant tapes which she logged and posted on a website www.evidencelocker [see Chapter 9 References for full reference] The point here is that her project was turned down when it was proposed in terms of an art project but was accepted when she rewrote the proposal and termed it public relations!
3 Whitehead, A.J. (1933) *Adventures of Ideas*. New York: Macmillan, pp. 304–5.
4 Whitehead 1993, A. N. (1993) *Adventures of Ideas*. New York: The Fress Press in Shapiro, S. Pulses of Emotion: Whitehead's Critique of Pure Feeling accessed online July 2008 at www.shapiro.com/othertexts/pulse.pdf

11 Manufacturing fear

1 Ellen Willis, 'Freedom from religion,' *The Nation*, 1 February 2001, http://www.thenation.com/doc/20010219/willis.
2 Heteronomy, in line with Castoriadis's theoretical framework, is "the condition where in a society the laws are imposed from the outside, from tradition, from God, nature, the laws of history or the market".
3 For a thorough discussion, see Henry Giroux, *Beyond the Spectacle of Terrorism: Rethinking politics and pedagogy in the society of the image* (manuscript).
4 Here he is paraphrasing Clausewitz's famous dictum that war is the continuation of politics by other means.

12 Militarizing higher education

1 Dwight D. Eisenhower, 'Military-Industrial Complex Speech, Dwight D. Eisenhower, 1961 – The Avalon Project at Yale Law School', The Avalon Project (1961). Available online at: http://www.yale.edu/lawweb/avalon/presiden/speeches/eisenhower001.htm.
2 More recently, the military-industrial complex has been defined through a conglomeration of social forces known as the 'Iron Triangle', and as James M. Cypher points out, it includes the following interest groups: 'One side of the triangle includes the 'civilian' agencies that shape US military policy – the Office of the President, the National Security Council, the Senate and House Armed Services Committees, and civilian intelligence agencies like the CIA and NSA. A second side includes the military institutions – the Joint Chiefs of Staff, the top brass of the Air Force, Army, Marines and Navy, the powerful 'proconsul' regional commands (known as 'CINCs'), and, in a supporting role, veterans' organizations like the American Legion and the Veterans of Foreign Wars. At the base of the triangle are the 88,000 private firms that profit from the military contracting system, and that use their sway over millions of defense workers to push for ever-higher military budgets'. James M. Cypher, 'The iron triangle: The new military buildup', *Dollars and Sense Magazine* (January/February 2002). Online: http://www.thirdworldtraveller.com/Militarization_America/Iron_Triangle.html.
3 Of course, at the time the National Defense Educational Act has been passed as part of the post-Sputnik legislation that linked national defence with federal investment in higher education. As Sophia McClennen points out in a brilliant essay in College Literature, the Soviet launching of Sputnik created a sense of vulnerability and opened the door for dynamics that further fuelled the rise of the military-industrial-academic complex. See Sophia McClennen, 'The geopolitical war on US higher education', College Literature 33: 4 (Fall 2006), pp. 43–75.

4   Cited in Kathryn Albrecht, '"Camp Justice": A sign of how we cherish our freedoms',
    Mountain Mail Newspaper (9 February 2006). Online at: http://www.mymountainmail.com/
    stories/opikkathrynalbrecht02–09-0620060306.php. The speech can be found in William
    J. Fulbright, 'The war and its effects: The military-industrial-academic complex,' *Super-
    State: Readings in the Military-Industrial Complex*, ed. Herbert I. Schiller (Urbana: University
    of Illinois, 1970).

5   Rebecca S. Lowen, *Creating the Cold War University: The transformation of Stanford* (Berkeley:
    University of California Press, 1997), p. 2.

6   Charles DeBenedetti and Charles Chatfield. *An American Ordeal: The antiwar movement
    of the Vietnam era* (Syracuse, NY: Syracuse University Press, 1990); Terry Anderson. *The
    Movement and the Sixties: Protest in America from Greensboro to Wounded Knee* (New York: Oxford
    University Press, 1995); Alexander Bloom and Wini Breines, eds *'Takin' It to the Streets':
    A sixties reader* (2nd edition). (New York: Oxford University Press, 2003).

7   There were dozens of plots by the US government to kill Castro. See William Blum,
    Killing Hope (Monroe, Maine: Common Courage Press, 1995), p. 189. Also see, *The Church
    Committee Report on Cuba*. Online: http://history-matters.com/archive/church/reports/ir/
    html/ChurchIR_0043a.htm

8   There is a distinguished body of literature written about the emerging historical relation-
    ship between the government, the military and higher education. See, for example, Roger
    L. Geiger, *To Advance Knowledge: The growth of American research universities, 1900–1940*
    (New York: Oxford University Press, 1986); Everett Mendelsohn, Merritt Roe Smith, and
    Peter Weingart, *Science, Technology, and the Military* (Dordrecht, The Netherlands: Kluwer,
    1988); Clyde W. Barrow, *Universities and the Capitalist State: Corporate liberalism and the
    reconstruction of American higher education, 1894–1928* (Madison: University of Wisconsin
    Press, 1990); Sigmund Diamond, *Compromised Campus: The collaboration of universities with
    the intelligence community, 1945–1955* (New York: Oxford, 1992); Stuart W. Leslie, *The Cold
    War and American Science: The military-industrial-academic complex at MIT and Stanford* (New
    York: Columbia University Press, 1993); G. Pascal Zachary, *Endless Frontier: Vannevar Bush,
    engineer of the American century* (New York: The Free Press, 1997); Christopher Simpson, ed.,
    Universities and Empire: Money and politics in the social sciences during the Cold War (New York:
    The New Press, 1998).

9   John Armitage, 'Beyond hypermodern militarized knowledge factories', *Review of Education,
    Pedagogy, and Cultural Studies* 27 (2005), p. 221.

10 While there are some excellent older analyses of the military-academic complex, more recent
    critiques are marginal to the literature on the military-industrial complex. Some recent
    analyses include: Sigmund Diamond, *Compromised Campus: The collaboration of universities
    with the intelligence community, 1945–1955* (New York: Oxford, 1992); Stuart W. Leslie, *The
    Cold War and American science: The military-industrial-academic complex at MIT and Stanford*
    (New York: Columbia University Press, 1993); G. Pascal Zachary, *Endless Frontier: Vannevar
    Bush, engineer of the American century* (New York: The Free Press, 1997); Rebecca S. Lowen,
    Creating the Cold War University: The transformation of Stanford (Berkeley: University of
    California Press, 1997); Noam Chomsky *et al.*, *The Cold War and the University: Toward
    an intellectual history of the postwar years* (New York: The New Press, 1998); Christopher
    Simpson, ed., *Universities and Empire: Money and politics in the social sciences during the cold war*
    (New York: The New Press, 1998); Cary Nelson, 'The National Security State', *Cultural
    Studies* 4: 3 (2004), pp. 357–61; John Armitage, 'Beyond hypermodern militarized know-
    ledge factories', *Review of Education, Pedagogy, and Cultural Studies* 27 (2005), pp. 219–39;
    Michael Perelman, 'The Role of higher education in a security state', *Thought and Action*
    (Fall 2005), pp. 179–86; and Greg McColm and Sherman Dorn, 'A university's dilemma
    in the age of national security', *Thought and Action* (Fall 2005), pp. 163–77.

11 Nicholas Turse, 'The military-academic complex', TomDispatch.com (29 April 2004).
    Available online at: http://www.countercurrents.org/us-turse290404.htm.

12　These figures are taken from Nicholas Turse, 'The military-academic complex'. See also Chalmers Johnson, *The Sorrows of Empire*, especially pp. 97–130.

13　Association of American Universities, *National Defense Education and Innovation Initiative: Meeting America's economic and security challenges in the 21st century* (January 2006). Online: http://www.aau.edu/reports/NDEII.pdf.

14　Marissa Carl, 'Spanier to head new FBI board', *The Daily Collegian* (19 September 2005). Online: http://www.collegian.psu.edu/archive/2005/09/09–19-05tdc/09–19-05dnews-05.asp.

15　Ibid.

16　Press release, 'FBI appoints National Security Higher Education Advisory Board', Federal Bureau of Investigation (15 September). Available at http://www.fbi.gov/pressrel/pressrel05/highered091505.htm.

17　Michael Perelman, 'The role of higher education in a security state', *Thought and Action* (Fall 2005), p. 179.

18　I have taken this question up of an emerging authoritarianism in the United States in two books. See Henry A. Giroux, *Against the New Authoritarianism: Politics after Abu Ghraib* (Winnipeg: Arbeiter Ring Publisher, 2005); and Henry A. Giroux, *America on the Edge: Henry Giroux on politics, culture, and education* (New York: Palgrave, 2006).

19　Jean Comaroff, 'Beyond the politics of bare life: AIDS and the neoliberal order,' unpublished manuscript (6 October 2005), p. 3.

20　Achille Mbembe, 'Necropolitics', trans. Libby Meintjes, *Public Culture* 15: 1 (2003), p. 11.

21　Giorgio Agamben, *Homo Sacer: Sovereign Power and Bare Life*, trans. Daniel Heller-Roazen (Stanford: Stanford University Press, 1998); Giorgio Agamben, *Remnants of Auschwitz: The witness and the archive*, trans. Daniel Heller-Roazen (Cambridge: Zone Books, 2002); Giorgio Agamben, *State of Exception*, trans. Kevin Attell (Chicago: University of Chicago, 2003); Foucault, *Society Must Be Defended* (Lectures at the College de France, 1975–1976).

22　Michael Hardt and Antonio Negri, *Multitude: War and democracy in the age of empire* (New York, NY: The Penguin Press, 2004), p. 334.

23　Ibid.

24　Giorgio Agamben, 'On Security and Terror', trans. Soenke Zehle, *Frankfurter Allegemeine Zeitung* (20 September 2001). Online: http://www.egs.edu/faculty/agamben/agamben-on-security-and-terror.html.

25　Zygmunt Bauman, *Wasted Lives*, p. 6.

26　Jane Mayer, 'A deadly interrogation' *The New Yorker* (14 November 2005), http://www.newyorker.com/fact/content/articles/051114fa_fact; and Seymour Hersh, *Chain of Command: The road from 9/11 to Abu Ghraib* (New York: Harper Collins, 2005).

27　Neil Smith, 'Global executioner', *South Atlantic Quarterly* 105: 1 (Winter 2006), p. 61.

28　Irene Kahn, Amnesty International Report 2005 (25 May 2005): Online: http://web.amnesty.org/library/Index/ENGPOL100142005. See also: Editorial, 'Torture in the U.S. Gulag,' *The Nation* (20 June 2005), p. 3.

29　Joshua Holland, 'The Mystery of the Marine Massacre in Iraq', *AlterNet* (1 June 2006). Online: http://www.alternet.org/story/36752.

30　Stephen Gray, *Ghost Plane: The true story of the CIA torture program* (New York: St. Martin's Press, 2006). For a personal narrative about the abuse and torture inflicted on an innocent Canadian citizen at the hands of the US government's extraordinary rendition program, see Maher Arar, 'The horrors of "Extraordinary Rendition"', *Foreign Policy in Focus* (18 October 2006). Online: http://www.fpif.org/fpiftxt/3636. For an excellent analysis of the role of academics in working with the CIA in developing physically brutal torture methods see Alfred W. McCoy, *A Question of Torture: CIA interrogation, from the cold war to the war on terror* (New York: Owl Books, 2006).

31　A Canadian public inquiry completely cleared Arar of any terrorist activities. See www.aracommission.ca/eng/AR_English.pdf.

32   Dana Priest, 'Wrongful imprisonment: Anatomy of a CIA mistake', *Washington Post* (5 December 2005), pp. 12–18.

33   See Dana Priest, 'CIA Holds Terror Suspects in Secret Prisons', *Washington Post* (2 November 2005), p. A01.

34   Anup Shah, 'Military Commissions At 2006–Unchecked Powers?' *Z Magazine* (2 October 2006). Online: http://www.zmag.org/content/print_article.cfm?itemID=11095&sectionID=1.

35   I take up the issue of the Bush administration's response to Hurricane Katrina as symptomatic of a new biopolitics of disposability in Henry A. Giroux, *Stormy Weather: Katrina and the politics of disposability* (Boulder: Paradigm Publishers, 2006).

36   Hardt and Negri, *Multitude*, p. 17.

37   I have borrowed this idea from the criticisms made of the Israeli Defense Force by the writer Yitzhak Laor. See Yitzhak Laor, 'You are terrorists, we are virtuous', *London Review of Books* 28: 16 (17 August 2006). Online: http://www.lrb.co.uk/v28/n16/print/laor01_.html.

38   William Sonnerberg, *Federal Support for Education: F Y 1980 to F Y 2003* (Washington: National Centre for Education Statistics, 2004). Online: http://nces.ed.gov/pubs2004/2004026.pdf.

39   James Sterngold, 'After 9/11 U.S. policy built on world', *San Francisco Chronicle* (21 March 2004). Online: http://www.sfgate.com/cgi-bin/article.cgi?file=/c/a/2004/03/21/MNGJ65OS4J1.DTL&type=printable.

40   Francis Fukuyama, 'The neocons have learned nothing from five years of catastrophe', *The Guardian/UK* (31 January 2007). Online: www.commondreams.org/views07/0131–26.htm.

41   Jim Wolf, 'US predicts bumper year in arms sales', *Reuters* (4 December 2006). Online: http://news.yahoo.com/s/nm/20061204/pl_nm/aero_arms_summit_arms_sales_usa_dc

42   Chalmers Johnson, "Republic or empire: A nation's intelligence estimate on the United States," *Harper's Magazine* (January 2007), p. 63.

43   Julian Borger and David Teather, 'So much for the peace dividend', *Guardian/UK* (22 May 2003). Online: http://www.commondreams.org/cgi-bin/print.cgi?file=/headlines 03/0522–01.htm.

44   James Surowiecki, 'Unsafe at any price', *The New Yorker* (August 7 and14, 2006),p. 32.

45   George Monbiot, 'States of war', *Guardian/UK* (14 October 2003). Available online: http://www.commondreams.org/views03/1014–09.htm.

46   Giorgio Agamben, 'On security and terror', http://www.egs.edu/faculty/agamben/agamben-on-security-and-terror.html.

47   This issue is brilliantly explored in Richard J. Bernstein, *The Abuse of Evil: The corruption of politics and religion since 9/11* (London: Polity Press, 2005).

48   C. Wright Mills, *The Power Elite* (1956; rpt. New York: Oxford University Press, 1993), p. 191.

49   See Joan Roelofs, 'Military contractor philanthropy: Why some stay silent', *CounterPunch. org* (25 January 2006). Available online at: http://www.counterpunch.org/roelofs01252006.html.

50   John Armitage, 'Beyond hypermodern militarized knowledge factories', p. 221.

51   Nicholas Turse, 'The military-academic complex'.

52   Daniel Golden, 'After Sept. 11 CIA becomes a growing force on campus'.

53   Kirsten Searer, 'ASU's Crow partners with CIA on research projects', *The Tribune* (30 March 2003). Online at: http://license.icopyright.net/user/viewFreeUse.act?fuid=MTU5NTM5.

54   Mark Clayton, 'Higher espionage', *The Christian Science Monitor* (29 April 2003). Available online at: http://www.csmonitor.com/2003/0429/p. 13s01-lehl.html.

55   Seth Rosenfeld, 'Secret FBI files reveal covert activities at UC Bureau's campus operations involved Reagan, CIA', *The Tribune* (30 March 2003). Online http://archives.econ.utah.edu/archives/marxism/2004w22/msg00213.htm.

56   See, for instance, John Prados, *Safe for Democracy: The secret wars of the CIA* (Chicago: Ivan

Dee Publishers, 2006).

57 For an extensive analysis of Senator Roberts' role as Chairman of the Senate Select Committee on Intelligence, see 'Sen. Pat Roberts (R-KS): Chairman of the Senate Cover-up Committee', *Think Progress* (8 March 2006). Online: http://thinkprogress.org/roberts-coverup/.

58 Editorial, 'Advice and assent', *Los Angeles Times* (19 February 2006). Online: http://www. truthout.org/cgi-bin/artman/exec/view.cgi/48/17831.

59 A description of the program can be found at the government website: www.intelligence. gov/0-prisp.shtml.

60 Roberto J. Gonzalez, 'We must fight the militarization of anthropology', *The Chronicle of Higher Education* 53: 22 (2 February 2007), p. B20.

61 George Packer, 'Knowing the enemy: Can social scientists redefine the "war on terror"', *The New Yorker* (11 December 2006). Online: http://www.newyorker.com/printables/ fact/061218fa_fact2.

62 Ibid.

63 Gore Vidal, *Perpetual War for Perpetual Peace* (New York: Nation Books, 2002).

64 Jorge Mariscal, 'Lethal and compassionate: The militarization of US culture', *CounterPunch* (3 May 2003). Available online at: http://www.counterpunch.org/mariscal05052003.html.

65 For information on the PAMO and their efforts to resist the militarization of OISE, see http://www.homesnotbombs.ca/oiseprotest.htm.

66 The work of the Media Education Foundation can be found online at: http://www.mediaed. org/about.

67 See 'No space wars: Songs for peace in space'. Online at: http://www.spinspace.com/cd/ artists.html.

68 Jacques Ranciere, 'Democracy, republic, representation', *Constellations* 13: 3 (2006), p. 299.

69 See, for example, the very powerful film, *'Sir, No Sir!'* at http://www.sirnosir.com/.

70 Andrew J. Bacevich, 'The normalization of war', *Mother Jones* (April 2005). Online: http:// www.motherjones.com/news/dailymojo/2005/04/bacevich.html.

Methodological discussion section iv

1 See the Homeland Security website: http://www.dhs.gov/xprepresp/. At the time of writing (20 April 2009) the level of threat is said to be 'elevated' and 'The threat level in the airline sector is High or Orange'.

2 See the photo album posted by *The Boston Globe*: http://www.boston.com/bigpicture/2009/04/ protests_at_the_g20_summit.html.

3 See article in the *Guardian* 5 April, 2009: http://www.guardian.co.uk/world/2009/apr/05/ g20-protest-ian-tomlinson.

4 See Paul Lewis' report, *Guardian* 21 April, 2009.

5 See Monbiot's blog, 1 April 2009: http://www.guardian.co.uk/environment/georgemonbiot/ 2009/apr/01/g20-policing-climate-protest-riot.

Index

eBooks – at www.eBookstore.tandf.co.uk

A library at your fingertips!

eBooks are electronic versions of printed books. You can store them on your PC/laptop or browse them online.

They have advantages for anyone needing rapid access to a wide variety of published, copyright information.

eBooks can help your research by enabling you to bookmark chapters, annotate text and use instant searches to find specific words or phrases. Several eBook files would fit on even a small laptop or PDA.

NEW: Save money by eSubscribing: cheap, online access to any eBook for as long as you need it.

Annual subscription packages

We now offer special low-cost bulk subscriptions to packages of eBooks in certain subject areas. These are available to libraries or to individuals.

For more information please contact webmaster.ebooks@tandf.co.uk

We're continually developing the eBook concept, so keep up to date by visiting the website.

www.eBookstore.tandf.co.uk